D0076282

Political Theory
A Thematic Inquiry

The Nelson-Hall Series in Political Science
Consulting Editor: Samuel C. Patterson
The Ohio State University

Political Theory
A Thematic Inquiry

James L. Wiser
Loyola University of Chicago

Nelson-Hall nh Chicago

Library of Congress Cataloging-in-Publication Data

Wiser, James L.
  Political theory.

  Includes bibliographies and index.
  1. Political science—History. I. Title.
JA81.W543   1986   320.09   86-863
ISBN 0-8304-1069-4

Copyright © 1986 by James L. Wiser

Reprinted 1987

All rights reserved. No part of this book may be reproduced in any form without permission in writing from the publisher, except by a reviewer who wishes to quote brief passages in connection with a review written for broadcast or for inclusion in a magazine or newspaper. For information address Nelson-Hall Inc., Publishers, 111 North Canal Street, Chicago, Illinois 60606.

Manufactured in the United States of America

10   9   8   7   6   5   4   3   2

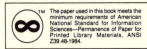
The paper used in this book meets the minimum requirements of American National Standard for Information Sciences—Permanence of Paper for Printed Library Materials, ANSI Z39.48-1984.

To my parents, Louis and Nita Wiser

CONTENTS

Contents

Contents

PREFACE

It has become commonplace to note that the most important and
creative works in political theory have been written during periods of historical and political crisis. This fact explains, in part,
the nature of the theoretical enterprise. Political theory arises in
response to an individual's experience of disorder. As such, it
begins with a perception of crisis, moves to the diagnostic analysis of its most important causes, and ends with the offering of
what is considered to be the most appropriate therapy. Consequently the best work in political theory necessarily reflects the
personal sensitivity, diagnostic skill, and therapeutic vision of
the analyst.

The fact that political theory begins as a response to the perception of disorder also explains, in part, the themes with which
it is typically concerned. The questions of the theorist are, in effect, the questions of the concerned citizen. As a member of a
specific historical community the theorist is simply asking in a
more radical fashion those very questions which are presented
to the citizen by the political issues of the day. To a certain extent the themes of political theory arise more or less spontaneously from the nature of political life itself. Describing the tradition of Western political theory, the contemporary philosopher
Eric Voegelin has written:

> As for the subject matter, it is nothing esoteric; rather, it lies not far
> from the questions of the day and is concerned with the truth of
> things that everyone talks about. What is happiness? How should
> man live in order to be happy? What is virtue? What, especially, is

the virtue of justice? How large a territory and a population are best for society? What kind of education is best? What professions, and what forms of government? All of these questions arise from the conditions of the existence of man in society. And the philosopher is a man like any other: as far as the order of society is concerned, he has no other questions to ask than those of his fellow citizens.[1]

The themes that are discussed in this book were selected because of their "spontaneous" character. They are questions which appear to arise from the very conditions of political life itself. As such, they are as relevant today as when they were first asked. Unlike mathematical problems which, when solved, are solved once and for all, political problems exhibit a certain open-ended quality. Each "solution" engenders a new set of problems, and thus the task of creating a decent and humane political order is never finished.

Although the questions and themes of political life may be universal, some thinkers have explored these issues in a particularly powerful fashion. Consequently their "answers" have served as benchmarks for those of us who are engaged in a similar inquiry. By contrasting and comparing such perspectives each of us may be better able to comprehend the significance of our own experience and thus more effectively participate in the reasoned political dialogue which is essential to a well-ordered society.

Acknowledgments

It would be impossible to list all of those who have helped me in my effort to understand the principles of political order. However I would like to acknowledge the special contribution of Michael B. Levy, Texas A&M University, and Roger Smith, College of William and Mary. They have read the manuscript in its entirety and have made a number of useful comments. Both invested considerable time and effort in this project. Their suggestions were extremely helpful, and their corrections were thoughtfully developed and graciously expressed.

I would like to thank Mary Margaret Kelly and Margaret Kransfelder for their patience and support during the preparation of this manuscript. Their professional skills were invaluable for the timely completion of this project.

Finally and as always there is Beth. Thank you.

Notes

1. Eric Voegelin, *Science, Politics, and Gnosticism*, trans. William J. Fitzpatrick (Chicago: Henry Regnery, 1968), pp.15–16.

PART
ONE

Political Theory:
Knowledge
or Opinion?

C H A P T E R 1

**Classical Political Science
and the
Discovery of Universal Reason**

The Athenian Crisis

As with many of our Western intellectual traditions, it is possible to trace the development of political science back to its origins in classical Greece. Commentators typically refer to Socrates (470–399 B.C.), Plato (427–346 B.C.), and Aristotle (384–322 B.C.) as providing the formative themes for the newly emerging discipline. Inasmuch as each of these thinkers was more or less directly involved in the politics of his day, it is not surprising that the character of the new discipline was strongly influenced by the realities of Athenian politics. Indeed, to a certain extent political science was created as a specific response to the disorder of Athenian political life.

Following its victory in the Persian wars (490–479 B.C.), Athens used its hegemony within the Delian League to establish its own imperial control over the Aegean area. However, after an initial period of prosperity and stability, Athens began to encounter increasing resistance to its rule. The city-state of Sparta, in particular, resented the imposition of Athenian authority, and in 431 B.C. the two powers entered into the prolonged battles of the Peloponnesian War. By 404 B.C. Athens was totally defeated; its empire had been dissolved, and the city's democratic regime was soon replaced by an oligarchy of thirty tyrants who were both sympathetic to and supported by Spartan interests. A year later, in 403 B.C., democracy was restored, but the Athenian city-state never regained its former prominence. In 322 B.C. the Athenian experiment in democratic self-rule was ended once and for all as the city was annexed by the expanding Macedonian Empire of Alexander the Great.

The lives of Socrates, Plato, and Aristotle spanned the period of Athens's rise and fall. As one would expect, it was a period in which the political issues of the day assumed an immediate importance. The growth and ultimate dissolution of the Athenian city-state were historical events that required an explanation. What were the principles that could account for Athens's earlier political success? Similarly, what actions were required if its collapse were to be delayed or even prevented?

The search for the answers to these and related questions was all the more urgent because of what appeared to be the failure of the Athenian aristocracy to respond adequately to the situation at hand. By the fifth century B.C., many had become convinced that a fundamental analysis of the new conditions was necessary precisely because the traditional assumptions of Athens's aristocratic order could no longer be accredited. For example, ancient aristocrats had argued that successful ruling depended upon the active presence of a noble spirit. This spirit, in turn, was associated with certain qualities that, according to the aristocratic argument, could only be transmitted through inheritance and then developed by special training. Typically, family lines were traced back to a divine or heroic ancestor whose original power was then passed on through each generation. From this perspective, then, the families of the aristocracies were set apart by the gifts they had inherited, and the excellence of any particular individual was explained ultimately in terms of his or her blood line. Although a program of education was important, it could be effective only if the student already had certain inborn qualities capable of responding to the educator's appeal. The education of one who lacked the necessary personal attributes was simply formal training, and formal training, according to the aristocrats, could never be an adequate substitute for the unique personal excellence of the landed nobility. This attitude is clearly expressed in the poetry of Pindar (522–443 B.C.). As a champion of the aristocracy, Pindar was careful to distinguish between that excellence which was truly innate and that which was merely learned:

But by innate excellence one mightily prevails; but he who hath *only* what he has learnt, *he, I say,* a man destitute of real worth, being of one spirit at one time and of another at another time, never descends with a sure foot, but tries at numberless excellences with a mind that completes nothing.[1]

The decline of Athens's political fortunes created a situation in which the traditional claims of its once-powerful artistocracy encountered an increasingly pervasive skepticism. If the aristocracy did indeed possess a particular form of excellence, it did not appear to be of the type that could in fact create an enduring political order. In short, the traditions of aristocratic Athens no longer offered the guidance or provided the substantive principles by which the society could be ruled. New principles were needed, and the political science of Plato and Aristotle was one attempt to satisfy this need.

In their writings, Plato and Aristotle sought to articulate an understanding of those principles of human and social order that could account for true political excellence. The name given to that understanding was political science (*politike episteme*) and it was, at first, only one of several theoretical responses to the Athenian situation.

The other major alternative was that provided by the Sophists. As groups of professional educators who traveled from city-state to city-state, the Sophists became an important cultural force during the fifth century B.C. Indeed such Sophists as Protagoras, Hippias, and Gorgias enjoyed an immense popularity among the politically ambitious sons of the newly rising commercial classes. As educators, the Sophists were concerned with developing a program of education that would replace the traditional aristocracy of birth with a new aristocracy of intellect. In doing so, they viewed education as a liberal rather than as simply a technical art. According to the Sophists, education was a process concerned with the shaping of both the intellect and the character of students. Breaking from the traditional preoccupation with the singular aristocratic hero, the Sophists attempted to develop a general understanding of human nature by exploring the common or universal structures of the rational mind. Accordingly, they investigated the form of language (grammar), the form of speech (rhetoric), and the form of thinking itself (dialectic). In addition to such formal studies, certain Sophists included the substantive sciences of mathematics, music, and astronomy.

In spite of these similarities, however, the Sophists did not succeed in developing a uniform curriculum. Different teachers emphasized different aspects of the program and, as a consequence, there was a fair amount of competition among the Sophists for students and the fees they paid. If there was a common theme to their work, however, it was the Sophistic concern for political excellence. As a group, the Sophists claimed to be able to teach political virtue. Such teachings necessarily included an examination of morality and therefore posed questions about the nature of life in general and of the good life in particular. Questions of this nature were precisely the type being asked by Plato and Aristotle. Thus, in one sense the philosophers were building upon the original Sophistic project. Yet at the same time, both Plato and Aristotle were critical of the Sophists and accused them of basing their teachings on half-truths. As opponents of Sophism, the philosophers presented themselves as the representatives of a true political science and sought to differentiate their own work from that of their contemporaries.

In his *Seventh Letter*, Plato described how his understanding of Athenian politics was deeply influenced by the tragic death of his teacher, Socrates. Socrates had been tried and condemned to death by the Athenian court. He had been charged formally with corrupting the youth of Athens and with dishonoring the official gods of the city. In addition, he was considered politically suspect, since several of his students were involved in a tyrannical plot against the democratic government of Athens. Found guilty, Socrates preferred death to exile and administered to himself the poison ordered by the court.

Plato's reaction to the death of Socrates influenced all of his philosophical writings. For Plato, Socrates had embodied the highest accomplishments of the human spirit, and his death raised a number of serious questions. How was it possible to explain the Athenian reaction to Socrates? Why was he treated as a mortal enemy of the state? What was it in his philosophy that provoked such anger and passion? In his attempt to answer these and similar questions, Plato was forced to examine the very nature of Socrates's approach to philosophizing.

Socrates never taught a positive doctrine. Unlike other teachers who claimed to know certain truths, Socrates was committed to an unending process of questioning and search. He was interested in asking about the nature of the good life in general and the role of human virtue in particular. Admitting his own ignorance about these things, he approached others who claimed to know and sought their advice. His experience, however, was always the same. Those who professed to know the nature of such virtues as courage, friendship, and piety inevitably failed to respond adequately to Socrates's request for the reasons that justified their positions. Eventually, the "self-evident" truths of these confident Athenians were revealed to be no more than unfounded opinion. From the perspective of the guardians of Athenian tradition, the Socratic style of questioning had the nihilistic effect of undermining popular confidence in the general beliefs of society. In this sense then, Socratic philosophy could appear to the dogmatically minded as politically dangerous.

The accusation that Socrates was somehow responsible for corrupting the youth of Athens was one that confused cause and effect. Socrates's questioning did not cause Athenian ignorance; on the contrary, it only called into question the Athenians' satisfaction with and acceptance of this very condition. In claiming to know that which they did not, the Athenians were in fact expressing their own willingness to continue as they were. Confident that their beliefs were true, they did not experience the need to explore further. Socrates on the other hand acknowledged his own ignorance and as a consequence, believed he was required to seek further for the truth. He challenged the popular assumptions of the day in order to provoke a similar desire for knowledge among his contemporaries. His quest, therefore, was not that of a nihilist who sought to destroy the truth, but rather that of a philosopher who wished to discover it. This distinction implies that the Socratic challenge to opinion presupposed a philosophical faith that such a challenge would eventually result in the discovery of knowledge. If opinion were all that exists, then one opinion is as good as another, and none can be criticized. If, on the other hand, there exists a standard of truth beyond opinion, then all opinions can be judged in terms of their adequacy vis-à-vis this higher standard. In his debates, Socrates attempted to make his opponents indirectly aware of the possibility of this higher standard by first pointing out the obvious inadequacies that existed within the realm of opinion. Plato, on the other hand, built upon this effort by turning his attention directly to the existence of the standard itself. In so doing, he sought to distinguish between the nature of opinion (*doxa*) on one hand and that of knowledge (*episteme*) on the other.

Book 6 of the *Republic* presents Plato's distinction between the material and the rational poles of reality. As bodily creatures, we are aware of the material world through the operation of our five senses. For example, we are able to perceive those objects which have shape and extension because of the faculty of sight. Without it, our appreciation of those particular aspects of reality would be greatly diminished. By bringing all our senses together, our bodies, which are themselves material, enable us to become aware of the many and various dimensions of the material world. Plato concludes that we have access to material reality because of our location or participation within it.

Similarly, according to Plato, there exists a pole of reality that transcends the strictly material dimension. This other dimension is the rational realm, and it too is given to us as an object for our awareness. Just as our bodies allow us to participate in the material realm, our souls (*psyche*)—which are of a rational nature—allow us to participate in that which transcends the material. For Plato, the soul is to the realm of ideas as the body is to the realm of the material. In other words, the soul is that faculty by which we participate in and thus become conscious of transcendent reason.

Central to Plato's metaphysics was his argument that the rational realm of ideas is, in fact, more real than the material realm of objective reality. As the realm of ideas, the rational dimension is composed of those unchanging and stable principles that define the nature of that which exists. For example, although people may disagree as to whether a particular policy is just or not, the idea of justice itself, according to Plato, is both constant and universal. As an idea, it belongs to the realm of the truly real, or in Plato's terms, the realm of the 'Is.' The material realm, on the other hand, is the realm of birth, growth, decay, and death. Within it, particular realities do not endure. Thus, rather than being stable and unchanging, the material realm is characterized by an ongoing process of growth and decay. In short, it is the realm of 'Becoming.' The material world is real, but its reality is only partially realized inasmuch as material things are always in a state of change. As such, they are more or less what they appear to be without ever achieving 'Being' itself. On the other hand, inasmuch as the rational realm does not change, its realities are complete, and thus they are, according to Plato, fully what they are intended to be. For example, every existing human being is real, yet not every particular individual achieves all the promise of his or her human nature. At any given moment, a person may to a certain degree fulfill his or her potential, but at no time does one achieve all that is humanly possible. In this sense, then, the idea of human nature is richer and more profound than any of its manifestations. Historically, existing individuals change, inasmuch as they rise and fall from the standard of human perfection. The standard itself, however, is unaffected by such changes. As an idea it exists beyond the material realm and is thus superior to it.

The human person, as body and soul, participates in both the realm of Becoming and the realm of Being. Thus, unlike other species, men and women exist in a state of tension between these two poles of reality. On one hand, the *realm of 'Becoming'* is the realm of images and things. It is therefore the realm of appearances, and Plato referred to our awareness of such appearances as opinion (*doxa*). On the other hand, the *realm of 'Being'* is the realm of ideas and the good. It is the realm of the rational idea, and Plato referred to our awareness of these ideas as knowledge or science (*episteme*). For Plato, then, opinion is distinguished from knowledge primarily in terms of the degree of being or completeness which characterizes the object of its interest. Opinions are based on appearances. Thus they, like appearances, are susceptible to change and are not grounded upon that which truly *is*. Knowledge, on the other hand, is an awareness of 'Being' itself. Thus, like 'Being,' it is unchanging, and its principles consequently can claim a universal validity.

In responding to the clash of opinions during his own day, Plato argued that it was possible to achieve an understanding of political order based upon the philosopher's rational insight into the order of Being itself. Inasmuch as this insight had to transcend the realm of appearances in order to participate in the realm of 'Being,' it claimed a status for itself superior to that of opinion. According to Plato, political opinions were based solely upon historical experience. As a consequence they lacked the proper grounding for a truly adequate understanding of political existence. Such opinions would be more or less appropriate to the degree to which they corresponded to the rational insight of the philosopher or scientist. Yet inasmuch as this very insight is not itself an object of opinion, those who remain within the realm of opinion are not capable of knowing to what degree such a correspondence may in fact exist. For Plato, the clash among opinions can never be resolved from within the domain of opinion itself. Opinion must be transcended, and that is precisely the claim that Plato made for his new science of politics. Only the philosopher who has a knowledge of those principles of order which inform the world of appearances but actually constitute the realm of ideas can possess that true measure according to which all action is to be judged. Before deciding what is best for a particular society, the statesman must first know what is good. Yet to know what the good actually is—as opposed to what it simply appears to be—is the defining characteristic of Platonic political science. Thus Plato's ultimate response to the disorder of Athenian politics was contained in his advocacy of the rule of rational insight. Specifically, political science was to replace public opinion as the source of Athenian civil culture. In personal terms, the philosopher was to become king:

> Unless . . . the philosophers rule as kings or those now called kings, and chiefs genuinely and adequately philosophize, and political power and philosophy coincide in the same place . . . there is no rest from ills for the cities . . . nor I think for human kind. . . .[2]

Aristotle's Response

A somewhat similar attempt to found the new science of politics upon the distinction between opinion and knowledge can be found in the work of Plato's most famous pupil, Aristotle. Like Plato, Aristotle recognized the distinction between knowledge and opinion, and it is a theme that appears throughout all of his work. However, unlike his teacher, who tended to equate all of science with the practice of philosophy, Aristotle offered a somewhat more complex understanding of the scientific enterprise. Whereas Plato had thought that all of science was essentially of one kind and therefore that the only important distinction was that between science and opinion, Aristotle argued on behalf of recognizing three distinct traditions of scientific inquiry: the theoretical, the practical, and the productive. As a consequence the new science of politics not only had to be differentiated from opinion, as Plato had argued, but at the same time, since political science was a practical science, it also had to be distinguished from its theoretical and productive counterparts.

According to Aristotle, those sciences he classified as theoretical were the most important. For him, a life devoted to the pursuit of theoretical inquiry represented the highest human achievement, and its realization became the goal of his ethical writings. As a group, the various theoretical sciences shared certain common features. First, the theoretical sciences only attempted to investigate certain types of objects. Specifically, they were concerned with understanding those realities over which humans could exercise no control. The realities they investigated existed independently of human choice; their properties were not the results of human activity; and their purposes were not established by human design. In Aristotle's terms, their principles of rest and motion were within themselves, and as such they were beyond human manipulation. Physics and theology would be examples of a theoretical science. As the study of divine causes, theology investigates a reality whose order is structured by principles that operate independently of human control. According to Aristotle, the divine exists; it can be known, but it cannot be used or commanded to act. Thus it is a reality that is an appropriate object for theoretical inquiry. Similarly, physics is the study of the natural world, and as such it seeks to comprehend a reality that cannot be other than it is. The laws of motion and change operate as they do regardless of whether their outcome is one that is preferred by the individual scientist. Thus, from Aristotle's perspective, the natural world lends itself to a truly theoretical analysis.

A second and related feature of the theoretical sciences refers to the attitude of the scientists themselves. Specifically, the theoretical sciences are those that one pursues for the sake of truth alone. Inasmuch as the realities the theorist investigates are beyond the realm of human control, the only realistic motive for pursuing theoretical inquiry is the potential satisfaction of the scientist's own intellectual curiosity. According to Aristotle, one engages in the study of mathematics or the various natural sciences for the sake of knowledge itself rather than for any pragmatic benefits that may eventually result from the inquiry.

Finally, Aristotle believed that, even though the various theoretical sciences are concerned with different objects, they nonetheless share a common logical structure. For him, the theoretical sciences are intended to systematize our knowledge of a particular subject matter. This project, in turn, requires that such knowledge be placed in an axiomatic form. The rules governing this effort are summarized in two of Aristotle's treatises, the *Prior Analytics* and the *Posterior Analytics*. Specifically, in the *Prior Analytics*, he developed the rules of logical deduction that should govern the derivation of scientific theorems from general axioms. In his *Posterior Analytics*, Aristotle examined the necessary character of the axioms themselves. In general he argued that a truly scientific understanding is possible only when two conditions are fulfilled. First, one must know the true, immediate, and prior causes of the phenomenon under investigation. And second, it must be the case that that which is known cannot of necessity be other than it is. Thus, for Aristotle, scientific theory produces knowledge of the universal, not the particular, and of the necessary, not the contingent.

If the only sciences were the theoretical sciences, then Aristotle's system would not support the Platonic distinction between political science and political opinion. In the study of politics, one is concerned with both the particular and the contingent, yet according to Aristotle, such qualities are not the appropriate concerns for a truly theoretical investigation. This problem is resolved, however, by Aristotle's recognition of two additional scientific traditions: the productive and the practical.

Unlike the theoretical sciences, both the productive sciences and the practical sciences are primarily concerned with the governance of human actions. Consequently, knowledge is not pursued for its own sake but rather as a means of directing individuals in the accomplishment of those tasks that they have set for themselves. Concerned with realities over which mankind can exercise a certain degree of control, the productive and practical sciences instruct individuals in order that they may act well as opposed to acting poorly.

Inasmuch as the productive sciences are concerned with those activities that result in the making of products, acting well is equivalent to working efficiently. In other words, the productive sciences are comprised of the various technologies by which an artisan transforms natural objects into useful products. Aristotle gave farming and engineering as examples.

Like the productive sciences, the practical sciences are also involved with the ordering of human action. Yet here the concern is not with the production of things. On the contrary, the practical sciences are those sciences that seek to instruct one in those activities through which his or her life can be properly fulfilled. Here the goal is to nurture and develop those potentialities whose realization constitutes the fulfillment of human nature. By instructing the individual how to act in order to acquire that which is good, the practical sciences seek human happiness as their goals. For Aristotle, there are two such sciences in particular: ethics and politics. Whereas ethics is the practical science concerned with teaching one how to act in order to achieve one's own individual good, political science is concerned with those activities necessary for the pursuit of the common good. Indeed, Aristotle's own *Nicomachean Ethics* and his *Politics* were intended to be examples of this type.

For Aristotle, political science is a science, and so its teachings can be differentiated from the beliefs of mere opinion. Yet, inasmuch as political science is one of the practical sciences, it does not manifest the same attributes as do its theoretical counterparts. For Aristotle, there is a truth to be found concerning particular moral questions. Therefore, the scientific comprehension of that truth can provide a standard against which the opinions of the day can be measured. For example, Aristotle believed that a morally wise person can easily discern that in a certain situation, courage requires that an individual act in a specific way. Such discernment, however, is a matter of experience, education, and practical judgment. As such, it does not lend itself to the same scientific procedures that Aristotle had developed for the axiomatic sciences.

Specifically, as a matter of practical judgment, political science cannot hope to achieve the same precision, clarity, or degree of generality that are characteristic of a truly theoretical inquiry. Questions concerning the good are complex because the reality they are investigating is truly complex. Similarly, inasmuch as political decisions will have different effects in different situations, the science of politics can only produce knowledge about what is good as a general rule and not about what is necessarily good in every case. Thus, although there is a truth concerning political and moral matters, it can only be portrayed in a rough and general sketch:

> For a well-schooled man is one who searches for that degree of precision in each kind of study which the nature of the subject at hand admits: it is obviously just as foolish to accept arguments of probability from a mathematician as to demand strict demonstrations from an orator.[3]

In all of his scientific work, Aristotle typically began his analysis with an examination of the various opinions that related to the topic of his inquiry. After reviewing the opinions of his predecessors, he then tested their adequacy either by appealing to concrete cases that demonstrated contrary evidence or by challenging the logic by which they were presented. As an attempt to correct the deficiencies of received opinion, this review was not simply an exercise in historical scholarship. Rather, for Aristotle, it was the necessary first step in an effort to move beyond the sphere of opinion and toward that of knowledge.

According to Aristotle, the practical realm is the realm of human action. Generally, individuals act for the sake of acquiring that which appears to them as good. However, just as there are particular goods that satisfy the many particular needs individuals have, so too is there a general good that satisfies the most inclusive of human desires. According to Aristotle, that inclusive desire is the desire for human happiness, because all individuals want to be happy. Inasmuch as politics is concerned with the pursuit of the highest good attainable by action, the ultimate purpose of political society is to secure those conditions that make happiness possible. The problem, of course, as Plato had shown, is that citizens disagree about the real meaning of happiness. Thus the political problem with which Aristotle's political science begins is the problem of public opinion:

> . . . let us discuss what is in our view the aim of politics, i.e. the highest good attainable by action. As far as its name is concerned, most people would probably agree; for both the common run of people and cultivated men call it happiness. . . . But when it comes to defining what happiness is, they disagree, and the account given by the common run differs from that of the philosophers. The former say it is some clear and obvious good, such as pleasure, wealth, or honor; some say it is one thing and others another, and often the very same person identifies it with different things at different times. . . .[4]

The problem this situation presents to Aristotle is a problem ultimately rooted in the distinction between appearances and reality. All individuals seek the good; yet what appears to someone as good may not actually be so. For example, it may seem good to a young child to eat only sweets, but this appearance is, in fact, indicative of a deeper ignorance about what the body actually needs in order to be healthy and thus what is, in fact, actually good for the body. This situation becomes even more complex, according to Aristotle, because oftentimes the decision as to what appears to be good is not the result of an explicit or rational judgment. Rather, "men . . . derive their concept of the good and of happiness from the lives they lead."[5] According to Aristotle, this is an understandable practice, yet he argued that "common" and "vulgar" people prefer the life of pleasure, while those who are active seek honor, and those who are contemplative enjoy the pursuit of science.

If human understanding were limited to the realm of appearances, there would be no possibility of resolving this clash of competing opinions. Yet Aristotle, like Plato, argued that human beings possess a faculty of rational insight by which they can apprehend being as it actually is and thereby transcend the level of mere phenomena. In the case of the theoretical sciences, this faculty is called rational intelligence (nous), and it enables one to apprehend those fundamental principles that are the universal propositions of the axiomatic sciences. In the case of the practical sciences, the equivalent faculty is prudence or practical wisdom (*phronesis*), and it enables one to deliberate correctly about what is good and advantageous—not in any partial or restricted sense, but in terms of the actual requirements of the good life itself. According to Aristotle, therefore, prudential wisdom enables an individual to gain that knowledge by which he or she can effectively bridge that gap which exists between appearance and reality. Having been transformed by an awareness of the good, persons of prudential wisdom learn to desire that which actually is good. Thus in this case, that which *seems good* is, in fact, that which actually *is good,* and as a consequence their decisions become the standards against which the opinions of others are to be measured:

> . . . must we not admit that . . . the object of wish is the good, but that for each individual it is whatever *seems* good to him? Thus what seems good to a man of high moral standards is truly the object of wish, whereas a worthless man wishes everything that strikes his fancy . . . [so in moral questions] a man whose standards are high judges correctly, and in each case what *is truly good will appear to him to be so.* Thus . . . the chief distinction of a man of high moral standards is his ability *to see the truth in each particular moral question,* since he is, as it were, the standard and measure for such questions.[6]

In arguing that the person of prudential wisdom is empowered to judge the various opinions about how one should act in order to be happy, Aristotle has, in fact, offered his solution to the Athenian crisis of his day. Like Plato, he believed that a knowledge of the good must replace one's opinions about it. Such a knowledge, in turn, was claimed by both the founders of classical political science to be the distinguishing characteristic of their teachings. Although their precise formulations differ, both Plato and Aristotle attempted to differentiate their work from that of the Sophists by appealing to the newly discovered power of human reason. Specifically they argued that it was possible for one to transcend the realm of opinion by participating in the actual order of being itself. Thus the classical conception of reason was, in fact, akin to an act of faith. The contemporary philosopher Eric Voegelin writes:

> A scientific analysis . . . makes it possible to judge of the truth of the premises implied by an opinion. It can do this, however, only on the

assumption that truth about the order of being—to which, of course, opinions also refer—is objectively ascertainable. And Platonic-Aristotelian analysis does in fact operate on the assumption that there is an order of being accessible to a science beyond opinion. . . . And indeed Platonic-Aristotelian analysis did not in the least begin with speculations about its own possibility, but with the actual insight into being which motivated the analytical process. . . .[7]

The Claims of Universal Reason

The previous discussion has focused upon the particular setting within which the discipline of political science first emerged, in order to emphasize two points. First, the nature of political science is due in part to the fact that the discipline originally developed as an explicit response to an experience of human and social disorder. As such, the study of political science has traditionally been characterized by a certain critical or practical intention. As a science, it seeks knowledge; yet the type of knowledge in which it is most interested is that which is either directly or indirectly capable of informing action. Second, political science is a creation within Western civilization. Thus, as is inevitable in such cases, it has borrowed extensively from the particular assumptions that inform this specific tradition. Given this, the student of political science must be sensitive to the larger cultural and intellectual environment within which the discipline operates. Without such an expanded perspective, it is difficult to appreciate either the assumptions with which political scientists work or the tasks to which they are dedicated.

On the other hand, the preceding summary of the particular historical and political situation within which Plato and Aristotle first attempted to construct the science of politics should not mislead one about the nature of their claims. Although political science emerged at a particular time and in response to a particular situation, its founders nonetheless claimed to be doing more than simply offering another set of specific opinions. As we have seen, political science actually originated in an effort to distinguish between the realm of opinion and that of knowledge. Even though the discipline emerged in a specific time and place, it claimed nevertheless that its teachings transcended the limitations of their specific origins. Plato and Aristotle, for example, grounded their political teachings on a philosophical understanding of the principles of human and social order. Thus, if they were correct, the validity of their ideas is not limited to the particular conditions of their own day. Although responding to a historical crisis, they claimed to have discovered a realm of transhistorical principle, and by doing so they thereby set the rational pursuit of universal truth as the objective for all political scientists. Indeed the work of such later thinkers as Augustine, Aquinas, Machiavelli, Locke, Hobbes, Rousseau, and J. S. Mill presents us with a continuing reaffirmation of this objective. Each in his own way sought to discover certain universal principles of political well-being. Each, therefore, claimed to write as a representative thinker, i.e., as one whose ideas were not simply the idiosyncratic expressions of his own private imagination.

How can such a claim to universal knowledge be justified? How is it that an individual's ideas can transcend the particular conditions within which they first emerged? In short, is a true political science possible? As we have seen, it was the assumption of the classical theorists that such a science is possible, and this assumption in turn was based upon the Greek discovery of universal reason.

Although Plato and Aristotle have been presented as the originators of classical political science, it is also true that at the same time they represent the culmination of another process that can be traced back through the early fragments of the pre-Socratic philosophers. In some respects, the work of Plato and Aristotle presupposed and built upon the prior discoveries of others. In particular it assumed and thus accepted the classical discovery of universal reason.

It may be helpful to examine the concept of universal reason in more detail because the term *reason* does not necessarily mean the same thing for us today as it originally did for the classical Greeks. Today, for example, reason is understood primarily as the ability to calculate. Given a certain goal or project, it becomes the task of reason to figure out the most efficient means for achieving the ends in view. Thus, in telling someone to act reasonably we are generally advising him or her to be circumspect and to calculate carefully both the current circumstances and the possible consequences of any action that may be undertaken. Such a conception of reason is often referred to as an instrumental one inasmuch as it understands reason to function primarily as an instrument or means for the achievement of other goals and purposes.

For the classical Greeks, however, such an instrumental understanding would be too restrictive and hence insufficient. For them reason was primarily a faculty of participation. As such it was the means by which individuals self-consciously inserted themselves into the common order of reality. By doing so, they were able to perceive that encompassing structure of which they were but a part and thereby attune themselves to the order of the whole.

It was the common field of reality which united all humans, and it was the faculty of reason which made this order apparent to all who participated within it. By illuminating the philosopher's experience of participation within reality, reason also illuminated the very same field in which all could potentially participate. Thus its claims were truly universal. According to the classical Greeks, the rational perspective was the human perspective per se, and all people shared in the one common order of reality precisely to the degree to which they were rational. Reason, therefore, was the common substance of our shared humanity.

An example of this understanding can be found in the fragments of Parmenides (circa 475 B.C.). In a poem written to his student Zeno, Parmenides compared the way of truth to the way of opinion. For our purposes, what is most important is the poet's insistence that thought or reason is necessarily related to 'Being' or the 'It is':

> To think is the same as the thought that IT IS: for you will not find thinking without Being.[8]

By this Parmenides is not arguing that individuals cannot make mistakes and that all thinking is necessarily correct; rather he is simply saying that it is only through the faculty of reason that people participate fully in reality; for where there is rational thought so, too, is there 'Being.' Reason is that which allows us to apprehend 'Being,' and thus we become fully a part of reality only if reason is allowed to order our life. For Parmenides, then, reason is not simply the power of calculation. Rather it is nothing less than a mode of human existence. It is the very condition of the human being when he or she is most fully in contact with the real: "For it is the same thing to think and to be."[9]

The classical Greeks' insistence that reason is the necessary and proper mode of human participation within reality serves to explain their faith in its universal authority. Inasmuch as reason allows us to participate in the common order of reality, it is only through reason that we are brought together in a community of shared meaning. In other words, it is only because we are rational that we are able to share in the truth of being. According to the Greeks, it is reason alone that unites humanity, and its truths, therefore, are necessarily universal.

This understanding is clearly reflected in the fragments of another pre-Socratic philosopher, Heraclitus (circa 500 B.C.). According to him, reason is the law of the universe that is common to all. It not only gives direction to everything that exists but it also orders a person's soul and thereby accounts for the faculty of thought that all individuals have in common. By following reason, one participates in reality and through this common mode of participation joins in the community of those who are truly united. Those who are not rational, however, fall away into the private dream world of the sleepwalker:

> To those who are awake, there is one ordered universe common [*to all*], whereas in sleep each man turns away [*from this world*] to one of his own.[10]

This classical Greek understanding of universal reason was accepted by both Plato and Aristotle. Thus their faith in the human ability to transcend the realm of opinion and enter the realm of knowledge was based upon a prior faith in the power of reason itself. As we have seen, reason for the classical Greeks was that faculty by which one could participate in the one common order of reality. Thus if political science were based upon reason, it could indeed claim to transcend the realm of the particular (opinion) and thereby enter into the realm of the universal (knowledge), because that movement is what defines the very power of reason itself. For Plato and Aristotle, political science was universally authoritative precisely because it was rational. Its teachings were based upon the very movement of reason, and as long as reason was understood in these terms, classical political science could claim scientific authority.

Notes

1. Pindar, "Nemian III," in *The Odes of Pindar*, trans. Dawson Turner (London: George Bell & Sons, 1885), p. 110.

2. Plato, *The Republic*, trans. Allan Bloom (New York: Basic Books, 1968), 5. 473d–473e.

3. Aristotle, *Nicomachean Ethics*, trans. Martin Ostwald (Indianapolis: Bobbs-Merrill, 1962), 1.3.1094b20–1095a.

4. Aristotle *Ethics* 1.4.1095a15–25.

5. Aristotle *Ethics* 1.5.1095b15–20.

6. Aristotle *Ethics* 3.4.1113a20–1113b.

7. Eric Voegelin, *Science, Politics, and Gnosticism*, trans. William J. Fitzpatrick (Chicago: Henry Regnery, 1968), pp. 17–18.

8. Parmenides of Elea, in Kathleen Freeman (ed.), *Ancilla to the Pre-Socratic Philosophers* (Cambridge: Harvard University Press, 1971), p. 44.

9. Parmenides, *Ancilla*, p. 42.

10. Heraclitus of Ephesus, in Kathleen Freeman (ed.), *Ancilla to the Pre-Socratic Philosophers* (Cambridge: Harvard University Press), p. 30.

Recommended Readings

Barnes, Jonathan. *Aristotle*. New York: Oxford University Press, 1982.

Hall, Robert W. *Plato*. London: George Allen & Unwin, 1981.

Hare, R. M. *Plato*. New York: Oxford University Press, 1982.

Jaeger, Werner. *Paideia: The Ideals of Greek Culture*. 3 vols. Translated by Gilbert Highet. Oxford: Oxford University Press, 1945.

Lloyd, G. E. R. *Aristotle: The Growth and Structure of His Thought*. Cambridge: Cambridge University Press, 1968.

Morrall, John B. *Aristotle*. London: George Allen & Unwin, 1977.

Snell, Bruno. *The Discovery of the Mind: The Greek Origins of European Thought*. Translated by T. G. Rosenmeyer. New York: Harper & Row, 1960.

Vernant, Jean-Pierre. *The Origins of Greek Thought*. Ithaca, N.Y.: Cornell University Press, 1982.

Voegelin, Eric. *Plato and Aristotle*. Baton Rouge: Louisiana State University Press, 1957.

C H A P T E R 2

![black bar divider]

Modern Political Science and the Discovery of History

The Continuation of a Rational Science of Politics

Every science establishes a set of standards that it uses to evaluate its own achievements. These standards, in turn, are derived either directly or indirectly from a larger set of metaphysical and epistemological assumptions that govern a particular culture's understanding of reality in general. Certain cultures sustain only certain sciences, and the legitimacy of a particular scientific tradition will depend upon its "fit" within the larger intellectual environment. For example, political science originally emerged within the context of Greek classical civilization. Its ambition to achieve a universally valid understanding of political order found essential support in the classical conception of universal reason. Given the Greek understanding of reality and of humanity's place within it, the classical attempt to transcend the realm of opinion in order to enter into the realm of knowledge appeared to be both a plausible and a legitimate undertaking. Thus the writings of Plato and Aristotle were appropriate to the intellectual environment within which they worked.

However, as this environment within the West changed, it became necessary for the various scientific traditions to adjust accordingly. For example, the Platonic and Aristotelian conception of political science would make little sense in a culture that denied the possibility of a nonmaterial dimension within reality. Thus as the larger intellectual environment changed, so too did the tradition of political science. While retaining the classical commitment to universal truth, postclassical political science sought to justify its claim by offering arguments different from those originally given by the Greeks. For example, the Italian Renaissance theorist Machiavelli (1469–1527) based his particular understanding of political reality on a reading of the general lessons of history. For Machiavelli, history continually repeats itself as if time were a great cycle through which every age and nation must inevitably move. Thus those political strategies that worked in the past will also work in the future, and the wise political leader will be the one who can learn from the example of others. For Machiavelli, therefore, political science is capable of discovering universal truth precisely because "the order [of human] motions and powers"[1] is no different today than it was yesterday or will be tomorrow.

Similarly the English philosopher Thomas Hobbes (1588–1679) was quite confident that his political research, as reported most systematically in his *Leviathan,* had achieved the same degree of precision, clarity, and rigor formerly found only in the natural sciences. Unlike Machiavelli, however, Hobbes structured his arguments according to the principles of mathematical reasoning. Like the geometrician, Hobbes built his universal science of politics by beginning with an analysis of the simplest elements of human psychology and then proceeding to the hypothetical construction of a complex and closed system. In doing so, he believed that he had created a science of politics whose principles were entirely self-evident and thus ultimately capable of forming that degree of popular consensus that is necessary for an enduring peace.

Finally, in the nineteenth century, the English utilitarian John Stuart Mill (1806–1873) attempted to reformulate the traditional teachings of English liberalism in order to incorporate the findings of philosophical empiricism. As a philosophy of science, empiricism taught that it was only possible to know those realities that were directly experienced through at least one of the five senses. Rejecting the belief in innate ideas, empiricism sought to redefine science in strictly materialistic terms. Accepting this challenge, John Stuart Mill attempted to formulate an ethical and political program that would be consistent with the empirical world view. His efforts to do so produced major reforms within both the Western liberal tradition in general and English society in particular.

As these examples show, Western political science has operated within a variety of intellectual contexts. Whether it was the spiritualism of Plato and Aristotle, the historicism of Machiavelli, the scientism of Hobbes, or the empiricism of Mill, there has always existed a specific set of metaphysical and epistemological assumptions within which the discipline was located. Yet in spite of such variety, certain themes have remained constant. In particular both classical and postclassical political scientists have attempted to discover universal truths based upon the principles of reason. Although the particular understandings of reason may have varied and although the specific political doctrines offered may have differed, each of the theorists discussed claimed that his teachings improved upon those of his predecessors. In short, each claimed that his analysis was not only different but also better. Such a claim implies, of course, the existence of a standard within reality against which the various interpretations can be measured. Thus, although postclassical political scientists may have rejected the spiritual metaphysics of Plato and Aristotle, each in his or her own way nevertheless retained the classical distinction between universal knowledge and particular opinion. In general, Western political science has expressed its faith in the power of universal reason. Yet, as with every act of faith, this commitment is susceptible to the doubt of the nonbeliever. For the modern political scientist this doubt is most clearly present in the challenge of ideology.

The Concept of Ideology

The term *ideology* was coined by the Frenchman Antoine Destutt de Tracy (1754–1836), whose book *Elemens d'ideologie* was first published in 1801. He used the term to refer to his "science of ideas." Influenced by the philosophical empiricism of John Locke and Etienne de Condillac, Tracy believed that it was possible to create a system of logic that would both explain the origin and development of ideas and at the same time assure the continuation of scientific progress. First, through a process of analysis, he reduced all ideas to their engendering experiences. Then he systematically removed all those that could not be traced back to a specific physical experience of the external world. Finally, he reassembled those ideas that remained in order to construct a scientific system which he claimed contained certain knowledge of both humanity and nature. Through this process of analysis, screening, and synthesis, Tracy hoped to create a methodological technique by which it would be possible to achieve perfect, complete, and certain knowledge for all time. Accordingly he exhibited a deep and lasting faith in the power of universal reason.

It is somewhat ironic, then, that the term *ideology* was subsequently appropriated by those who were the most radical critics of the concept of universal reason as it was then understood by Tracy and his followers. Indeed, as the term is currently used, it signifies a denial of the very goal that Tracy originally envisioned for his science of ideas.

Ideology and the Theory of Prejudices

The current meaning most often associated with the term *ideology* presents a radicalization of the theory of prejudices, which was first developed in the seventeenth and eighteenth centuries. This tradition, in turn, was inspired by Francis Bacon's (1561–1626) analysis of what he termed the "idols of the mind." Bacon's critique of the Western intellectual tradition differed from that of previous critics in that it represented a total rejection of the available sources. Rather than first correcting and then building upon the existing traditions of Western science, Bacon believed that it was necessary for modern science to totally reject its past and start anew. His own plans for this new science and the novel civilization it would make possible were to be developed in a work he did not live to complete, *The Great Instauration*. His intentions, however, were clearly expressed in its proem:

> There was but one course left, therefore, to try the whole thing anew upon a better plan, and to commence a total reconstruction of sciences, arts, and all human knowledge raised upon the proper foundations.[2]

To achieve this, Bacon recommended the construction of a new scientific method that would be experimental in design and operate inductively. His own efforts to outline such a procedure were extremely influential, and he is regarded as one of the founders of modern science. As important as this may be, however, it was Bacon's specific critique of the intellectual traditions of the past that contributed most directly to the theory of prejudice in the eighteenth century.

In rejecting the entire tradition of Western science, it became necessary for Bacon to explain how the errors of the past actually developed. If the sciences were so fundamentally erroneous, how could such mistakes have been made so often and by so many? On one hand, Bacon rejected the skeptical argument that the mind was by its very nature incapable of knowing reality. On the other hand, this faith in the potential power of reason led him to an investigation of those external impediments that he believed had prevented the human mind from realizing its full potential. In particular he called attention to the weaknesses of the deductive method, the inadequacy of syllogistic logic, and the distorting powers of the "idols of the mind."

According to Bacon, the idols are specific "notions" or "phantoms" that occupy the mind and have the effect of distorting its perception of reality. Thus, rather than simply recording impressions from the outside world and seeking only to reflect accurately what is already there, a mind under the influence of the idols actually distorts and confuses its materials by impressing upon them its own peculiarities:

> . . . that as an uneven mirror distorts the rays of objects according to its own figure and section, so the mind, when it receives impressions of objects through the sense, cannot be trusted to report them truly, but in forming its notions mixes up its own nature with the nature of things.[3]

For Bacon there were four classes of idols in particular. The *idols of the tribe* were those distortions that are common to the species in general and therefore appear in almost all the work done by individuals. For example, human nature, according to Bacon, seems to require a high degree of order and regularity. Accordingly it is common for a thinker to create a sense of order amidst actual disorder either by assuming the existence of final causes in nature or by projecting a pattern of relationships on to what are in fact irregular events. Similarly the *idols of the cave* are those projections that are rooted in the specific personalities of individual thinkers. For example, some tend to draw distinctions where in fact they don't exist, while others attempt to unify that which in reality should remain distinct. At the same time, some are attracted to what is new and novel, while others respect the ancient and traditional. In each case the results of the inquiries reflect not only the actual facts of the situation but also those particular qualities and characteristics that the observers bring to their studies. In such cases, according to Bacon, the resulting information is too subjective and thus lacks that degree of objectivity that is necessary if one is to achieve a truly disinterested understanding of reality.

Bacon referred to both the idols of the tribe and the idols of the cave as "innate" idols because he believed they are inherent in the very nature of the human mind itself. Being part of human nature, these idols can never be totally removed. By being aware of their distorting presence, however, one can mitigate their effects by subjecting one's work to the rigorous discipline that is part of the scientific method.

The final two classes of idols are similar to one another inasmuch as they are both "adventitious." Rather than springing from the very nature of the mind itself, both the *idols of the market* and the *idols of the theater* are produced by external circumstances. They arise from the false teachings of the past and can be completely controlled simply by replacing such traditions with the doctrines of modern science. For example, the idols of the market are those misunderstandings that result from the improper use of language. By naming things improperly or by creating ill-founded abstractions, one creates an artificial and inappropriate language and thus confuses a natural understanding of things. By paying more attention to how we speak and by following rules that require that we communicate with precision and clarity, it is possible, according to Bacon, to overcome such limitations.

Finally, the idols of the theater are those specific errors that were part of the powerful but nonetheless erroneous scientific traditions of the past. Referring specifically to the work of Aristotle, Pythagoras, Plato, and Gilbert, Bacon rejected the teachings of premodern science as unrealistic and even fanciful. Such idols of the theater, he believed, could be abolished simply by creating a new civilization based upon the doctrines of modern science. Indeed, Bacon's own attempt to found such a new order is contained in his posthumously published utopia, *New Atlantis*.

By emphasizing the social, affective, and psychological impediments that interfere with the pursuit of knowledge, Bacon succeeded in questioning all forms of naive rationalism. Given his arguments, it is clear that an individual's ideas can no longer be considered the simple products of pure reason. On the contrary, our ideas are influenced by a variety of arational factors which, unless disciplined, can interfere with and at times actually oppose the disinterested pursuit of truth. For his part, Bacon was quite confident that such a discipline was available in his newly created method of scientific induction.

Modern Political Science and the Discovery of History

Consequently he saw the destruction of the idols as only the first step in an otherwise positive intellectual program.

In his writings, Bacon was careful to distinguish his critique of natural philosophy from both a critique of religion and a critique of the ethical and political realm. His discussion of the idols and of the failure of traditional knowledge does not include an attack upon either the church or the state. Bacon's own caution on this matter, however, could not prevent his followers from extending his original arguments into precisely those areas he himself had avoided. Indeed, in the eighteenth century the French *philosophes* succeeded in expanding Bacon's theory of the idols into a general theory of prejudices that had obvious political and social implications. The *philosophes* used the term *préjugé* to refer to an entire complex of antirational beliefs that supported the selfish interests of specific groups within French society. Thus in the works of such writers as Helvetius (1715–71) and Holbach (1723–89), Bacon's original analysis of natural philosophy is transformed into a radical critique of class society.

Like many of his Enlightenment colleagues, Helvetius believed in the existence of a natural social and political order whose principles can be understood and proven by unaided reason. That such a natural order is not in fact realized by any given society can be explained as a consequence of the social effect of common prejudices. Captured by their prejudices, most individuals are ignorant of both the true principles of political order and their own disadvantageous situation within society. Consequently, rather than forming their beliefs according to the dictates of reason, they naively adopt the biases, preferences, and opinions sponsored by the powerful social organizations of their day. These organizations, in turn, are concerned with promoting their own special interests, and thus they promulgate only those beliefs that promise to serve their needs.

As a consequence, what the citizens believe to be the time-honored truths of their particular society are, according to the *philosophes*, actually prejudices used to justify the privileges of the powerful and the wealthy. According to Helvetius, both religious dogma and traditional political theory are particularly susceptible of being used in this way. As a theorist, then, he sought to unmask such prejudice and thereby expose the realities of superstition and power to the light of rational analysis:

> Opinion, they say, rules the world. No doubt there are instances where general opinions have overruled sovereigns. But what has

this to do with the power of truth? Does it prove that general opinion is the product of truth? No; experience shows, on the contrary, that almost all moral and political questions are decided by the powerful not by the reasonable. If opinion rules the world, in the long run it is the powerful who rule opinion.[4]

Karl Marx

There is an obvious relationship between Helvetius's desire to unmask the prejudices of his day and Marx's own attempt to expose the ruling ideas of society as essentially the ideas of the ruling class. Like the Enlightenment *philosophes*, Marx wished to challenge the naive rationalism of his contemporaries, and he did so by describing the class-related functions of what at first glance is a set of neutral ideas. In spite of these similarities, however, it is still necessary to differentiate between the Enlightenment concept of prejudice and the Marxist notion of ideology. First, and somewhat ironically, Marx (1818–83) argued that Enlightenment rationalism itself was an example of false thinking. In particular, he accused the rationalists of being naively unaware of the historical and therefore contingent presuppositions that necessarily influenced their own work. For example, Helvetius had written of a natural order whose principles could be discovered by unaided reason and consequently were believed to be valid for all citizens and at all times. Marx, on the other hand, argued that the so-called natural insights of the rationalists were in fact the cultural products of their own particular age. Consequently what they had considered to be universal truths were in actuality the particular beliefs of a specific period. As such they reflected the historically unique conditions and changing needs of that particular time and were not in fact the universally valid principles the *philosophes* had originally sought.

Second, the Enlightenment theory of prejudice was intended to expose particular distortions of the truth. As a consequence, the *philosophes* sought to replace specific superstitions with the correct teachings of reason. They did not, however, doubt the power or the independence of reason as such. Marx's notion of ideology, on the other hand, was much more inclusive. His concern was not so much with particular falsities as with the general relationship between consciousness and being. Whereas the *philosophes* sought to unmask particular prejudices, Marx wished to analyze the structure of false consciousness in general and thereby explain why it is that we have come to see the world through partial and distorted lenses.

Marx's analysis of ideology is closely associated with his understanding of human history. Marx's theory of history, referred to as *historical materialism*, entailed a particular understanding of the relationship between being and consciousness. Specifically, according to Marx, humanity's existence as a social entity determines the various forms of human consciousness. Summarizing this understanding, Friedrich Engels (1820–95), Marx's collaborator, wrote:

> Just as Darwin discovered the law of development of organic nature, so Marx discovered the law of development of human history: the simple fact, hitherto concealed by an overgrowth of ideology, that mankind must first of all, eat, drink, have shelter and clothing before it can pursue politics, science, art, religion, etc.; that therefore the production of the immediate material means of subsistence and consequently the degree of economic development attained by a given people or during a given epoch form the foundation upon which the state institutions, the legal conceptions, art, and even the ideas on religion, of the people concerned have been evolved, and in the light of which they must, therefore, be explained, instead of *vice versa*, as had hitherto been the case.[5]

Unfortunately Engel's explanation somewhat oversimplified Marx's own position. In his *A Contribution to the Critique of Political Economy* of 1859, Marx introduced the concepts of *superstructure* and *substructure* in an attempt to clarify his own position. He referred to the substructure as the sum total of the "relations of production which correspond to a finite stage of development of their material productive forces" and to the superstructure as "the legal, political, religious, aesthetic, or philosophical—in short ideological, forms" of social consciousness.[6] The difficulty in understanding Marx's position arises from a certain ambiguity as to what precisely should be included in his understanding of the substructure and what is the exact relationship between a particular substructure and its superstructural counterpart. Is the substructure simply composed of the existing instruments of production, or does it also include the social context within which such instruments function and which is itself an expression of human consciousness? Is the relationship between the substructure and its superstructure a strictly causal one, or is it somewhat less determinant and consequently more akin to a relationship of affinity? Marx was not always consistent in his treatment of these issues, and consequently commentators have disagreed as to the most accurate interpretation of his argument.

Granting these difficulties, however, it is still possible to gain a general understanding of Marx's conception of ideology by examining *The German Ideology,* an early work which he co-authored with Friedrich Engels, his colleague and sponsor. In this work, Marx presented an overview of his materialist understanding of history. In general, he argued that an adequate explanation of the process of social and historical change can only be found in an examination of the way in which individuals produce their life in common. Whereas the activity of material production (the substructure) is fundamental, the ideas, concepts, and institutions by which this activity is organized and comprehended (the superstructure) is secondary. Consequently, an accurate understanding of history requires that historians focus their attention primarily upon those activities that actually determined its course—i.e., the social relations among individuals during the process of production. Rather than examining theoretical abstractions, the study of history, according to Marx, should begin with an analysis of the empirical realities of life. In particular it should examine the efforts of individuals to produce those means necessary for the satisfaction of their basic material needs. According to Marx, this primary effort informs all that humanity does. The way in which individuals satisfy their needs determines the way in which they can live, and the way in which they live determines who they shall become. Every activity, therefore, is ultimately based upon this primary undertaking, and to understand these activities it is necessary to comprehend their specific relationship to the process of production:

> The production of ideas, of conceptions, of consciousness, is at first directly interwoven with the material activity and the material intercourse of men, the language of real life. Conceiving, thinking, the mental intercourse of men, appears at this stage as the direct efflux of the material behavior. The same applies to mental production as expressed in the language of politics, laws, morality, religion, metaphysics, etc. of a people. . . . Life is not determined by consciousness, but consciousness by life.[7]

Marx's critique of his idealist opponents was based upon his belief that they ignored the true relationship between ideology and practice. According to Marx, ideology is a necessary intellectual derivative of primary economic practices. Those before him, however, had failed to acknowledge this fact. They either believed that ideas somehow existed in an objective sphere beyond the realm of practice, or they held to the illusion that consciousness itself actually enjoys a certain causal efficacy vis-à-vis concrete historical reality. In either case, according to Marx, such interpretations fail to appreciate the true meaning of historical change. For Marx, history is neither the story of the rise and fall of empires, nor that of the growth of the idea of freedom, nor that of the conquest of paganism by Christianity. Indeed, these events may have happened, but they occurred only at the level of the superstructure and as a consequence were causally insignificant for determining the long-run fate of humanity. According to Marx, the true meaning of history as the dialectical development of the forces of production becomes apparent only if one succeeds in penetrating to an examination of the substructure itself. In his effort to do so, Marx focused his analysis upon an examination of the history of property. He did so because he believed that the forces of production were most evident in the various forms of ownership that structured the social division of labor. In his *German Ideology,* he offered the following scheme, which he believed described the four periods of human history.

1. *Tribal ownership.* In this earliest period of history, the means of production were extremely primitive. Tribes relied upon fishing, hunting, and basic agriculture. Although the division of labor was minimal, slavery existed; and the social structure was essentially an extension of the family.

2. *Ancient communal and state ownership.* In this more advanced economy, several tribes came together to form a town. With the emergence of towns, there developed a division between material and intellectual labor and a subsequent tension between the needs of the city and those of the country. Within the cities, distinct manufacturing and commercial interests emerged, while in the countryside, some peasants lost their land and were thus forced to become agricultural workers. Slavery existed, but the slaves were owned by the community in general and not by individuals. Private property began to emerge, but it was still subordinate to the dominant forms of communal ownership.

3. *Feudal or estate ownership.* Although a separation between industry and commerce existed, the division of labor within feudalism remained relatively simple. Property was based upon the community and organized either as feudalities in the countryside or guilds in the cities. Both forms, however, were restricted by the limited conditions of production, whereby industry was based upon traditional crafts, and agriculture consisted of the small-scale and primitive cultivation of the land. Feudalism was an essentially agricultural economy and relied primarily upon the labor of serfs. Politically, feudal communities were organized as monarchies.

4. *Capitalism.* With the development of capitalism, industrial production replaced agriculture as the most important source of economic wealth. As the division of labor became more complex, a new class of merchants arose which encouraged the development of big industry and heavy manufacturing. The proletariat, or industrial wage laborers, replaced the serfs as the most important producing class, while the owners of industry, or bourgeoisie, began to introduce mechanization and automation into the manufacturing process. As trade expanded, the increasing competition for foreign markets required that the manufacturing states undertake a policy of colonization in order to sell their goods and acquire cheap labor from abroad.

Marx's understanding of historical evolution was related to his conception of ideology inasmuch as he believed that with each new economic substructure there also appears a new and more appropriate ideological superstructure. A change in the dominant ideas, beliefs, and concepts of a society can therefore be explained in terms of its evolving substructural base. New ideas emerge because they are required by the newly developing forces of production. Thus, in *The Poverty of Philosophy* Marx wrote:

> In acquiring new productive forces men change their mode of production; and in changing their mode of production, in changing the way of earning their living, they change all their social relations. The hand-mill gives you society with the feudal lord; the steam mill, society with the industrial capitalist. The same men who establish their social relations in conformity with their material productivity, produce also principles, ideas, and categories in conformity with their social relations. Thus these ideas, these categories, are as little eternal as the relations which they express. They are historical and transitory products.[8]

Although the above statement was specifically directed against the writings of the French anarchist Proudhon (1809–1865), its general relevance is quite clear. For Marx, the traditional belief in the possibility of achieving universal truth within a class society was obviously untenable. Past ideas have been appropriate only in terms of that specific substructure which first produced them and of which they were a more-or-less-necessary reflection. According to Marx, the so-called natural order of Enlightenment political philosophy was not a universally valid discovery, as Helvetius had originally believed. It was instead a particular intellectual product of the capitalist age and appeared meaningful only within the context of that specific period. Similarly from Marx's perspective, Plato's and Aristotle's claim to have founded a science of politics based on the principles of universal reason could only be accredited by the particular form of consciousness typical of an ancient slave society. The "truth" of classical political science was thus a partial truth at best. Given the transitory nature of its historical base, classical political science could reflect and comprehend only conditions similar to those of its own substructure. Yet inasmuch as Western history has moved beyond such a substructure, the teachings of classical political science represent an ideology irrelevant to the concerns of the present.

Marx's critique of the ideological consciousness of his predecessors is not limited to the charge of partiality. For Marx, ideological thinking is not only time bound and narrow, but at the same time fundamentally biased and distorted. It is, as he termed it, a product of false consciousness.

Since ideology is a creation produced in conformity with the material and social relations of a particular period in history, it necessarily reflects those same qualities that are characteristic of its substructure. Specifically, inasmuch as the socioeconomic substructure of a class-divided society is characterized by the presence of irrationality and alienation, so too will these conditions be present within the superstructure. As we have seen, Marx differentiated among four distinct socioeconomic substructures. Yet, as different as the ancient tribal society was from its modern, capitalistic counterpart, each of the precommunist forms of society shared in a fundamental and common weakness, for according to Marx, all noncommunist societies depend upon a systematic process of class exploitation. Whether this exploitation is that of the slaves by their masters, serfs by their lords, or the proletariat by the capitalists, the very existence of such a situation is indicative of a certain historical immaturity and attests to the presence of human and social alienation. For Marx, life within such an environment is actually "prehuman" and its intellectual products necessarily exhibit distortions typical of a false or immature form of consciousness.

In addition to reproducing social and economic immaturity at the intellectual level, ideological thinking also serves an exploitive purpose. By masquerading as an "objective" set of truths, ideological thinking necessarily distorts the reality of mankind's actual condition. By treating the destructive features of alienated existence as if they are necessary and proper characteristics of a natural or inevitable order, ideological thinking serves to justify that exploitation that is intrinsic to class rule. In short, every ideology necessarily promotes the selfish interests of the ruling classes:

> The ideas of the ruling class are in every epoch the ruling ideas, i.e. the class which is the ruling material force of society is at the same time its ruling intellectual force. . . . The ruling ideas are nothing more than the ideal expression of the dominant material relationships, the dominant material relationships grasped as ideas; hence of the relationships which make the one class the ruling one, therefore, the ideas of its dominance.[9]

Marx's understanding of historical materialism had as one of its effects the binding of ideas to history; yet inasmuch as he held a progressivist view of historical evolution, he could look forward to a future in which false ideologies would eventually disappear and be replaced by the insights of true consciousness. This expectation, in turn, was supported by Marx's understanding of revolution. In the *Communist Manifesto* he wrote, "The history of all hitherto existing society is the history of class struggles."[10] As we have seen, Marx believed that every society is based upon a fundamental class antagonism involving the exploitation of the oppressed. In time such antagonisms become open class struggles leading to revolutionary warfare. Such revolutions, in turn, result in the creation of new and more efficient forms of social organization. Thus, for example, Marx argued that capitalism was the result of that class warfare between the nobility and the bourgeoisie that brought about the destruction of the feudal order. Similarly he predicted that the future communist society would first come about only after the successful conclusion of the apparently imminent proletarian revolution. In each case where a class revolution was in fact capable of transforming the social order, it was only because the objective material conditions for such a transformation had already been realized. According to Marx, then, class revolution was not something that could simply be wished to completion; rather, certain objective conditions had to be met. Specifically, a society is considered ripe for revolution only when its productive and technological capabilities have so expanded as to have outgrown those particular institutions and practices by which they are currently organized and administered. Indeed it was precisely such an imbalance between the "forces and forms of production" that Marx believed characterized the condition of capitalism in his own day.

Like its predecessors, the proletarian revolution would destroy the society of the past and thereby create the society of the future. Yet, unlike its predecessors, it would do so in such a way as actually to transform the human condition itself. It would, according to Marx, be the first "total revolution." Although Marx refused to speculate about the exact organization of the future communist society, he did nonetheless suggest several essential characteristics. For example, in mature communism, there would be no state, and as a consequence the citizens would be free to govern themselves. At the same time, each individual would produce according to his or her abilities and be rewarded according to his or her needs. Thus freed from the necessity of earning a wage, people would work, not as a compulsory activity, but rather as a means to express their creative skills and abilities. Similarly, with the common ownership of the social means of production there would be no private property; and as a consequence, all class divisions would necessarily disappear. The traditional division of labor thus would be replaced by a more fluid situation in which each person could work in a variety of careers depending upon his or her changing needs.

As important as these institutional changes would be, however, they would not constitute the real achievement of the communist revolution. For Marx, communism would not be simply one more set of institutional relationships; rather it would represent the culmination of a long historical development in which humanity would finally achieve the full realization of its natural potential and power. Specifically, in communism Marx foresaw an end to human alienation. Those problematic conditions that had characterized so much of human history would disappear as social and personal existence finally achieved their full and perfected form. The complete and radical nature of this hoped-for transformation is evident in the following statement by Marx:

> . . . there is communism as the positive abolition of private property
> and thus of human self-alienation and therefore the real reappropria-
> tion of the human essence by and for man. . . . It is the genuine solu-
> tion of the antagonism between man and nature and between man
> and man. It is the true solution of the struggle between existence and
> essence, between objectification and self-affirmation, between free-
> dom and necessity, between individual and species. It is the solu-
> tion to the riddle of history and knows itself to be this solution.[11]

Given Marx's understanding of the structure of consciousness,
the humanization of the substructure necessarily leads to a corresponding humanization of the superstructure. With the success of the
proletarian revolution, the false forms of ideological consciousness
will be replaced by a consciousness capable of true knowledge. For
Marx, then, ideology appears to be a specific form of untruth created
by the division of labor and necessarily associated with the existence
of the class system. As history "corrects" these conditions, so too will
it "correct" ideological false consciousness. Until that time, however, there seems to be little justification for accrediting the possibility of a universally valid science of politics. Whether such a skepticism rightfully applies to Marxism itself is, of course, a question
implicit within Marx's own arguments. Indeed, if Marx's understanding of prerevolutionary ideological consciousness is correct,
what then is the status of his own ideas? As products of the prerevolutionary era, can they claim a universal validity? Or is Marxism itself
simply another form of ideology?

Karl Mannheim

One of those who raised these and similar questions most forcefully
was the Hungarian-born sociologist Karl Mannheim, (1893–1947).
Influenced by both German historicist philosophy and Marxist sociological analysis, Mannheim accepted the general thesis of Marx's critique of abstract rationalism. Like Marx he insisted that any adequate
analysis of ideas must include an examination of the specific historical, social, and political conditions within which they first emerged.
Yet unlike Marx he was not willing to draw the politically useful distinction between prerevolutionary false consciousness and its post-
revolutionary corrected forms. According to Mannheim, all thought
was existentially determined and, as a consequence, none could

rightfully claim for itself a special or nonideological status. Thus by radicalizing Marx's own arguments, Mannheim created a theory of total ideology that he termed the "sociology of knowledge":

> As long as one does not call his own position into question but regards it as absolute, while interpreting his opponent's ideas as a mere reflection of the social positions they occupy, the decisive step forward has not yet been taken. . . . But since, in such an instance, one is interested merely in a sociological analysis of the opponent's ideas, one never gets beyond a highly restricted, or what I should like to call a special, formulation of the theory. In contrast to this special formulation, the general form of the total conception of ideology is being used by the analyst when he has the courage to subject, not just the adversary's point of view, but all points of view, including his own, to the ideological analysis.[12]

The task Mannheim set for the sociology of knowledge was to provide an analysis of the necessary relationship between the structure of knowledge on one hand and the structure of its underlying sociohistorical situation on the other. His own best effort to meet this challenge is found in his *Ideology and Utopia,* published in English in 1936. As a sociologist, Mannheim emphasized the importance of social groups. Consequently the primary unit of analysis for the sociology of knowledge was the group and not the individual. From this, all forms of individual behavior—including thinking—were to be traced back to that particular set of social groups that created and encouraged such activity. Strictly speaking, according to Mannheim, isolated individuals don't think; people in groups do. Thus if one is to comprehend the full significance of an idea, one must first locate that idea vis-à-vis the specific historical goals of a concrete social group. Like Marx, then, Mannheim understood ideas as the intellectual manifestations of underlying social interests, and similarly he wished to penetrate to an analysis of the "real" substructure of human consciousness. Unlike Marx, however, he believed that such a substructure included more than one's class identification. On the contrary, there existed a wide variety of economic, geographical, political, and occupational groups. Each was identified by its own shared character, and each sought to acquire that power by which to serve its own selfish interests:

> . . . they [humans] act with and against one another in diversely organized groups and while doing so they think with and against one

another. These persons, bound together into groups, strive in accordance with the character and position of the groups to which they
belong to change the surrounding world of nature and society or attempt to maintain it in a given condition. It is the direction of this
will to change or to maintain, of this collective activity which produces the guiding thread for the emergence of their problems, their
concepts, and their forms of thought.[13]

Focusing primarily upon the history of political thought, Mannheim classified all political ideas either as *ideologies* or as *utopias*.
Ideologies are the shared ideas of the dominant groups or classes
within a given society. As such they function to legitimate the status
quo and are so immediately bound to the interests of the ruling classes
that they actually fail to recognize those facts that would undermine
the rulers' sense of domination. As a result, ideological thinking ob-
scures the real condition of society and is, in this sense, a form of false
consciousness. Utopias, on the other hand, are the theories and ideas
of the aspiring or oppressed groups. Committed either to the destruction or the transformation of the status quo, utopian thought focuses
exclusively upon those aspects of social reality that threaten the given
order. As a consequence it, too, is incapable of providing an adequate
diagnosis of the actual situation. Like ideological thinking, utopian-
ism is a form of false consciousness. According to Mannheim, then,
the difference between an ideology and a utopia is not the same as the
traditional difference between truth and error. Traditionally, to speak
of truth and falsity is to imply the existence of a single objective standard within reality against which various opinions can be measured.
For Mannheim, however, all historical—i.e., nonstatic or
nonmathematical—knowledge is "relational." Its "truth" or "falsity" can only be formulated with reference to the position or perspective of the observer. Thus the value of a particular statement is
determined by the utility of its contribution to the group perspective.
Inasmuch as all groups are engaged in a continual struggle for power,
ideas actually become weapons in the service of a group's arational
interests. Consequently, for Mannheim, it is not the love of wisdom
that guides the search for truth but rather the more fundamental desire of one group to dominate another. Just as superficial intellectual
differences can often be reduced to more fundamental philosophical
disagreements, so too can these philosophical disagreements be reduced further to an underlying competition among ultimately antagonistic interest groups:

We may regard competition as such a representative case in which extra-theoretical processes affect the emergence and development of knowledge. Competition controls not merely economic activity through the mechanism of the market, not merely the course of political and social events, but furnishes also the motor impulse behind diverse interpretations of the world which, when their social background is uncovered, reveal themselves as the intellectual expressions of conflicting groups struggling for power.[14]

Mannheim's concept of total ideology offers several obvious challenges to the classical understanding of political science. First, classical political science presupposed the universal authority of philosophical consciousness. As we have seen, classical thinkers such as Plato and Aristotle had argued that reason allowed one to discover the transcendent principles of order, and in so doing, enabled the philosopher to create a form of human and social order within his or her own political society. From Mannheim's perspective, however, such a project is necessarily ill-conceived; what Plato believed to be universal truth is, according to Mannheim, really the ideological bias of the Athenian aristocracy. Rather than transcending the realm of the particular as Plato had claimed, classical political science actually preserved it by creating for the Athenian status quo its appropriate intellectual form.

Second, as we have seen, classical political science was created in response to a specific political problem, i.e., the need to find a way by which to judge among the inevitable variety of political opinions. Both Plato and Aristotle had argued that a philosophically informed political science provided such a measure. Yet if Mannheim is correct, the classical solution is obviously inappropriate. So, too, is the Marxist; for as Mannheim argued, there is no compelling reason to exempt proletarian consciousness from the analysis of total ideology. All political thinking, according to Mannheim, is rooted in the existential context of group struggle. Given this, one must ask if there can ever be any solution to the problem of disagreement which does not violate the central principle of "relationism." Mannheim believed that there can, and he developed this solution in his discussion of the intellectual.

Mannheim's argument that all thinking possesses an inherently ideological character necessarily undermines any appeal to verisimilitude. Accordingly, one cannot differentiate among opinions in terms of how closely they resemble the truth unless one can first achieve an objective understanding of the truth against which the opinions in question may be tested. The ability of reason to do this, however, is precisely what Mannheim denied. Given this, it may appear that Mannheim's sociology of knowledge necessarily leads to a radical relativism in which all opinions are to be treated equally and none is to be preferred to another. Mannheim, himself, however, refused to accept this conclusion. Indeed, he believed that it is possible to show that some intellectual perspectives are in reality superior to others and that this in turn could be established according to the principle of fecundity. Specifically, opinions that are more comprehensive and thereby potentially more fruitful are to be preferred to those that are more restricted and thereby less promising:

> It is natural that here we must ask which of the various points of view is the best. And for this too there is a criterion. As in the case of visual perspective where certain positions have the advantage of revealing the decisive features of the object, so here pre-eminence is given to that perspective which gives evidence of the greatest comprehensiveness and the greatest fruitfulness in dealing with empirical materials.[15]

Fortunately, according to Mannheim, cultural and educational developments within modern society have had the effect of creating a new class of intellectuals characterized by this ability to create such comprehensive and fruitful perspectives. Relatively unaffected by the traditional structures of social reality, the modern intelligentsia forms an almost classless stratum which, as a consequence, is more or less socially unattached. This freedom, in turn, allows the intellectual to develop a sympathetic appreciation for a variety of perspectives—each of which is associated with a particular set of group interests. By appreciating a number of perspectives, the intellectual is able to develop a synthetic viewpoint on the total situation of his or her society, and from that position he or she can suggest those compromises and coalitions that are necessary for a peaceful and stable social order. For Mannheim, then, the ideal political regime would be one that is ruled by the intelligentsia.

At first glance, it may appear that Mannheim's solution to the diversity of political opinions is similar to that of Plato and Aristotle. Indeed, Plato's philosopher-king, Aristotle's mature person of practical wisdom, and Mannheim's intellectual all appear to be characterized by an attitude of openness that distinguishes their thinking from the opinions and beliefs of their fellow citizens. Yet the differences between the classical person of wisdom and Mannheim's intellectual are important ones, and by recognizing them one can appreciate the different claims being made by classical political science on one hand and by modern political ideology on the other.

Plato's philosopher-king is empowered to rule because of his understanding of the order of Being. This knowledge, in turn, informs his very life and enables him to serve as a living model for others. He is open, but he is open to the reality of Being itself, and this openness allows him to participate in that right order that is potentially available to everyone. Mannheim's intellectuals, on the other hand, do not claim to know the order of reality. What they know is simply a variety of opinions about that order. Their openness, therefore, is not toward the oneness of Being but rather toward the diversity of history. It is the Intellectuals' sympathetic appreciation of many interests rather than their knowledge of the transcendent source of order that supports their claim to power. From Plato's perspective, then, Mannheim's intellectual remains a captive of the realm of opinion. From Mannheim's perspective, however, Plato's philosopher-king is simply an advocate of narrowly defined and ultimately selfish group interests.

Notes

1. Machiavelli, *Discourses on the First Ten Books of Titus Livius,* trans. Christian E. Detmold (New York: Random House, 1950), p. 105.

2. Francis Bacon, *The New Organon and Related Writings* (Indianapolis: Bobbs-Merrill, 1960), p. 4.

3. Bacon, *Organon*, p. 22.

4. As quoted in Hans Barth, *Truth and Ideology*, trans. Frederic Lilge (Berkeley and Los Angeles: University of California Press, 1976), p. 35.

5. Friedrich Engels, "Speech at the Graveside of Karl Marx," in Robert Tucker (ed.), *The Marx-Engels Reader*, 2d ed., (New York: W. W. Norton, 1978), p. 681.

6. Karl Marx, "A Contribution to the Critique of Political Economy," in David McLellan (ed.), *Karl Marx: Selected Writings* (New York: Oxford University Press, 1977), p. 389.

7. Karl Marx and Friedrich Engels, "The German Ideology," in McLellan, *Writings*, p. 164.

8. Karl Marx, "The Poverty of Philosophy," in McLellan, *Writings*, p. 202.

9. Karl Marx and Friedrich Engels, "German Ideology," in McLellan, *Writings*, p. 176.

10. Karl Marx and Friedrich Engels, "The Communist Manifesto," in McLellan, *Writings*, p. 222.

11. Karl Marx, "The Economic and Philosophical Manuscripts," in McLellan, *Writings*, p. 89.

12. Karl Mannheim, *Ideology and Utopia*, trans. Louis Wirth and Edward Shils (New York: Harcourt, Brace, & World, 1936), p. 77.

13. Mannheim, *Ideology*, p. 4.

14. Mannheim, *Ideology*, p. 269.

15. Mannheim, *Ideology*, p. 301.

Recommended Readings

Barth, Hans. *Truth and Ideology*. Translated by Frederic Lilge. Berkeley and Los Angeles: University of California Press, 1976.

Carlsnaes, Walter. *The Concept of Ideology and Political Analysis*. Westport, Conn.: Greenwood Press, 1981.

Connolly, William E. *Political Science and Ideology*. New York: Atherton Press, 1967.

Cox, Richard, ed. *Ideology, Politics, and Political Theory*. Belmont, Calif.: Wadsworth Publishing Co., 1969.

Germino, Dante. *Beyond Ideology: The Revival of Political Theory*. New York: Harper and Row, 1967.

Plamenatz, John. *Ideology*. New York: Praeger, 1970.

Seliger, Martin. *The Marxist Conception of Ideology: A Critical Essay*. New York: Cambridge University Press, 1977.

Shklar, Judith, ed. *Political Theory and Ideology*. New York: Macmillan, 1966.

C H A P T E R 3

Contemporary Political Science
and the
Appeal to Natural Science

Ideology and the Threat of Relativism

The theory of ideology as developed in Marx's *The German Ideology* was originally intended as a critique of certain idealistic teachings within the works of Ludwig Feuerbach (1804–72) and Max Stirner (1806–56). At the same time it had the more immediate political aim of presenting Marx's own understanding of socialism to the various members of the Communist Correspondence Committees which he and Engels had founded earlier. On one hand, then, the arguments of *The German Ideology* were intended to be quite specific and, as such, were designed to present a historical materialist alternative to the crude materialism of Feuerbach, the naive rationalism of German idealism, and the romantic individualism of Stirner. Yet at the same time the logic of the argument Marx used for his own specific purposes could easily be expanded to include a number of issues that he himself never specifically intended. As an example, we have already seen how Mannheim extended Marx's critique of ideology to include the ideological analysis of Marxism itself.

Similarly it soon became apparent that one of the possibilities implicit within the theory of ideology was that of a radical moral and epistemological relativism. Although both Marx and Mannheim had attempted to provide a special epistemological status for the perspective of certain groups—e.g., Marx's proletariat and Mannheim's intellectual—a thoroughly consistent application of their own logic could easily be used to deny the legitimacy of such a strategy. An ex-

43

ample of such a radicalized relativism can be found in the writings of the French communist Paul Nizan (1905–40). Interpreting Marx's theory of historical materialism to mean that human consciousness was not structured according to its own unique principles but rather was dependent upon those of a different order, Nizan believed, as did Mannheim, that all thinking is purely instrumental. In short, thought serves the material interests of the thinker; "It does not serve the True (which does not exist) nor the Eternal (which does not exist)."[1] However, if neither the True, the Universal, nor the Eternal exists, how then does one establish the adequacy of one's own arguments? Apparently Marx would have done so by referring to their "proletarian" character, while Mannheim would have necessarily emphasized their empirical fecundity and conceptual promise. Yet, as a radical relativist, Nizan denied the need for such a justification. According to him, our arguments can never in fact be justified; rather, as expressions of specific material interests, they can only be asserted:

> To this I would reply only that I do not like being put on the spot in this way. I personally have no intention of asking Reason if I am right. . . . Our school teachers taught us that every sequence of thought begins with certain axiomatic statements. . . . And so we will have our axioms, and we do not have the slightest desire to prove that they are valid.[2]

It should be apparent that Nizan's denial of the existence of any standard by which one's basic beliefs can be justified implies at the same time a denial of the possibility of a universal science of politics. If the True, the Universal, or the Eternal does not exist, any challenge to the validity of a specific opinion is meaningless and without consequence. At the same time, if every opinion is to be permitted, then no opinion may be denied; and each individual is thereby entitled to hold to whatever values he or she may choose to adopt. For Nizan, all ideas have become simply weapons in the struggle for power. By denying an idea's intellectual substance and thus its possible claim upon us, Nizan has in fact deprived us of the possibility of ever differentiating the practice of political science from the techniques of political propaganda.

Nizan's critique of Western culture is as bold as it is clear. However, to a large degree, he has simply developed that logic of ethical and epistemological relativism which is already implicit within the modern theory of ideology itself. If, as traditionally believed, the universal validity of our ideas depends upon their foundation in reason and if, as the theory of ideology maintains, that foundation is itself based upon a deeper, more powerful, and yet ultimately irrational force, then the quest for a general science of politics is in vain. Given this challenge to the traditional understanding of political science, it is not surprising that many contemporary political scientists have reacted to this situation by seeking to establish a more certain grounding for their discipline.

Some, such as Eric Voegelin and Leo Strauss, have attempted to reintroduce the perspective of the classical tradition by carefully reexamining its most important documents. By showing what the classical thinkers actually taught and by presenting the reasons for these teachings, they hoped to demonstrate the relevance of this tradition for the modern age. Others, however, have turned to an altogether different source and use as their model for political inquiry the practices of modern natural science. Thus, rather than attempting to recapture the classical age, these thinkers prefer to explore that cultural revolution which was partially responsible for its demise—i.e., the modern scientific revolution of the seventeenth century.

It is generally argued that the modern scientific revolution found its philosophical support in the writings of Francis Bacon (1561–1626) and Rene Descartes (1596–1650). Even during Descartes's own lifetime, such political thinkers as Thomas Hobbes (1588–1679) began to call attention to the remarkable progress the natural sciences were making. Unlike such "moral sciences" as ethics and politics, which appeared to Hobbes to be no further developed in the seventeenth century than they were in ancient Greece, the physical sciences had made obvious and important progress. This being the case, it appeared to many that the natural sciences should be used as a model for the restructuring of the moral and political sciences. Specifically, it was hoped that political science would adopt those precise methods of inquiry and proof that had appeared to work so well for the natural sciences in general and for physics in particular. During the eighteenth and nineteenth centuries this spirit of "scientism" (or the appeal to natural science as a model for all forms of human inquiry) was an important feature of the Enlightenment tradition associated with Voltaire (1694–1778), Diderot (1713–84), and D'Alembert (1717–83). More recently, in the twentieth century, this same appeal to the spirit of scientific reasoning has been an important characteristic in the work of the German sociologist Max Weber (1864–1920) on one hand and on the other in the teachings of a group of American social scientists who are loosely referred to as "members of the behavioral movement."

Max Weber

The writings of Max Weber have exerted a profound influence upon much of contemporary social science. A prolific scholar, Weber wrote on a wide variety of topics, including such themes as the development of capitalism, the sociology of religion, the history of law, and the apparently related processes of secularization, rationalization, and disenchantment within the modern world. These and other substantive themes were explored in such books as *The Protestant Ethic and the Spirit of Capitalism; The Religion of China: Confucianism and Taoism; Ancient Judaism; General Economic History;* and his most important work, *Economy and Society.* In addition to such substantive and relatively concrete issues, Weber was also deeply concerned about the more formal aspects of the disciplines within which he worked. Specifically he was preoccupied with the question of methodology and sought to discover a set of methods that would establish the scientific character of sociological and political inquiry.

On one hand Weber acknowledged both the impossibility of writing a truly presuppositionless history and the inevitability of theoretical distortions arising from the subtle influence of unconscious motives, irrational beliefs, and social prejudices. On the other hand, he believed that it was possible nonetheless to develop a methodology that could guarantee an essential degree of social-scientific objectivity. In general he built this program upon the recognition of three key distinctions:

1. Methodological individualism as opposed to methodological holism.
2. The construction of ideal types as opposed to the formulation of general laws.
3. The recognition of facts as opposed to the advocacy of values.

As a methodological individualist, Weber focused upon those specific and deliberate actions by which individuals attempted to influence the behavior of others. In doing so, he rejected the holistic attempt to interpret the meaning of a part in terms of its contribution to the whole and sought instead to explain the meaning of the whole by reducing it to its constitutive particulars. For example, according to Weber, such concepts as "state," "association," or "church" are understood to be categories of human interaction, the meaning of which can best be explained by reducing them to the specific actions of their individual participants.

Weber's effort to understand that which is unique, specific, and individual also served to establish his preference for the ideal type as his chief diagnostic tool. The ideal type is a pure-case construction by which Weber attempted to summarize the common features of associated empirical phenomena. Thus he could write of "the capitalist," "the bureaucrat," or "the sociologist" as an ideal type by comparison with which actual individual capitalists, bureaucrats, or sociologists can be described and explained. The ideal type as such never really exists but is rather a logical construction by which the common attributes of those individuals who actually do exist can be recognized as "typical" of that classification. In this respect his methods differed from both those of the natural scientists and those of the social scientists who imitated the former in their quest for the formulation of general laws. According to Weber, the physical sciences seek to discover and formulate invariable natural laws and, as a result, are necessarily concerned with an examination of that which is both universal and abstract. At the same time, those social scientists, like Marx, who imitate the natural scientist by attempting to deduce a particular event from the operation of a general historical law are, according to Weber, bound to misunderstand the specific and unique character of those phenomena they are seeking to explain. Unlike the natural sciences, therefore, the social sciences, according to Weber, are properly concerned with the particular and concrete rather than with the universal and abstract:

> The type of social science in which we are interested is an *empirical science* of concrete reality. Our aim is the understanding of the characteristic uniqueness of the reality in which we move. We wish to understand on the one hand the relationships and the cultural significance of individual events in their contemporary manifestations and on the other, causes of their being historically *so* and not otherwise.[3]

Of the three distinctions Weber offered in his attempt to establish a scientific methodology for the study of politics, perhaps the most controversial, and yet at the same time the most influential, was that of the fact-value dichotomy. Although this position did not originate with Weber himself, his own presentation of the traditional arguments has been a particularly influential one.

For Weber, the factual is that portion of reality that is empirically verifiable. Values, on the other hand, are simply the preferences, tastes, and desires people express as they choose those ends they seek to attain. Rather than being objective realities that can be studied impartially and dispassionately, values are in effect the products of human will and consequently remain "real" only in view of those very passions that first created them.

Weber believed that just as modern natural science has properly refused to investigate formal and final causation, so too should the social sciences refrain from debating the intrinsic worth of specific value preferences. Whereas facts are empirical givens, values are the results of a decision or a choice; consequently the two categories have a different logical status. Fact can be analyzed according to a specific methodological process, and the accuracy of any factual account can be tested, confirmed, or refuted by others. Values, on the other hand, exist as preferences, and inasmuch as there is no principle in nature according to which one may rationally discriminate among preferences, there is no scientifically acceptable way of justifying certain values over others. In this sense, then, Weber believed that the social sciences were to be value free. When values clash, reason must remain silent if it wishes to remain scientific:

> "Scientific" pleading is meaningless in principle because the various value spheres of the world stand in irreconcilable conflict with each other.[4]

Given this argument, Weber restricted the task of the social sciences to "the analytical ordering of empirical reality."[5] Compared to the more ambitious project found in classical political science, Weberian social science offers a more limited set of expectations. Yet, by limiting the range of science, Weber also believed that he was securing its objectivity and power. Modern social science, according to Weber, can aid people by developing their ability for rigorous and methodical thought. At the same time, by accurately examining the facts of a specific situation, modern social science allows one to gain a certain power over reality and thereby achieve a degree of control over his or her own destiny. Finally, Weberian social science can improve our ability to calculate which means would most effectively accomplish the ends we may happen to choose. At the same time, however, if one were to ask, "But which ends should we choose?" or "Which ends are necessary for the good life?" Weber's reply would be both sober and straightforward:

> Under these internal presuppositions, what is the meaning of science as a vocation now after all these former illusions, the "way to true being," the "way to true art," the "way to true nature," the "way to true God," the "way to true happiness," have been dispelled? Tolstoi has given the simplest answer, with the words "Science is meaningless because it gives no answer to our question, the only question important for us: "What shall we do and how shall we live?" That science does not give an answer to this is indisputable.[6]

Given this, the contrast between Weberian social science and classical political science could not be clearer. As we have seen, classical political science was created in an effort to answer the practical question, "How should we live?" That question, in turn, both set the focus for and guided the investigations of the classical analyst. Weberian social science, on the other hand, begins by refusing to accept the scientific relevance of such questions.

What it loses in scope by this act of theoretical closure, it hopes to offset by its gains in precision and objectivity. As a consequence, Weberian political science is presented by its advocates as an alternative to both the potential dogmatism of classical reason and the implicit relativism of modern ideology.

The Behavioral Movement

Weber's own attempt to provide a scientific foundation for the social sciences was only one of several factors that would eventually influence the development of behavioralism within American political science. Like Weber, many American political scientists had felt the need for a new and more empirically rigorous approach to the study of political reality. Traditionally much of American political science had focused upon the analysis and description of political institutions. However, at the beginning of the twentieth century, some, such as Charles E. Merriam, began to advocate the systematic study of political behavior as a complement to the traditional and more formal analysis of governmental institutions. This recommendation appealed not only to academics but also to government officials, who were interested in the possibility that such an approach would allow one to predict certain forms of political behavior and thereby aid in the rationalization of the policy process. By the end of the Second World War, research produced by those within the behavioral movement had achieved such a level of recognition that it was able to compete successfully for research support from such important organizations as the Social Science Research Council and the Carnegie, Rockefeller, and Ford foundations. Indeed with the development in the 1950s of such new research techniques as the "survey method," which allowed one to study political attitudes and to analyze the behavior of individuals rather than simply relying upon aggregate data, the behavioral movement had managed to establish itself as a significant, if not dominant, tradition within American political science.

Although behavioral political scientists display a wide variety of interests and consequently do not constitute a united school, there are nonetheless certain common characteristics that express the nature of the movement. For example, behavioral political science is, in general, concerned with the analysis of individual or small-group behavior. As a result, its most productive work has been in such fields as voting behavior, political participation, and political psychology. At the same time, behavioral political science is also committed to the development and refinement of new research techniques. Thus sample surveying, research experimentation, and content analysis are specific examples of behavioralism's general effort to develop new methods that address the problems of observation and verification and provide thereby for a greater degree of quantification and testing. Finally, inasmuch as behavioralism is a modern expression of the scientistic tradition, the truly distinctive feature of the behavioral movement is to be found in its explicit attempt to imitate the practices of natural science. For example, the behavioralist political scientist David Truman writes:

> More narrowly, and perhaps more accurately, the phrase [behavioral sciences] refers to those bodies of knowledge, in whatever academic department they may be found, that provide or aspire to provide "verified principles" of human behavior through the use of methods of inquiry similar to those of the natural sciences.[7]

In general the behavioral movement understands the characteristic feature of modern natural science as being its commitment to an essentially empirical methodology. As such, behavioralism too distinguishes between facts on one hand and values on the other. Whereas the former lend themselves to the methods of the natural sciences, the latter do not and are, as a consequence, beyond the scope of a rigorously empirical scientific analysis. Thus, for example, Robert Dahl writes:

> The empirical political scientist is concerned with what *is*, as he says, not with what *ought* to be. Hence he finds it difficult and uncongenial to assume the historic burden of the political philosopher who attempted to determine, prescribe, elaborate, and employ ethical standards—values, to use the fashionable terms—in appraising political acts and political systems. The behaviorally minded student of politics is prepared to *describe* values as empirical data; but qua "scientist" he seeks to avoid prescription or inquiry into the grounds on which judgments of value can properly be made.[8]

As Dahl's statement clearly shows, behavioralism understands the scientific enterprise as one solely concerned with the description and possible prediction of empirical events. Accordingly, as a scientist one may describe the fact that certain values exist and at the same time attempt to analyze the actual consequences that may follow from the adoption of certain commitments. But a person who attempted to discuss the essential merit of a particular value or to argue for the intrinsic superiority of one set of values over another would at that point no longer be able to claim the authority of science. From this perspective, then, the political scientist as scientist is incapable of speaking to the question of whether any given value or end is superior in kind to another. Although an individual may be vitally concerned with such a question as a citizen, as a scientist he or she is not in a position to contribute meaningfully to a discussion of this nature. Thus, whereas classical political science understood itself as both arising from and being guided by the practical political questions facing the citizenry, modern behavioral political science posits a necessary distinction between the realm of theory (the analytical ordering of empirical facts) and the realm of practice (the engaged pursuit of specific values). Indeed it argues that, unless such a distinction is carefully maintained, political science will collapse into a form of political ideology. In developing this distinction between the political scientist as understood by the behavioralists and the political citizen, David Truman wrote:

> Seen in these terms, is an interest group inherently ''selfish''? In the first place such judgments have no value for a scientific understanding of government or the operation of society. . . . Judgments of this kind are and must be made by all citizens in their everyday life but they are not properly a part of the systematic analysis of the social process. . . . Evaluations such as this may be made of particular groups, depending on the observer's own attitudes, but . . . they will not facilitate one's understanding of the social system of which the groups are a part.[9]

Clearly then for Truman the judgment as to the intrinsic desirability of a particular set of values, goals, or interests is not grounded in reason but rather depends upon the personal and therefore subjective attitudes of the observer. In view of this, value judgments, as essentially subjective assessments, can make no real contribution to the scientific understanding of politics. Whereas the judgment of values is a matter of attitude or opinion, the systematic analysis of facts is a proper concern of reason. For the behavioralist, a failure to recognize this fundamental distinction is potentially a threat to the very possibility of doing political science itself.

As an approach to the study of political reality, behavioralism has produced several significant achievements. First, behavioral political science has increased our ability to explain the behavior of political actors under specific assumptions and within controlled situations. Second, behavioralism has allowed us to predict more accurately how political actors, including mass electorates, are likely to behave in a given situation. And third, the behavioral movement has developed within the discipline as a whole an increased appreciation of the importance of methodological rigor and conceptual clarity.

At the same time, however, behavioralism has also been shown to have certain, and perhaps unavoidable, limitations. For example, behavioralist political science has tended to underemphasize the analysis of political institutions and other large-scale processes. Second, the behavioralist concern to test ''if-then hypotheses'' has led it to ignore the importance of historical studies and to favor instead the analysis of abstract models. In its effort to find the ''average,'' the ''recurrent,'' and the ''replicable,'' behavioralism must overlook the singularities and contingencies within a given historical context. In doing so, however, its results may appear somewhat "unreal" and out of touch with the actual practices of political life. Finally, critics of the behavioralist movement have focused upon some of the consequences that arise from its refusal to enter into the investigation of value questions. For example, some have argued that by ignoring questions of value, behavioralism offers thereby an implicit endorsement of the status quo. Rather than being value-neutral, as its advocates had claimed, behavioralism actually functions as a conservative and thus committed political force. Others have argued that by slavishly following the model of the natural sciences, behavioralism has been forced to concentrate upon relatively insignificant political issues that lend themselves to manipulation by empirical research techniques, or it has had to ask the wrong kinds of questions in order to avoid involving itself in a discussion of value claims. In short, behavioralism is portrayed as having willfully removed itself from the practical and immediate concerns of political life.

In response, the advocates of behavioralism simply point to the authority of empirical science. The scientific method is above all else a discipline. As such it imposes a certain routine and form upon the activity of human inquiry. Although this requires both a loss of spontaneity and a narrowing of focus and interest, it is nonetheless the only way of assuring the precise, clear, and rigorous knowledge characteristic of the scientific disciplines. By restricting its concern to the realm of the factual, behavioral political science attempts to "save" at least a part of political reality as a proper object for human reason. Whether this part is significant or whether it is all that can be saved are, of course, questions that continue to be debated within political science today.

The New Philosophy of Science

As we have seen, both Weber and the behavioralists hoped to respond to the challenge of modern ideology and improve upon the traditional tenets of Western political science by referring to the more recent experience of modern natural science. Whereas the behavioralists wished to directly imitate the practices of the natural scientists, Weber was careful to distinguish between the natural scientist's use of general laws and his own use of ideal types. On this point, therefore, there are significant differences between the two positions. Yet at the same time Weberian social science and contemporary behavioralism share several common assumptions. For example, both schools of thought accept the empiricist distinction between fact and values and admit to the noncognitive nature of the latter. Similarly both the Weberian and behavioral forms of social science emphasize the importance of scientific objectivity and methodological rigor. Both assume, therefore, that scientific truths can be made explicit and consequently tested, affirmed, or rejected. Finally both schools expect scientific knowledge to be impersonal, compelling, and logically specifiable.

In spite of their differences, therefore, both Weberian social science and modern behavioralism have accepted the modern or "critical" understanding of scientific knowledge. In doing so, they share in an interpretation of modern science that has dominated Western thinking since the scientific revolution of the seventeenth century. Recently, however, this "critical" perspective has come under increasing scrutiny and is now being challenged by philosophers and historians of science alike.

The critical understanding of modern science emerged in the seventeenth century in an effort to correct the perceived limitations of dogmatic philosophy and medieval culture. Its two most important representatives were Francis Bacon (1561–1626) and René Descartes (1596–1650).

In chapter 2 we examined Francis Bacon's theories of the "idols of the mind." Bacon took some of the first steps toward a relativist approach to political thought, maintaining that conclusions were unavoidably tainted by personal and social prejudices. He believed a new, more rigorous scientific method would help correct matters. To Bacon, medieval science was based upon an inadequate logic and informed by insufficient data. Its concepts were the results of uncorrected sense impressions, based on experience rather than experiments, and its method depended upon the traditional application of inadequate deductive syllogisms. To correct this situation Bacon offered a new form of science which was inductive rather than syllogistic and experimental rather than experiential. The modern scientist, in Bacon's understanding, begins by first observing the facts of nature and then, through a process of induction, attempts to generate concepts and hypotheses, which are eventually confirmed by repeated testing. This entire process is governed by the rules of a logically specifiable methodology and results in a knowledge that is universal, certain, and explicit.

Like Bacon, the French philosopher René Descartes also felt himself compelled to reject the claims of traditional Western science. Rather than generating an agreed-upon set of fundamental truths, the scientific tradition of his day, according to Descartes, was characterized by its complexity, plurality, and doubt. Its logic was discursive rather than investigative, and its mathematical systems were limited and unnecessarily abstract. In response Descartes developed his own understanding of the new scientific method. Whereas Bacon's version of the new science was empirical and inductive, Descartes' was both rationalistic and deductive. Accordingly he argued that the rational intuition of first principles was more important for science than the mere accumulation of factual information. If properly mastered, the Cartesian method promised to generate truths that were clear and distinct, certain and indubitable, and therefore universally persuasive and self-evident.

As different and distinct as Bacon and Descartes were (one an empiricist, the other a rationalist) they both agreed as to modern science's fundamentally critical nature. This critical interpretation of science emphasized the fully explicit character of scientific findings.

In this view, scientists follow a detailed set of methodological rules which allow them to present their findings in a clear and concise form. Their experiments can then be repeated by others and their conclusions thus tested for accuracy. Scientific truth, therefore, is fully explicit truth; its principles are open to critical examination, and its authority depends solely upon the verifiability or falsifiability of its results. The truths of science are understood to stand alone—i.e., their validity does not depend upon the personal, historical, or social circumstances within which they first emerged. On the contrary the authority of a scientific statement is to be found solely in its evidence, which is held to be specifiable in principle and thus capable of being examined in critical detail.

As we have seen, scientism argues that all forms of true knowledge will necessarily reflect those qualities believed to be the defining characteristics of scientific truth. Accordingly, inasmuch as scientific truth is understood to be fully explicit and thus specifiable in principle, scientism holds that a given tradition of speculation will qualify as scientific only to the degree to which it is able to achieve a similar condition.

Given this understanding of modern science, it is not difficult to see why such thinkers as Max Weber or those associated with the behavioral movement in general have attempted to limit political science to an analysis of the empirical realm. For such persons a discussion of values, unlike the examination of facts, is neither "self-evident," "certain," nor "objective." Ethical decisions are obviously a matter of personal evaluation. Their authority is, in part, dependent upon the quality or skill of the person who is making the judgment. This judgment, in turn, is accepted as legitimate only within a community that acknowledges a particular individual's authority and is, as a result, willing to follow that person in trust. It would appear then that, inasmuch as a discussion of values seems to rely upon authority, personality, and trust, such a discussion could not qualify as truly scientific—at least not as science is understood within the critical tradition.

Recently philosophers and historians of science have begun to challenge this critical interpretation of modern science. In particular the work of such thinkers as Michael Polanyi, Norwood Hanson, and Paul Feyerabend has begun to undermine the traditional conception of scientific reason as explicit truth.

One example of this new approach has been particularly influential among contemporary political scientists: the work of the physicist and historian Thomas Kuhn. In *The Structure of Scientific Revolutions* Kuhn investigated the process of scientific evolution and was led by his evidence to break with what had by then become the dominant view of scientific change. Traditionally it has been argued that science progresses incrementally through the slow and steady accumulation of data; scientists can thus correct their earlier work by refining their theories in view of the more recent information available to them. Yet, according to Kuhn's studies, this view of science as a cumulative process fails to account adequately for certain episodes in the history of science. For example, the traditional view of science tends to emphasize the sufficiency and power of the scientific method. Kuhn and others, however, argued that the history of science is replete with examples wherein the scientific method fails to dictate the substantive conclusions to important issues. Thus, when two schools of thought disagree on a serious issue, both commonly have followed the dictates of the scientific method. They disagree, not because one is methodologically incorrect, but rather because the two have developed incommensurable ways of seeing the world and thus cannot appreciate each other's perspective. In such a situation the scientific method by itself is incapable of deciding which interpretation is superior. Indeed the eventual winner is often determined by other factors that are "apparently arbitrary . . . [and] compounded of personal and historical accident."[10] According to Kuhn, a theory of science that fails to acknowledge such events fails thereby to explain the actual development of science as it really occurs in history.

Similarly Kuhn notes that the traditional interpretation of science argued that science progresses according to a process of confirmation and falsification, whereby facts are collected either to support or to challenge the dominant theory. Yet Kuhn's studies indicated that the situation is actually quite different. Rather than simply assimilating new facts to fit its theories, science actually develops through a process of confrontation wherein entire packages of facts and theories are challenged by alternative sets, each of which is able to produce evidence entirely consistent with its own world view. In short, the history of science according to Kuhn is the history of revolution.

In his attempt to account for this history, Kuhn introduces the concepts of "normal science" and "scientific revolutions." Normal science is that activity that is practiced by a community of scientists when they are bound together by their commitment to a specific set of generalizations, models, and exemplars (*paradigms*). A paradigm, or set of beliefs, both defines for the scientists the problems on which they will work and specifies the methods and techniques by which they will proceed. At the same time, the governing paradigm both isolates a certain class of facts that it considers to be the most revealing and establishes those theories it feels to be the most helpful and thus in need of greater articulation. In short, a scientific paradigm establishes that web of beliefs, expectations, and procedures from within which the scientific community works and by which it defines its world view. Typically, then, normal science is concerned with refining and defining the postulates of that particular paradigm that has been adopted by the community of scientists of that day. It is an activity that builds upon a specific set of traditions as defined by a particular historical community. At the same time, those who represent that community use their authority to enforce compliance with its traditions and to suppress or explain away those discoveries that would challenge its operating assumptions.

Nonetheless, according to Kuhn, the history of science provides many examples wherein the dominant paradigm comes under attack and eventually gives way to a challenger. An example would be the struggle between the Ptolemaic and Copernican conceptions of the universe. Typically this happens when certain anomalies develop that finally cannot adequately be explained by the dominant paradigm. If these persist, a sense of crisis may develop, and if the crisis is severe enough, it may eventually lead to the development of an alternative paradigm designed to solve the problems at hand. At that moment in which the scientific community substitutes a new paradigm for its traditional one, it ceases to practice normal science and engages instead in a scientific revolution. According to Kuhn, such revolutions involve the wholesale substitution of one paradigm for another. After this occurs, the new paradigm then becomes the model for the normal science of the future:

> The transition from a paradigm in crisis to a new one from which a new tradition of normal science can emerge is far from a cumulative process, one achieved by an articulation or extension of the old paradigm. Rather, it is a reconstruction of the field from new fundamentals. . . . When the transition is completed, the profession will have changed its view of the field, its methods, and its goals.[11]

According to Kuhn, then, science does not evolve by objectively measuring its theories against the established facts of nature. Rather, it develops by shifting from one paradigm—which is complete with its own facts, theories, and goals—to another that is equally self-sufficient. Since any two paradigms are to a certain extent incommensurable, inasmuch as each suspends selected universal principles of the other, this shift between paradigms is never simply the result of a strictly logical calculation. If two paradigms are in fact incommensurable and thus cannot be strictly compared, there can be no truly neutral proof that requires the acceptance of one paradigm over another. Given this, the decision to shift paradigms cannot be explained in exclusively methodological terms. Such a decision includes the essentially evaluative, and hence personal, judgments of the scientists involved, and so it entails a wide variety of logical, psychological, and sociological elements.

Various scholars have studied the history of science in an attempt to examine the nature of the decision by which a particular scientific community replaces one paradigm with another. Not surprisingly there is a fair amount of disagreement. Some like Michael Polanyi[12] and Imre Lakatos[13] have emphasized the rational but not necessarily logical qualities of such a decision. On the other hand others, like Paul Feyerabend,[14] point to the aesthetic and essentially subjective nature of such moments. For our purposes it is not necessary to enter into the details of this debate. It is more important that we recognize what these studies have in common. Specifically, the image of natural science that is emerging from this new work shows that science necessarily incorporates into its practices such extramethodological features as tradition, personal judgment, and community authority. Referring to the inadequacy of the traditional critical view, Thomas Spragens has written:

> In short, the remarkable success of natural science is not attributable to the demonstrability of its theories, for they do not possess such definitive certainty. It is not attributable to their logicality, for logical rigor, though it is important and necessary in science, is clearly an insufficient cause of scientific advance. And it is not attributable to the existence of some cookbook set of scientific methods, for these are not only insufficient but trivial.[15]

Unlike the older view of science as the impartial, skeptical, and neutral examination of the facts, this newer interpretation emphasizes the importance of the scholarly community's commitment to specific traditions and models. According to this interpretation, the natural sciences have succeeded, not in spite of the fact that they trust in their traditions, but rather precisely because they do so. As an attempt to explore the possibilities and the limitations of its governing paradigms, science is concerned primarily with the interpretation of tradition and not with the direct investigation of neutral facts. As we have seen, Weberian social sciences and modern behavioralism have argued that value judgments have no proper role within the scientific study of politics. They base this argument on a specific interpretation of science that posits the possibility of fully explicit knowledge. However, if the revised understanding of science is correct, the process by which we make our value judgments is essentially the same as that by which we derive our understanding of factual information. In short, both efforts are basically acts of interpretive judgment. Although facts and values may be different aspects of reality, the mechanisms by which we come to know them are essentially the same. This being the case, then, there is nothing in the logic of science itself that would require the rejection of value statements.

The work of Kuhn and others provides yet another example of an attempt to respond to the challenge of ideology by appealing to the authority of modern science. Unlike the traditional appeal of critical science, however, this new interpretation seeks to open rather than to limit the scope of human inquiry. In this sense, then, it is, in its own peculiarly modern way, akin to the spirit of classical reason. By rejecting the principle of a universal and self-sufficient methodology, it once again bases science upon human experience rather than upon logical procedure. In doing so, however, it, too, becomes susceptible to the ideologue's argument that, given the fundamentally historical structure of all human experience, the very possibility of a universal truth must be called into question.

Notes

1. Paul Nizan, *The Watchdogs: Philosophers and the Established Order*, trans. Paul Fittingoff (New York: Monthly Review Press, 1971), p. 91.
2. Nizan, *Watchdogs*, pp. 96–97.
3. Max Weber, "Objectivity in Social Science and Social Policy," in *Max Weber on the Methodology of the Social Sciences*, edited and translated by Edward Shils and Henry A. Finch (Glencoe, Ill.: The Free Press, 1949), p. 72.
4. Max Weber, "Science as a Vocation," in *From Max Weber*, edited by H. H. Gerth and C. Wright Mills (New York: Oxford University Press, 1958), p.147.
5. Weber, "Objectivity," p. 54.
6. Weber, "Vocation," p. 143.
7. David Truman, "The Impact on Political Science of the Revolution in the Behavioral Sciences," in *Behavioralism in Political Science*, edited by Heinz Eulau (New York: Atherton Press, 1969), p. 39.
8. Robert Dahl, "The Behavioral Approach in Political Science: Epitaph for a Monument to a Successful Protest," in Eulau, *Behavioralism*, p. 86.
9. David Truman, *The Governmental Process: Political Interests and Public Opinion* (New York: Alfred A. Knopf, 1951), p. 38.
10. Thomas Kuhn, *The Structure of Scientific Revolutions* (Chicago: University of Chicago Press, 1962), p. 4.
11. Kuhn, *Structure*, pp. 84–85.
12. Michael Polanyi, *Personal Knowledge: Towards a Post-Critical Philosophy* (New York: Harper & Row, 1964).
13. Imre Lakatos, "Falsification and the Methodology of Scientific Research Programmes," in *Criticism and the Growth of Knowledge*, edited by Imre Lakatos and Alan Musgrave (New York: Cambridge University Press, 1975).
14. Paul Feyerabend, *Against Method* (London: NLB, 1975).
15. Thomas A. Spragens, Jr., *The Irony of Liberal Reason* (Chicago: University of Chicago Press, 1981), p. 370.

Recommended Readings

Bendix, Reinhard. *Max Weber: An Intellectual Portrait*. Berkeley and Los Angeles: University of California Press, 1977.

Brown, Harold. *Perception, Theory, and Commitment: The New Philosophy of Science*. Chicago: University of Chicago Press, 1979.

Charlesworth, James, ed. *The Limits of Behavioralism in Political Science*. New York: American Academy of Political and Social Science, 1962.

Crick, Bernard. *The American Science of Politics: Its Origins and Conditions*. London: Routledge & Kegan Paul, 1959.

Eulau, Heinz, ed. *Behavioralism in Political Science*. New York: Atherton Press, 1969.

Freund, Julien. *The Sociology of Max Weber*. New York: Pantheon Books, 1968.

Giddens, Anthony. *Capitalism and Modern Social Theory: An Analysis of the Writings of Marx, Durkheim, and Weber*. New York: Cambridge University Press, 1971.

Gould, James A., and Vincent V. Thursby, eds. *Contemporary Political Thought: Issues in Scope, Value, and Direction*. New York: Holt, Rinehart and Winston, 1969.

Harre, Rom. *The Principles of Scientific Thought*. Chicago: University of Chicago Press, 1970.

Kuhn, Thomas. *The Essential Tension: Selected Studies in Scientific Tradition and Change*. Chicago: University of Chicago Press, 1977.

MacRae, Donald G. *Max Weber*. New York: The Viking Press, 1974.

Scheffler, Israel. *Science and Subjectivity*. New York: Bobbs-Merrill, 1967.

PART ONE: Summary

Since political science is an established discipline of the contemporary university, one may easily overlook the fact that its most fundamental assumptions are in fact disputed. Our beliefs and opinions about political life constitute a part of that very reality which the political scientist is examining. That is, the assumptions that govern the practice of political science are themselves the proper object for a theoretical inquiry. One of the most basic questions concerns whether it is possible to acquire objective and universally valid knowledge about political reality. If not, how can one responsibly choose among the variety of opinions characteristic of any political debate?

In the chapters of part 1 we have examined three distinct attempts to confront these issues. Although the arguments were arranged in chronological order, it would be misleading to assume that the discipline as a whole has moved from that position represented in chapter 1 as classical political science, into and through a period of ideological consciousness as described in chapter 2, and finally accepting the contemporary perspective as summarized in chapter 3. A close study of contemporary political science reveals that no such consensus exists. Rather, all three perspectives retain their advocates and, as a consequence, the debate concerning the status of political science continues today.

In simplified terms, the issue of this debate centers upon one's understanding of the range of human reason. Contemporary advocates of the classical position begin from the assumption that the power of reason extends beyond the realm of immanence and thereby enables one to comprehend, although perhaps only partially, those transcendent principles that structure the order of human and social reality. This knowledge, in turn, allows one to attune history to the measure of 'Being' itself.

Those contemporary political scientists who are influenced by the work of Marx and Mannheim question the validity of these classical assumptions. From their perspective, the so-called universal truths of the Western tradition are partial and particular insights at best or false and exploitive prejudices at worst. This evaluation, in turn, is based upon a belief that the range of reason is radically limited by its historical context. Human consciousness may be able to articulate the spirit of the age, but reason cannot transcend the bounds of history. Consequently the ''truths'' of any particular time or place are limited in their application, and political scientists should be most cautious about imposing their beliefs, values, and attitudes upon those whom they are studying.

The success of modern natural science offers powerful evidence that reason is able to transcend somewhat the limits of its particular situation and aspire, thereby, to the attainment of universal truths. The fact that physicists working in such diverse cultures as the American, the Russian, or the Chinese are able to communicate with one another and agree upon certain fundamental postulates attests to the consensus-building power of the scientific method. At the same time, however, as we have seen, the natural sciences are able to function as they do precisely because they have reached a prior agreement that limits the range of reason to strictly empirical phenomena. The scientistic distinction between fact and value secures the realm of the factual by first prohibiting the theoretical anaylsis of value issues in their own terms. From the perspective of the advocates of this tradition, the precision and clarity achieved by this exclusion compensates one for those costs associated with the closure of intellectual perspective. As a disciplined mode of inquiry, science depends upon the principles of exclusion and selectivity.

Contemporary political science is characterized by the fact that all of the traditions we have examined remain influential within the discipline today. The fact that each of these traditions denies one or more of the fundamental principles of the others means that their mutual coexistence within a common discipline is somewhat paradoxical. This paradox is one of the first issues to be faced by a student of politics. One's understanding of the questions that can legitimately be asked and of the answers that can validly be accepted will depend to a great part on how he or she resolves this issue.

PART
TWO

Human Nature and Politics

CHAPTER 4

The Discovery of the Soul

Introduction

In 1838 John Stuart Mill, the English philosopher, wrote:

> But they were destined to renew a lesson given to mankind by every age, and as always disregarded—to show that speculative philosophy, which to the superficial appears a thing so remote from the business of life and the outward interests of men, is in reality the thing on earth which most influences them, and in the long run overbears every other influence save those which it must itself obey.[1]

Mill's statement, which was written originally to honor the work and influence of Jeremy Bentham and Samuel Coleridge, attests to the general fact that, as a self-conscious being, the human person necessarily acts in such a way as to reveal his or her most fundamental assumptions about the nature of reality and the proper place of humanity within it. Unlike other animals, which appear to react in an immediate and direct way to their environment, the individual's relationship to reality is mediated by a complex set of concepts, beliefs, and expectations by which the human experience is first organized and thereby ultimately made meaningful. Thus, as Mill argued, those who provide us with the concepts by which we structure our thinking actually exercise the power of forming and directing our understanding of "the business of life."

This influence of ideas upon reality is especially clear in the realm of politics. For example, the way in which a society organizes itself politically unavoidably reflects the values, commitments, and expectations of those who are its active members. To a significant degree, therefore, the political character of a particular society can only be understood in terms of those underlying assumptions and beliefs that together form its dominant culture. Indeed, the importance and variety of such cultural traditions explain in part the difficulty that many nations have in living with or even understanding one another. For example, it is interesting to note how such a relatively concrete concept as "democracy" can take on a variety of meanings depending upon the specific cultural context within which it is developed.[2] Similarly, such a relatively abstract idea as the "common good" or "political justice" displays an even greater variety of meanings as expressed by one tradition or another.

One of the most important assumptions within any political culture is that which is concerned with defining human nature. Inasmuch as each society seeks to promote the good of its members, each must necessarily operate, at least tacitly, according to some concept of human nature. Without an appreciation of who the human is and of what is required for each to live as fully as is humanly possible, it would be difficult to determine either the appropriateness of a society's goals or the validity of its claims. The very activity of governing, like conducting a personal life, requires that one decide which actions, interests, and desires are to be encouraged and which are to be restrained. Such decision making presupposes the existence of a measure according to which such determinations can be made. Typically such a standard is found in a particular tradition's dominant understanding of human nature.

The Mythological Background

A major, if no longer dominant, tradition within contemporary Western culture is one that first emerged from a blending of the classical Greek and early Christian civilizations. The historical relationship between these two sources has not been without its tensions. Yet for many, such as Thomas Aquinas, the thirteenth-century philosopher and theologian, it was possible to understand each of them as contributing in its own way to a common civilizational order. Thus, without attempting to diminish some of the important differences that distinguish the Christian tradition from its pagan counterpart, it is possible to discover certain themes common to both. One is a specific understanding of human nature that emphasizes the spiritual integrity of the human soul.

The classical Greek and Christian understanding of "the human soul" could become authoritative in the West only after it first succeeded in breaking from the then-dominant mythological understanding of human nature. Some scholars, such as the German philosopher Karl Jaspers, have argued that a similar and roughly simultaneous rejection of the mythological world view also occurred in the civilizations of India and China.[3] It is sufficient for our purposes, however, to focus primarily upon the Greek and Christian experiences of the West.

An example of the ancient (preclassical) Greek view of human nature can be found in the poetry of Homer. Although it is not possible to give precise dates to Homer's epics (which perhaps were composed between 750 B.C. and 700 B.C.), there is no doubt about their singular place within ancient Greek culture. Indeed, Homer's epics, the *Odyssey* and the *Iliad*, are more than just samples of an ancient poetic art. They are instead the repositories of those shared experiences that constituted Hellenic consciousness. Through them the Greeks learned of their gods, their history, and their heroes. The poetry of Homer served to inform the Hellenic conception of reality, and, by analyzing the view of human nature they represent, one can gain an appreciation of the self-understanding of the ancients.

In exploring the meaning of ancient mythology, it is important to avoid reading the materials in a strictly literal fashion. The myth is, above all, a specific form of symbolic art. As such its symbols were created to give expression to a particular range of human experience. Just as artists use paint in order to communicate their experience of love, beauty, or joy, so too poets create verbal symbols in order to articulate those experiences that they are seeking to preserve for themselves and share with others. Given this, the adequacy of any particular set of symbols can only be measured in terms of its ability to communicate clearly those experiences by which it was first engendered. Those who read the ancient myths as if they were primitive, yet erroneous, attempts to give a scientific explanation of reality inevitably fault them for failing to achieve the more sophisticated understandings of modern science. Yet those who do so fail to appreciate the fact that the truth of mythical poetry can be determined solely in terms of the adequacy with which it expresses its own proper and peculiar form of experience. Consequently it is not particularly useful to compare one set of symbols with another.

Inasmuch as specific symbolic traditions are created in order to explore particular segments within the range of human experience, specific sets of symbols may be more or less incommensurable. For example, it is difficult to compare the symbols of ancient myth with those of modern science (e.g., $E = MC^2$) because each in its own way is exploring a different field within the realm of human experience. It is best, therefore, to analyze each symbol system in its own terms. Specifically, in reading Homeric poetry one should "give in to" the symbols in such a way as to sympathetically recreate those particular experiences that the author was originally attempting to communicate. In short, by reading the *Iliad* and the *Odyssey* it is possible to gain an appreciation of the ancients' understanding of themselves, god, nature, and society.

The symbols of Homeric poetry were created in an attempt to express the ancient experience of reality in its *cosmological* form. For the ancients, all of reality existed as a *cosmos*—a single, ordered, hierarchically structured whole that included all that existed and hence all that could be known. Accordingly, humanity, nature, society, and the gods were experienced as living within the single continuum of a unified cosmic reality. In short, being was experienced as whole and complete; and inasmuch as there were no absolute divisions according to such an understanding, everything was eventually related to everything else. Eric Voegelin, the philosopher, has summarized the ancient cosmological experience in the following terms:

> The cosmos of the primary experience is neither the external world of objects given to a subject of cognition, nor is it the world that has been created by a world-transcendent God. Rather, it is the whole . . . of an earth below and a heaven above—of celestial bodies and their movements; of seasonal changes; of fertility rhythms in plant and animal life; of human life, birth and death; and above all . . . it is a cosmos full of gods. This last point, that the gods are intracosmic, cannot be stressed strongly enough. . . . The numbers are not important, but rather the consciousness of divine reality as intracosmic or transmundane. . . . This togetherness and one-in-anotherness is the primary experience that must be called cosmic in the pregnant sense.[4]

As Voegelin has stated, the ancient cosmological experience of reality was one that accredited the immediate and powerful presence of the divine among all things. According to this perspective, the cosmos is structured by sacred forces, and everything that exists—including the human person—can only be understood in terms of its specific relationship to those sacred principles. Since the ancients experienced themselves as part of the cosmos, they too could be understood only in terms of those sacred forces that acted upon them and penetrated to the very core of their being. Rather than seeing themselves as the agents of their own actions, the ancients understood their behavior as being simply the result of a larger play among cosmic forces that acted upon and through them to produce the results intended. Indeed, according to the cosmological view, even an individual's thoughts and emotions are experienced as coming from the outside and thus originating not in one's own personality but ultimately in the act of a god. The classicist Bruno Snell has summarized this perspective in the following terms:

> Mental and spiritual acts are due to the impact of external factors and man is the open target of a great many forces which impinge on him and penetrate to his very core . . . man has not yet awakened to the fact that he possesses in his own soul the source of his power; . . . [rather] he receives them as a natural and fitting donation from the gods.[5]

In short, the ancients did not yet understand themselves as having what we today would consider to be a personality. As such they had not yet discovered that spiritual center or inner source of energy that would allow them to understand their actions, thoughts, and desires as expressions or manifestations of their own integral personality. As an articulation of natural or sacred currents the individual was at most a nodal point, but certainly not yet a "self."

Given the self-understanding of the ancients, it was obvious to them that an adequate explanation of any significant human event required that the investigation proceed until one could expose those specific sacred forces which actually controlled the situation. Inasmuch as an individual was incapable of any truly original action, logic required that all events be ultimately traced back to their divine source. Then and only then could the real meaning or significance of the events be made clear.

An example of the mythological attempt to elucidate the meaning of history can be found in Homer's *Iliad*. In general the *Iliad* describes an episode within the Trojan War. Specifically it is the story of the

Greek prince Achilles who at first withdraws from but then eventually reenters the siege of Troy. The Trojan War itself was an event which depicted the rise of Western power, as represented by the forces of Greece, over and against the traditional power of the East, represented by the city of Troy. Later historians, such as Thucydides (circa 471 B.C.–400 B.C.) would explain this war in terms of the imperialistic ambitions of the Greeks, who were attempting to establish a commercial empire in the eastern Mediterranean. Such an explanation, however, is distinctively postmythological because it assumes that the meaning of such events can be fully accounted for in terms of a strictly human calculation regarding political and economic interests.

For the ancients, however, such an explanation was not available, because it presupposed a vision of human nature that they in fact did not share. In the cosmological world, individuals were not capable of significant historical decisions. Thus the only acceptable explanation of such an important event as the ten-year siege of Troy was one that could expose the divine forces at work.

This, in fact, was accomplished by the "Myth of the Golden Apples" wherein the Trojan prince Paris was called upon to judge which of three goddesses (Hera, Athena, or Aphrodite) was the most beautiful. His decision on behalf of Aphrodite set into motion a chain of events that culminated in the Trojan War and the eventual fall of Troy. More important, however, was that this story explained to the Greeks how the war between Troy and Greece was but a manifestation at the human level of an underlying conflict among the goddesses themselves. From this perspective it was the very cosmos which was at war. Humans, in turn, were simply participants within the larger divine drama, which was not settled until Zeus himself restored order among the warring gods.

As an episode within the Trojan War, the story of Achilles displays a similar structure. In his opening sentence, Homer says:

> An angry man—there is my story: The bitter rancor of Achilles, prince of the house of Peleus, which brought a thousand troubles upon the Achaian host. Many a strong soul it sent down to Hades, and left the heroes themselves a prey to dogs and carrion birds, while the will of God moved on to fulfillment.[6]

A modern commentator might regard Homer's reference to the will of god as simply a poetic device. Yet, as we have seen, such a

reference is actually required by the very logic of the ancient mythological mind. For the ancients, the death of thousands of Greeks was
necessarily meaningless unless one could understand the real and
therefore the divine causes that ultimately required such an event.
This was, in part, the purpose of Homer's *Iliad*. When Achilles withdraws from the battle because of his jealous feud with the Greek general Agamemnon, Homer asks, "What god, then, made the feud between them?" And then Homer answers his own question, "Apollo,
son of Leto and Zeus."[7] Thus it would appear that, for the cosmological mind, even one's deepest emotions had to be explained in terms
of their particular role within that divine drama that was, in fact, the
true subject of Homeric poetry. Having analyzed both the *Iliad* and
the *Odyssey*, Werner Jaeger, the classicist, concluded:

> But Homer does not, like modern authors, see every action from
> within, as a phenomenon of human consciousness. In his world,
> nothing great happens without the aid of a divine power. . . . Homer
> . . . presents all human actions as guided by the gods. . . . If we
> study the instances of divine intervention in the epics, we can trace a
> development from the occasional interference of the gods . . . to the
> constant spiritual guidance of a great man by a divinity, as Odysseus
> is guided by the perpetual inspiration of Athena.[8]

Lacking an appreciation of themselves as distinct personalities, the
ancients had not yet discovered within themselves the existence of
the human soul. This, in turn, had an obvious influence upon the
ways in which they organized their public life and practiced the art of
politics.

Cosmological Politics

Inasmuch as all significant historical events were understood as resulting from divine action, it was only logical for the ancients to assume that politics, too, had a divine or sacred character. As the gods
controlled history, so too did they determine the fate of any particular
political society. Within such a perspective, political leaders were
able to claim a certain divine authority. Their laws or pronounce-
ments were understood as equivalent to sacred revelation and, as a

consequence, the claim of a society upon its members was nearly absolute. In the words of Eric Voegelin, politics was "divinized."[9]

The divinization of ancient politics can be illustrated by examining the war songs of the Spartan poet Tyrtaeus (eighth century B.C.). His songs were originally intended to instill in the citizens of Sparta a spirit of self-sacrifice and patriotism as they faced the increasing hardships of the Messenian War. They did so by reminding the Spartans that each individual's good was necessarily subordinate to the common good of the community as a whole, and that in the present circumstances patriotism was the most important of the virtues. For our purposes, however, these songs are interesting primarily because they provide us with a good example of cosmological politics.

For example, in the second song Tyrtaeus reminds the Spartans that their community can trace its origin back to the man-god Hercules and that as a consequence it has enjoyed the continuing favor of Zeus himself. Similarly, in the sixth song Tyrtaeus remarks that the city of Sparta was given to its people by Zeus. Rather than being a strictly secular institution organized by citizens in order to serve their mundane interests, Sparta was, in fact, a divine donation or gift. Finally, in song ten Tyrtaeus refers to the laws of Sparta as "oracles and perfect words of a god" and claims that the Spartan form of government was specified in an act of revelation which decreed ". . . that divinely-honoured kings should rule the senate."[10]

In this perspective, where laws are seen as revealed truths and the regime is established according to a divine commandment, it is clear that the authority of the state appears to be absolute. Accordingly, disobedience would be akin to an act of sacrilege, and a challenge to the laws of society would imply at the same time an impertinent questioning of divine wisdom. In short, existence within an essentially closed cosmos necessarily implies the existence of an equally closed society.

The Collapse of the Cosmos:
The Classical View of Human Nature

As we have seen, the cosmological view of reality did not evolve according to a set of preconceived intellectual hypotheses. It was rather an attempt to give symbolic expression to a particular type of human experience. Specifically, the ancients' compact experience of the immediate and overwhelming presence of the divine required a theory of human nature compatible with the basic structure of this world view. However, if the human experience of the basic structure of reality changes, so too must those traditional theoretical symbols by which people had previously attempted to "capture" this experience. Remarkably, such a change and its accompanying theoretical innovations appear to have occurred at the beginning of the classical period. This, in turn, can be documented by an analysis of newly developing poetic symbols.

The myth was the uniquely appropriate symbolic form for expressing a belief in cosmological reality; as different basic experiences began to emerge and receive public accreditation, so did new forms. For example, the tradition of epic poetry was eventually replaced by that of the lyric. And if one reads such lyric poets as Sappho, Anacron, and Archilocus (seventh century B.C. to sixth century B.C.), one notices a new concern for the subjective and emotional life of the individual. Since such a concern could not be expressed in the language of the myth, Sappho and others were forced to create a new literary form in order to communicate their particular interest in the individual as such. Whereas Homer was interested in the story of Achilles primarily because it allowed for his analysis of the larger cosmological order, the lyric poets focused their attention directly upon the individual and his or her unique emotional life. For Sappho, the individual possessed a certain intrinsic interest; as a consequence she used the lyric as a device by which to explore the individual aspects of the human personality. Although the lyric poets were still influenced by the traditions of Greek mythology, they nonetheless examined for the first time that primitive sense of individuality that arises from one's experience of emotional upheaval. In assessing the Greek lyrists, Bruno Snell has written:

> That life on earth is imperfect and sorrowful is known even to Homer; even his heroes share in the deeprooted imperfection of man. But his gods endow everything under their sway with its particular essence and ensure its continued existence. These gods also sustain the world of the lyrists; any rebellion against them is out of the question. . . . In the expression of their private sentiments and demands the early lyrists try to reproduce those moments in which the individual is all of a sudden snatched out of the broad stream of life, when he senses that he is cut off from the ever-green tree of universal growth. Such are the moments which furnish man with his first glimpse of the soul.[11]

Human Nature and Politics

The full exploration of the inner self was an achievement reserved for Greek tragic poetry. In the writings of such authors as Aeschylus, Sophocles, and Euripides, the human soul emerges as the foundation for all thought, action, and emotion. The characters within a tragedy are presented as independent agents who must agonize over their decisions and wrestle with problems whose solutions depend entirely upon their own insight, character, and ability. In tragic poetry, then, the individual has finally emerged as a morally responsible actor who is capable of a personal commitment to the principles of justice. As the myth was created to explore one's experience of cosmological necessity, and as the lyric was used to express the human reality of emotional dislocation, so, too, tragic poetry allowed one to articulate the existence of a binding moral order. Inasmuch as a person's own soul was now recognized as the source of life, the individual became increasingly independent of those divine and earthly forces that might influence his or her decision. Indeed, it is as if the individual personality actually emerges in the human struggle to make the right choice among difficult alternatives. In this sense, then, Sophocles's Antigone is much more real to us than Homer's Achilles can ever be. We come to know Antigone because we have actually seen her personality develop as she struggles to choose between her obedience to the law of god and her loyalty to the laws of her king.

This formal shift from epic to lyric and then to tragic poetry was the literary expression of an essentially substantive movement. During this time, the search for the meaning of reality became increasingly inner directed. Whereas the ancients had looked to the external forces of the cosmos for the ground of being, the new poets were looking directly within the individual. In this effort, they discovered within the person a source of energy (the *psyche* or soul) that could convincingly explain those experiences that were increasingly characteristic of human existence. Rather than understanding themselves as simply a part of the external cosmos, the tragic poets proclaimed the discovery of a second dimension. In short, the poets had discovered an inwardness or depth within each person which allowed him or her to open up beyond the closed order of the cosmos and thereby to participate in that which transcended it. This discovery of the soul was first formulated in philosophical terms by Heraclitus. His method was one of meditation ("I searched within myself")[12] and it resulted in the discovery of an essentially unbounded (i.e., open) soul which operated according to principles hitherto unknown within cosmic nature:

The Discovery of the Soul

> You could not in your going find the ends of the soul, though you travelled the whole way: so deep is its Law. . . . The soul has its own Law which increases itself.[13]

The Greek discovery of the soul received its clearest symbolic representation in the philosophy of Plato. In one sense, then, Plato's work represents the final culmination of that experiential and literary evolution that we have previously traced through its epic, lyric, and tragic forms. This evolutionary discovery of an inner dimension within human nature required that the view of reality found in the ancient myth be rejected. Whereas the ancients had experienced reality as a single, ordered, and compact whole, the classical Greeks had discovered the existence of a second dimension whose reality could not be incorporated into the cosmological framework. Since this inner dimension was experienced as a reality whose existence could not be denied, its acceptance implied a direct challenge to the cosmological world view. As an outcome, the compact symbolization of the single cosmos was eventually replaced by one that postulated the existence of two distinct levels within reality itself. According to this more highly differentiated view, reality contains both an immanent dimension (the material world of time and space) and a spiritual one which both transcends the former and is structured according to its own specific principles of order.

According to the mythological world view, the gods, humans, and animals live together on the single plane of an all-encompassing cosmos. Thus the co-presence of mankind, the gods, and the animals creates a unified field of existence within which there are no true gaps or voids. The myth explains all of reality because everything is equally at hand—even the sacred ground of being itself.

With the discovery of the human soul, however, the classical Greek became conscious of a second dimension within reality. The existence of such a dimension, in turn, had the effect of displacing mankind, the gods, and the animals from their previous locations. Since the cosmos was no longer one, its members were no longer equally co-present. For example, the classical Greeks argued that animals are necessarily and exclusively worldly creatures. Lacking reason, they were believed to be incapable of participating in that which is spiritual, while at the same time, their lack of self-consciousness was understood to limit their world to that of their own immediate physical environment. Similarly, such classical Greeks as Parmenides, Plato, and Aristotle understood their gods to be essentially spiritual beings. Inasmuch as the gods were removed from the limitations of physical nature, they were understood to be complete, perfect, and unchanging. Being beyond change, they were, as a result, beyond the world, and as such were perceived as purely transcendent beings.

Within this perspective, both the animals and the gods appear to have their own "proper" place within reality. The situation for the human person, however, is somewhat more complex. Having both body and soul, the human belongs in principle to both the material and the spiritual realm. On one hand, the body allows and indeed requires the individual to participate in the concerns of the world. Thus, as material creatures, individuals cannot in fact ignore the mundane yet legitimate needs of their animallike nature. Yet on the other hand, humans also possess a rational soul which opens them to the transcendent reality of the spirit. By referring the individual to a dimension of reality beyond that of the merely material, the soul thereby creates a set of distinctly spiritual needs. In short, the classical Greeks understood human nature as being simultaneously godlike and animallike. As both a spiritual and worldly creature the human person is, in effect, pulled in two different directions at the same time. Bound to the earth yet yearning for the transcendent, humanity discovered its soul by acknowledging the reality of this existence-in-tension.

Perhaps the most dramatic presentation of this experience can be found in the "Cave Allegory" in Book 7 of Plato's *Republic*. In it, Plato describes a situation wherein cave dwellers are bound in such a way that they are facing the front wall of a cave against which shadowy images are being projected. Because of their bindings, the inhabitants of the cave are unable to comprehend their true situation and, as a consequence, assume that the images they see are in fact real. As the allegory proceeds, one prisoner is mysteriously freed from the chains and dragged out of the cave into the light of day. Although at first stunned by the power of the sunlight, the prisoner eventually adjusts and begins to perceive the vivid colors, beauty, and richness characteristic of the outside world. By comparison, the "reality" within the cave is remembered as dark, restrictive, and ultimately unattractive. Consequently, the prisoner wishes to remain outside but must eventually return and, once back, faces the difficult task of readjusting to the former situation.

This readjustment is difficult for at least two reasons. First, having experienced the more beautiful reality of the world outside the cave, the prisoner is no longer satisfied with the things of the cave. He perceives the shadowy images for what they really are—i.e., pale imitations of those true realities that exist beyond. Second, in attempting to communicate these experiences to the fellow cave dwellers, the prisoner encounters extreme resistance. The others have never experienced the process of conversion and release to which the prisoner refers. Therefore, it is difficult for them to understand or even make sense of the experiences described. At the same time, by calling their attention to the existence of a superior reality beyond the cave, the prisoner is necessarily questioning the adequacy of that shared reality to which all the cave dwellers are habitually committed. In time, the cave dwellers are so offended by the prisoner's constant challenges that they put him to death.

Plato's cave allegory can be interpreted on a number of levels, from the specific to the most general. At one level, the prisoner can be seen as representing the person of Socrates. As the "gadfly of Athens" Socrates was eventually executed because of his constant challenging of popular opinion. At a second level, the prisoner may be understood as representing all those who practice the art of philosophy. As noted earlier, Plato understood philosophy as the all-consuming effort to leave the realm of opinion (the cave) in order to encounter the reality of 'Being' itself (the external world). Yet inasmuch as the philosopher represents the fullest and most complete expression of that potential for reason that is common to all people, the prisoner of the cave may also be understood as a symbol for humanity in general.

At this third and most general level, the cave can be understood as representing the material world, while the reality beyond is that of the spiritually transcendent. Accordingly, the prisoner's liberation from the cave actually represents the soul's awakening to the reality of the spirit, while at the same time his return symbolizes the necessary material foundation of our bodily nature. In this interpretation, then, the returned prisoner represents not only Socrates or the philosopher, but also the human condition at large. As body and soul, humans are both material and spiritual. As material creatures, they cannot escape from the cave itself. Yet at the same time, as spiritual creatures, they discover that the things of the cave are not enough. The body requires the goods of the earth, while the soul requires the goods of the spirit. As a consequence, humanity is both *in* the cave but not totally *of* the cave; it is rather existence-in-tension.

The Mutual Search:
The Christian View of Human Nature

In spite of the significant differences between the paganism of the classical Greeks and some of the central tenets of Christian theology, there is nonetheless a striking compatibility between their respective views of human nature. Saint Augustine's admiration of Plato and Saint Thomas Aquinas's appropriation of Aristotle are only two examples of Western Christianity's sympathetic appreciation of classical Greek philosophy. Indeed, Christianity's ability to assimilate much of Greek pagan culture accounts, in part, both for the historical preservation of the Hellenic tradition and its eventual influence within modern European civilization. This sympathy is especially evident in the Christian view of human nature. The Greeks discovered the soul, and in so doing they succeeded in defining human nature primarily in terms of the individual's relationship with the transcendent. As we have seen, Plato understood the soul to be that faculty which allowed one to transcend the mundane world and thereby participate in the spiritual ground of being itself. In similar terms, Plato's student Aristotle referred to the human soul as that godlike reality within persons that elevated them above the purely animal realm and thereby established their unique humanity. For Aristotle, then, individuals are fully human precisely because they are partly divine. In summary, the Greek discovery of the soul implied that one's humanity consists in his or her ability to seek the divine. From the Christian perspective, obviously, such an understanding is entirely appropriate. It could easily be incorporated into the new Church tradition.

At the same time, although the Greek understanding of the soul was appropriate, from the Christian perspective it was not yet complete. The Christian view of human nature sought to build upon the Greek experience by supplementing rather than replacing the pagan understanding. According to the Christian perspective, the Greeks were correct insofar as they were true to their experience of the individual's rational quest for the transcendent. Yet inasmuch as Christianity accredited a distinct and unique encounter with the divine—one not available to the earlier Greeks—so, too, did it amend the Greek tradition in an effort to incorporate its own more recent experiential data.

It is difficult to speak precisely of the Christian view of human nature. Since Christianity has evolved within a number of cultural and historical contexts, and given the doctrinal differences among those religious bodies that claim to represent the Christian tradition, it is not easy to specify a common set of dogmas about which all Christians would completely agree. Indeed there have been and continue to be significant theological, philosophical, and political differences among the various Christian churches. However, having said this, it is still possible to suggest a general and therefore necessarily abstract Christian understanding of human nature. This, in turn, may be demonstrated by briefly examining two important Christian symbols: the Incarnation and grace.

There are numerous interpretations of the Incarnation within Christianity, and they differ greatly. For example, there is a long and contentious debate concerning the precise relationship between Christ's humanity on the one hand and his divine or Godlike qualities on the other. Without entering into the details of this argument, one can suggest that the symbol of the Incarnation is at the very least an expression of the Christian experience of a specific divine inrush into human history. Accordingly, for Christians, Christ's birth, life, and death were manifestations of God's desire to become directly involved in the affairs of humanity. Whereas for the classical Greeks, the only relationship between the individual and god was that which was established by a person's rational yearning to encounter the transcendent ground of being, the Christians claimed to have experienced a similar movement on the part of God himself. Thus, just as the individual sought the divine, so, too, did God seek the individual. This mutual and reciprocal bond established between the person and God is symbolized by the fact that, for Christians, Christ is simultaneously an expression of their highest aspirations and of God's power and intention. As a mediator, Christ is understood to represent God and the individual to one another and as a consequence is the culmination of the quest of each for the other. This experience of a mutual quest is clearly present in the writings of Saint Augustine. For example, in his *Confessions*, Augustine addressed God in the following terms:

> So I set about finding a way to gain the strength that was necessary for enjoying You. And I could not find it until I embraced the *Mediator between God and man, the man Christ Jesus, who is over all things, God blessed forever*, who was calling unto me and saying: *I am the Way, the Truth, and the Life*; and who brought into union with our nature that Food which I lacked the strength to take. . . .

For Your Word, the eternal Truth, towering above the highest parts of Your creation, lifts up to himself those that were cast down. He built for Himself here below a lowly house of our clay, that by it He might bring down from themselves and bring up to Himself those who were to be made subject. . . .[14]

Another way of illustrating this feature of the Christian tradition is to compare Aristotle's discussion of friendship with the Christian experience of divine love. In his *Nicomachean Ethics*, Aristotle had argued that true friendship presupposed a certain equality among friends. Accordingly if either party is noticeably inferior to the other, it will be impossible for them to establish a real friendship based upon mutual respect. Aristotle argued, therefore, that the relationship between the individual and god can never be characterized as one of friendship. Inasmuch as the gods are superior to humans, the minimal degree of equality can never be achieved. As a result, the relationship is necessarily one-sided. The philosophers' love of divine wisdom motivates them to undertake their quest; but the gods themselves remain unmoved.

The Christian experience, on the other hand, is quite different. Not only do Christians understand God as the proper object of their love, but at the same time, they experience the active presence of his love for them. In Christianity the relationship between God and the human is not only one of possible friendship but also one of a mutual and personal love. For Christians, God's love for them is the necessary and sufficient cause that explains the creation, redemption, and salvation of the world. In traditional terms, the philosopher's desire for the divine is balanced by the experience of God's love for his creation. Once again the relationship between man and God is pictured as being reciprocal.

The fact that the Incarnation argues for the mutual bonding of the mundane with the transcendent does not imply, however, that both parts of this reciprocal movement are of equal importance. On the contrary, the Christian symbol of grace suggests the existence of a radical inequality. Specifically, the human yearning for God is not nearly as important as is God's quest for individuals. This dependence upon God's prior action is associated with the Christian understanding of sin. As fallen creatures, individuals cannot perfect themselves. They are in need of salvation, and the offer of salvation is something that flows from the abundance of God's love for them. It is not something that can be earned. In this emphasis on humanity's soteriological nature, Christianity moves beyond the classical discussion of philosophical virtue. For the Greek, an individual's fulfillment is achieved in the practice of philosophy and thus is dependent upon the inculcation of the intellectual virtues. For Christianity, however, such an undertaking is not enough. Even the philosophers fail of necessity to achieve true human fulfillment because their very humanity is now understood as being in need of redemption. Without denying the importance of the intellectual virtues, Christianity necessarily subordinates them to the beatitudes. In short, the example of the philosopher is replaced by that of the saint.

The understanding of human nature that emerged within the Christian tradition both appropriates and expands upon the classical Greek conception. The human soul is no longer understood as simply the source of an individual's quest for the divine. It is that and more. For Christianity, the soul is also the sensorium of transcendence. It is both that which seeks God and that which receives His action. Consequently the binding of the person to the transcendent assumes an even greater intensity for the Christian than for the Greek. As individuals become increasingly aware of the transcendent character of their origin and goal, it soon becomes apparent that they will have to rethink the nature of their commitment to the world in general and to politics in particular.

Political Consequences of the Classical and Christian Views of Human Nature

With the collapse of the cosmological world view, the classical Greeks were forced to reconsider their traditional attitudes toward political reality. The ancient understanding of politics as a godlike or sacred activity was no longer acceptable to a culture that differentiated between the mundane and the transcendent poles of existence. To this culture, a god or the absolute existed as a transcendent reality and was, as a result, no longer understood as involved in an immediate way with political events. By losing its divine character, therefore, politics came to be understood as a strictly human affair. In Platonic terms, it became a matter of the cave, while in Christianity it was relegated to those secondary concerns associated with the earthly pilgrimage. As the results of a strictly human undertaking, laws and political institutions are deprived of their sacred or absolute authority. Instead of being treated as equivalent to divine revelation, they now appear as the pragmatic results of the all-too-human process of deliberation and decision making. Whereas at one time laws may have been considered as absolutes, from within the classical and Christian perspectives, they stand under constant judgment and are thus in need of continual justification.

By positing the existence of a higher spiritual order, the classical-Christian tradition also established a means by which the "laws of the cave" can be evaluated. As we have noted, the transcendent realm was understood to be structured according to its own appropriate principles. These principles were described differently by different theorists. For example, Plato would refer to the laws of reason, while Christian theorists, such as Thomas Aquinas, would appeal to the laws of God. In each case, it was argued that the principles so described could be used as a standard against which all political laws should be measured. Accordingly a particular society's understanding of justice can be compared to the principles of transcendent justice as such; and, as Plato did in his *Gorgias*, such a comparison can then be used to question the adequacy of any particular society's attempt to approximate the just order. Similarly Thomas Aquinas had argued that if a specific political law violates the universal principles of the divine law, the specific law will, in fact, forfeit its legal character and thereby lose its claim upon the citizens. In both cases, a particular law's ability to demand one's uncritical obedience is called into question. Thus, rather than being obligated to uncritically obey all political laws, the citizen is now in the position to evaluate the very legitimacy of the legal system itself.

Finally the classical-Christian understanding of human nature has had the effect of questioning the amount of importance assigned to political activity within the cosmological perspective. Although politics can contribute to the achievement of the good life and is therefore a noble undertaking, it can no longer demand the totality of one's commitment. Having a soul implies that the individual has a spiritual destiny, and inasmuch as that destiny is considered to be higher than any strictly mundane calling, it necessitates the subordination of all other concerns—including the concerns of politics. For Plato, the life of wisdom (philosophy) is superior to either the life of honor (politics) or the life of wealth (business). Consequently the fully good person will refuse to be totally committed to either of the two inferior vocations. By elevating philosophy, Plato necessarily limited the appeal of politics. Similarly, for the Christian, the salvation of one's soul is the most important concern. Whereas politics or the state may care for one's material and cultural needs, the church alone can satisfy one's spiritual needs. Thus for thinkers such as Augustine and Aquinas, the church is superior to the state, and by its very existence it places a limit upon what the state can legitimately do. As the concerns of the cave give way to the needs of the soul, politics inevitably loses its former prestige and authority.

Notes

1. John Stuart Mill, "Bentham," in *John Stuart Mill: Utilitarianism, On Liberty, Essay on Bentham,* ed. Mary Warnock (New York: New American Library, n.d.), p. 78.

2. See C. B. MacPherson, *The Real World of Democracy* (New York: Oxford University Press, 1972).

3. Karl Jaspers, *The Origins and Goal of History,* trans. Michael Bullock (New Haven: Yale University Press, 1953).

4. Eric Voegelin, *The Ecumenic Age* (Baton Rouge: Louisana State University Press, 1974), pp. 68–69.

5. Bruno Snell, *The Discovery of the Mind: The Greek Origins of European Thought,* trans. T. G. Rosenmeyer (New York: Harper & Row, 1960), pp. 20–21.

6. Homer, *The Iliad,* trans. W. H. D. Rouse (New York: New American Library, 1950), p. 11.

7. Homer, *The Iliad,* p. 11.

8. Werner Jaeger, *Paideia: The Ideals of Greek Culture,* Vol. 1, trans. Gilbert Highet (New York: Oxford University Press, 1939), p. 51.

9. Eric Voegelin, *The New Science of Politics* (Chicago: University of Chicago Press, 1952), pp. 76–106.

10. Tyrtaeus, "War-Songs," in *The Idylls of Theocritus, Bion, and Moschus and the War-Songs of Tyrtaeus,* ed. Rev. J. Banks (London: Henry G. Bohn, 1853), p. 336.

11. Snell, *Mind,* pp. 64–65.

12. Heraclitus, "Fragments," in *Ancilla to the Pre-Socratic Philosophers,* ed. Kathleen Freeman (Cambridge: Harvard University Press, 1971), p. 31.

13. Heraclitus, "Fragments," pp. 29, 32.

14. F. J. Sheed (ed.), *The Confessions of Saint Augustine,* Books 1–10 (New York: Sheed & Ward, 1942), p. 122.

Recommended Readings

Cochrane, Charles Norris. *Christianity and Classical Culture.* New York: Oxford University Press, 1957.

Finley, M. I. *The World of Odysseus.* 2d ed. New York: Penguin Books, 1979.

Frankfort, Henri, *et al. Before Philosophy: The Intellectual Adventure of Ancient Man.* New York: Penguin Books, 1949.

Griffin, Jasper. *Homer.* New York: Hill and Wang, 1980.

Jaeger, Werner. *Early Christianity and Greek Paideia.* New York: Oxford University Press, 1969.

Kantorowicz, Ernst. *The King's Two Bodies: A Study in Medieval Political Theology.* Princeton, N.J.: Princeton University Press, 1957.

Kenny, Anthony. *Aquinas.* New York: Hill and Wang, 1980.

Meagher, Robert. *Augustine: An Introduction.* New York: Harper & Row, 1979.

Vernant, Jean-Pierre. *Myth and Society in Ancient Greece.* Translated by Janet Lloyd. Atlantic Highlands, Humanities Press, 1980.

Voegelin, Eric. *The New Science of Politics.* Chicago: University of Chicago Press, 1952.

C H A P T E R 5

The Assertion of the Self

Introduction

Both the classical Greek and Christian understanding of human nature emphasize the priority of the human soul. The soul, as we have seen, is that source of spiritual energy that allows one to participate in the order of reality even unto its transcendent ground. Persons who believe in this concept understand themselves as part of a larger whole whose order provides those universal principles according to which each individual is to structure his or her own particular way of life. From this perspective, the rational or divine order is that standard against which each person is to be measured and those who fail to meet this test are to be judged accordingly. In short, in the classical Greek and Christian perspective, the well-ordered persons are those who have found and maintained their proper and peculiar place within the hierarchy of Being. As a consequence, attunement to the whole rather than individual differentiation is the accepted hallmark of human goodness.

This classical Greek and Christian concern that individuals find their appropriate place within the established order of reality necessarily influenced traditional attitudes toward both ethics and politics. For example, in the field of ethics, the predominant concern was with the inculcation of virtue. Such classical thinkers as Plato and Aristotle recommended that their students first select for themselves appropriate persons whose conduct could serve as a model of proper ethical behavior. Having done so, they were then consciously to imitate the actions of such models until they themselves habitually behaved in such an exemplary manner. In short, classical ethics is an ethics of imitation, and the chief task of the moral educator is to designate those models that are particularly appropriate for the time. As we have seen, Plato argued that the only true model is that of the philosopher-king, while Aristotle suggested the additional possibility of the "mature person," or *Spoudaios*. In neither case, however, is the individual expected to act in a truly autonomous or original manner. On the contrary, living the good life is essentially a matter of faithfully imitating those who have mastered its principles. It thus presupposes a "master-apprentice" relationship.

Christianity's ethical tradition is somewhat more complex because of the moral legalism found within its Jewish heritage. Nonetheless, Christianity did appropriate certain features from the classical Greek perspective. For example, in Roman Catholicism selected individuals are elevated to the status of sainthood and then presented to the faithful as models to be honored and imitated. Similarly, such Christian works as *The Imitation of Christ* by Thomas a Kempis (1380–1471) argue that the true Christian is not simply a member of the institutional church but rather one who is capable of imitating the life of Christ by sharing in his personal commitment to poverty and charity. Thus, like the Greeks, Christians are encouraged to follow the example of others and, if necessary, to transform themselves so as to better do so.

A similar emphasis upon individual transformation is also evident within the Greek and Christian understanding of politics. Inasmuch as traditional ethics seeks the moral transformation of the historical individual, traditional politics tends to equate the art of ruling with the art of education. The well-ordered society is to educate its citizens in such a way that they conform to its preferred models. For example, Plato argued in his *Republic* that the various regimes of his day could be classified according to their particular understanding of the "good citizen." Thus, regimes can be classified as timocracies, oligarchies, democracies, or tyrannies according to whether they encourage their citizens to pursue fame, wealth, freedom, or order, respectively. From Plato's perspective, of course, the best society is that which teaches its citizens to pursue wisdom, and all others are judged according to how closely they approximate this goal.

In a similar manner, Aristotle believed that moral virtue is acquired through habituation and that the most important habits of any particular society are those determined by the law. Consequently the primary concern of the true legislator is to establish those laws that result in the formation of both the good citizen and the good person. In short, like Plato, Aristotle assumed that the business of politics is moral education.

This argument that the art of politics is simultaneously the art of education is also evident in the work of selected Christian political thinkers. Although Christianity expanded somewhat the classical list of virtues to include faith, hope, and charity, it still believes that the purpose of society is to transform its citizens in such a way as to make them more appealing to God. In view of this, Thomas Aquinas wrote:

> Therefore, since man, by living virtuously is ordained to a higher end, which consists of the enjoyment of God . . . then human society must have the same end as the individual man. Therefore it is not the ultimate end of an assembled multitude to live virtuously, but through virtuous living to attain the possession of God.[1]

Similarly it was in this spirit that the Christian philosopher Erasmus (1466–1536) wrote his famous treatise *The Education of the Christian Prince*. In it Erasmus sought to create a "likeness of the perfect prince" which could then serve as a model for actual princes who, in turn, were the authoritative personalities for their own people. The purpose of this, of course, was to create true Christians, i.e., those who embraced Christ in their hearts and emulated him in their deeds.

The classical Greek and Christian understanding of the person as a rational and spiritual participant within a preestablished hierarchy assumes the existence of a transcendent order. Reality is experienced as a meaningful and ordered whole, and individuals discover their true nature by adjusting themselves to those principles that are its source. Generally such an experience of wholeness is more easily accredited during a time of social harmony and political stability than during a period of cultural disruption and rapid social change. For example, the Christian view of human nature was particularly influential during the early and high Middle Ages. Beginning with the founding of the Holy Roman Empire in about 800 A.D. and continuing well into the twelfth century, "civilized" Europe understood itself as a single society constituted by the spiritual power of Christ, i.e., as the *Sacrum Imperium*. Being both holy and an empire, medieval Europe did not distinguish strictly between religious, moral, and political categories. The citizens of the empire were considered simply as "the faithful," and to this extent, the modern distinction between church and state did not yet exist. All the faithful were simultaneously members of both the single Church and the one empire. Thus, rather than being separate and distinct institutions, each serving its own specific ends, the Church and the state were understood as complementary aspects of a single and essentially harmonious society. United in one society and seeking one end, the faithful were encouraged to organize their everyday life in view of their common and transcendent spiritual destiny. Inasmuch as the order of society was understood as a microcosm of the order of creation, all individuals could easily acquire an understanding of their role in God's plan. Describing this situation, the historian J. Huizinga has written:

> The functions or groupings, which the Middle Ages designated by the words "estate" and "order" are of very diverse natures. They are, first of all, the estates of the realm, but there are also the trades, the state of matrimony and that of virginity, the state of sin. At court there are the "four estates of body and mouth": bread-masters, cup-bearers, carvers, and cooks. In the Church there are the sacerdotal orders and monastic orders. Finally, there are the different orders of chivalry. That which, in medieval thought, establishes unity in the very dissimilar meanings of the word, is the conviction that every one of these groupings represents a divine institution, an element of the organism of Creation emanating from the will of God, constituting an actual entity, and being, at bottom, as venerable as the angelic hierarchy. . . . The estates of society cannot but be venerable and lasting, because they have been ordained by God.[2]

In the compact world of medieval Europe, the Christian understanding of human nature, on one hand, and the hierarchical organization of feudal society, on the other, served to reinforce one another and thereby mutually sustain the view of reality as a harmonious whole. When this feudal order began to collapse, however, its underlying assumptions soon came under increasing scrutiny. For example, during the late Middle Ages, the Holy Roman Empire faced a series of political crises with the eventual result that the centralized monarchies of France, England, and Spain broke from the traditions of feudal politics and established thereby the beginnings of the modern nation-state. Similarly the cultural integrity of medieval Christendom was repeatedly challenged by the recurrence of popular spiritual movements which evolved outside of the formal structures of the

Church. At first the social forces represented by these movements could be contained within the official Church institutions. In time, however, they erupted to inspire the Reformation of Luther and Calvin. In short, the medieval order was fractured and, as a consequence, the traditional representation of reality as an ordered whole appeared increasingly questionable.

As feudal civilization eventually collapsed, the traditions, principles, and beliefs by which individuals had hitherto structured their lives eventually lost their basis in experiences. Deprived of such social and communal coordinates, individuals were of necessity referred back to their own personal resources. Consequently it appeared that if the meaning of life could not be found in the principles of an all-encompassing and stable order, perhaps it could be secured within the immanent structures of one's own existence. In short, the individual "self" was discovered.

As a "self," each person came to be seen as an autonomous, dignified, and essential being whose worth could be attributed to his or her own unique individuality. For a person understood as a "soul," virtue depended upon subordination to previously established principles. With the discovery of the "self," however, the principles of the traditional view were increasingly experienced as unnecessary constraints upon one's fundamental nature. Whereas at one time the idea of a "coherent universe" or of a "transcendentally grounded order" was welcomed as a necessary basis for psychic harmony, the modern "self" tends to regard such ideas as both burdensome and oppressive. For postfeudal individuals, the authentic self is its own creation. Rather than being determined by the will of another, the free self is required to accept only those principles that it, itself, has created. In short, the postfeudal age calls for the liberation of human individuality. Or in more traditional terms, it seeks to replace the model of the "well-ordered soul" with that of the "open self." There is perhaps no clearer early expression of this intention than that found in the work of Pico della Mirandola. In 1484, Pico retold the creation story in *Genesis* in a distinctively modern fashion:

> Therefore He (God) took up man, a work of indeterminate form; and placing him at the midpoint of the world, He spoke to him as follows: "We have given to thee, Adam, no final seat, no form of thy very own, no gift peculiarly thine, that thou mayest feel as thine own, have thine own, possess as thine own the seat, the form, the gifts which thou thyself shalt desire. A limited nature in other crea-

tures is confined within the laws written down by Us. In conformity
with thy free judgment, in whose hands I have placed thee, thou art
confined by no bounds; and wilt fix limits of nature for thyself . . .
Thou, like a judge appointed for being honorable, art the molder and
maker of thyself; thou mayest sculpt thyself into whatever shape
thou dost prefer. . . .[3]

Pico's celebration of individuality goes far beyond anything intended by such classical thinkers as Plato or Aristotle. For them, persons are free to develop their potential, but this potential itself is
strictly defined and limited by the set ends of human nature. For example, according to Plato, an individual is free to become a philosopher, but the actual nature of philosophical existence is fully established by the transcendent structure of reality itself. Pico, on the other
hand, refused to allow such prior determinations. According to him,
humans differ from the animals not because they have a different end
but rather because, unlike the animals, they have no particular end at
all. Humans are, in fact, autonomous; they decide for themselves who
they will become and, in so doing, express the open potential of their
free nature. This celebration of the autonomous self is characteristic
of the modern age in general, and it found one of its strongest advocates in the nineteenth-century Englishman John Stuart Mill. In his
On Liberty Mill wrote:

There is no reason that all human existence should be constructed on
some one or small number of patterns. If a person possesses any tol-
erable amount of common sense and experience, his own way of lay-
ing out his existence is the best, not because it is the best in itself but
because it is his own mode.[4]

It is obvious that an understanding of human nature that rejects
"some one or small number of patterns" for human existence must
also reject both an ethical system based on imitation and a political
system that seeks the moral transformation of its citizens. Just as the
discovery of the soul required a rethinking of the cosmological conception of politics, so too did the discovery of the self require an alternative to the classical Greek and Christian traditions. That, in turn,
has been provided by the theorists of classical liberalism.

Classical Liberal Theory of Human Nature

Liberalism first emerged as an important political movement during the seventeenth century. It originated in England and was but one of several major intellectual and social developments of its day. For example, it was also during this period that modern science successfully freed itself from the assumptions and restrictions that had characterized its medieval predecessor. In the writings of such Englishmen as Isaac Newton (1642–1727) and Francis Bacon (1561–1626), the traditional practices of medieval science were replaced by a new method both empirical and experimental in nature. Modern science views nature as being simply matter-in-motion. Nature, as a consequence, is understood to have no intrinsic purpose and thus is fully available for human manipulation. As we shall see, both the modern view of science and the modern view of nature have had significant impact upon liberal political thinking.

Similarly in the seventeenth century, English capitalism began to emerge as a new and eventually dominant form of economic organization. With the development of machine technology, industry and commerce began to displace agriculture as the most important segment of the English economy. Eventually such changes seemed to require that both the traditional restraints upon free trade and the time-honored restrictions upon innovation in manufacturing give way to the practices of the open market. In time, as the English middle class succeeded in acquiring an increasingly larger share of Britain's economic power, it also began to insist that it be allowed to determine its own political fate. This demand, in turn, soon resulted in a long series of constitutional conflicts between Parliament and the king. Traditionally the English monarchy had enjoyed the support of the landed nobility. Thus, as the middle class became more powerful, it attempted to use Parliament as its own way of controlling the crown's power. This tension between the royalists and the parliamentarians came to a head between 1648 and 1688. After a series of bloody wars which included the execution of King Charles I, the principle of parliamentary sovereignty was finally accepted when William and Mary assumed the throne at Parliament's invitation in what has become known as the "Glorious Revolution of 1688." Given these events, liberalism can be understood as a specific and concrete response to the intellectual, economic, and political changes within seventeenth-century England. It was, however, a response made in the name of universal principles, and as such it made a claim that, if correct, is still of importance for us today.

The two most important seventeenth-century English liberal philosophers were Thomas Hobbes (1588–1679) and John Locke (1632–1704). Although they are both classified as liberal, there are significant differences in their political teachings. Hobbes favored the creation of an absolute sovereign who could rule without constitutional limitations. Locke, on the other hand, preferred a much more restricted form of government. Consequently, in the English Civil War Hobbes supported the monarchy, while Locke favored the forces of Parliament. In spite of these important differences, however, both thinkers are classified as liberal philosophers because both began from the assumption that human nature was best understood according to the model of the autonomous self. Locke's *Second Treatise of Government* (1690) was a particularly influential elaboration of this perspective and presents an important example of the classical liberal world view.

Locke wrote his *Second Treatise* in order to present an alternative to the then-popular theory of political absolutism. In making his case, he argued that a proper understanding of the nature of political power could best be achieved by examining the way in which it first came about. Employing an essentially analytical method, Locke sought to reduce the complexity of historical reality by examining the more simplified existence of individuals in a prepolitical state of nature.

For Locke, natural persons exist as essentially complete and autonomous individuals. They enjoy their full faculties of reason and will and at the same time possess a series of natural rights which protect them from the inappropriate claims of others. Living according to their nature, such individuals exist in a prepolitical condition characterized by the complete absence of political authority. In a famous phrase, Locke summarized: "Men living together according to reason without a common Superior on Earth, with Authority to judge between them, is *properly the State of Nature.*[5]

In describing this state of nature, Locke emphasized two qualities in particular. First, the state of nature is a state of perfect equality. No individual can claim rightfully to exercise political authority over another; as a consequence, each is obligated to obey only those laws to which he or she has previously consented. Second, the state of nature is a state of perfect freedom. Individuals are free both to order their own actions and to dispose of their own property and persons as they alone see fit. Assuming that they act within the limits of natural reason, individuals are, as a consequence, free to act independently of and without regard for any other person. Locke insisted, however, that this state of natural freedom is not at the same time a state of license. Indeed for him, the state of nature is a state of natural law. In particular, the laws of nature require that everyone take such action as is necessary for self-preservation. This implies, in turn, that individuals be allowed to pursue those goods necessary for their life, liberty, and health. At the same time, since all individuals have a natural right to their life, liberty, and property, none can legitimately interfere with the rightful pursuits of another unless their own preservation is thereby threatened.

It is obvious from what we have seen that Locke's understanding of natural law was decidedly different from that of the classical Greek and Christian traditions. The natural law perceived by the Greeks is primarily a source of duty. It compels persons to resist the demands of their lower nature in order to allow them to actualize the implicit possibilities of their higher nature. The law, therefore, is an instrument of instruction that educates individuals by referring them to a standard of excellence beyond that of their primitive or elemental nature. For Locke, on the other hand, the natural law is not primarily a source of duty in the classical sense. On the contrary, in his theory it serves as the theoretical basis for individual rights. Instead of obligating individuals to transcend their primitive nature, Locke's natural law secures for them those very claims by which they can best preserve it. From this perspective, nature is understood to be teaching the principle of self-preservation. Rather than demanding a transformation of the "soul," it requires instead the indefinite continuation of the free and individualized "self." For Locke, nature intends that individuals simply continue to be that which they already are. In this sense, the natural self is assumed to be fundamentally complete and fulfilled. Inasmuch as individuals are conceived of as being complete and whole in nature, they are not, as a consequence, in need of those refinements or virtues that society alone can contribute to their development. Indeed, society may be a convenience but it is not a necessity; therefore, it can make no necessary claim over and against the individual. The political scientist C. B. Macpherson has described the classical liberal view of human nature as that of "possessive individualism":

> [The] possessive quality [of modern liberal-democratic theory] is found in its conception of the individual as essentially the proprietor

of his own person or capacities, owing nothing to society for them. The individual was seen neither as a moral whole, nor as part of a larger social whole, but as owner of himself. The individual, it was thought, is free inasmuch as he is proprietor of his person and capacities. The human essence is freedom from dependency on the wills of others and freedom is a function of possession.[6]

Being naturally complete, individuals nevertheless enter into civil society in order to preserve and advance their interests in the pursuit of life, liberty, and material wealth. These particular interests, however, are already established by the natural needs of dissociated individuals and are, in this sense, logically prior to society itself. The fulfillment of these preestablished needs sets the goals by which a particular society is to be judged. According to Locke, individuals are prior to society inasmuch as their specific interests both explain society's origin and define its purpose. This assumption is especially evident in Locke's understanding of the necessity of consent and the framing of the social contract.

If, as Locke assumed, all persons are by their nature free and equal, how then is it possible to justify the existence of a political arrangement that allows some individuals to rule others? As we have seen, the Greek tradition justified such a condition by denying the original premise. In this tradition, some are superior to others by nature—e.g., the virtuous are superior to the nonvirtuous, and, as a consequence, have a natural claim to rule. Similarly, Christianity and especially those traditions heavily influenced by Saint Paul argue that God actually ordained the institution of political rulership and therefore necessarily commanded the practice of civil obedience. For Locke, however, such arguments violate the principles of our natural condition. In his own analysis of Scripture, Locke found that God had indeed given Adam dominion over things but that this dominion did not include the power to rule over other humans. On the contrary, since all share in a common human nature, all individuals are naturally equal and thus born into a state of freedom. Indeed, even the right of parents over their children is only a claim that they be honored in return for their having fulfilled their obligation to care for the young: it is not a right to political dominion. If neither God nor nature has established some as superior to others, then according to Locke there remains only one legitimate source of political authority—i.e., consent. Individuals must agree to take themselves out of the state of nature and establish thereby those structures of authority characteristic of political society in general. In short, for reasons of convenience and inclination, individuals contract with one another to form a political society:

> Men being, as has been said, by Nature, all free, equal, and independent, no one can be put out of this Estate, and subjected to the Political Power of another, without his own Consent. The only way whereby any one divests himself of his Natural Liberty, and puts on the bonds of Civil Society is by agreeing with other Men to joyn and unite into a Community for their comfortable, safe, and peaceable living amongst another, in a secure Enjoyment of their Properties, and a greater Security against any that are not of it.[7]

According to Locke, political authority exists because individuals want it to, and individuals want it to exist because of the conveniences political society makes possible. From this perspective, political society exists for the sake of individuals; their interests are, in effect, both the source and the goal of the community. Everyone by nature seeks life, liberty, and property; yet while in the state of nature, the pursuit of such goods is difficult because there is neither an established law nor an established judge to regulate the competition that inevitably arises. Hence individuals conclude that it is in their own interest to submit to the authority of a common legislative and executive power serving as a neutral umpire. As a neutral umpire, the government has no interests of its own but rather seeks only to mediate among competing individual interests according to those impartial laws that have been established by the consent of the governed.

Classical Liberal Politics

As a political doctrine, Locke's teachings have been extremely influential throughout the Western world. In particular they had a decisive impact upon the thinking of the leaders of the American Revolution, as the language of the Declaration of Independence makes clear. At the same time, however, inasmuch as Locke claimed to have understood the universal principles of human nature, the standards of liberal politics should be able to transcend their specific Anglo-American context. If this is so, it should be possible to describe the principles of the liberal polity without necessarily limiting ourselves to an examination of either British or American history.

Foremost among these principles is that of a fundamental respect for the integrity of the autonomous individual. For liberalism, the individual is the basic element out of which all societies are constructed. Thus it is the individual rather than the family, tribe, or association who serves as the basic unit for all liberal analysis. From this perspective, the common good of society is essentially the aggregate of those particular goods that constitute the discrete interests of its individual members. Thus, in the words of the nineteenth-century liberal philosopher, Jeremy Bentham (1748–1832):

> The Community is a fictitious *body*, composed of the individual persons who are considered as constituting as it were its *members*. The interests of the community then is what?—the sum of the interests of the several members who compose it.[8]

If, as Bentham argued, the public interest is nothing but the sum total of the private interests of society's individual members, then it follows that society may serve no purpose other than that which is established for it by the desires of its constituents. To this extent, then, the individual is prior to society in a second and even more inclusive sense. Not only do individual needs constitute the foundations upon which society rests, but they also establish the purpose and direction for every legitimate social movement. The individual is both the *terminus a quo* and the *terminus ad quem* of the community. As we have seen, John Locke argued that individuals in the state of nature created society in order to realize those specific interests that were originally operative in the state of nature itself. Rather than pursuing conventional goods whose actualization would draw one out of his or her natural condition, liberal society seeks to satisfy more efficiently those needs that are already in existence. In short, liberal politics is a politics of preservation and not one of transformation. As such, its highest principle is that of individual freedom.

Inasmuch as liberalism assumes the reality of the autonomous self, it must allow each person the liberty of defining what the self shall become. Whereas the classical Greek and Christian views of human nature argue on behalf of a preexisting normative order to which each individual should be attuned, the liberal view of human nature requires that each be allowed to express and live by his or her own particular understanding of the good life. Instead of seeking to impose a uniform set of virtues and thereby implying the superiority of a particular way of life, liberal politics accepts the plurality of lifestyles and thereby seeks the maximization of personal freedom. Summarizing this perspective, the twentieth-century English philosopher Isaiah Berlin wrote:

> Most modern liberals, at their most consistent, want a situation in which as many individuals as possible can realize as many of their ends as possible without assessment of the value of these ends as such, save in so far as they may frustrate the purposes of others. They wish the frontiers between individuals or groups of men to be drawn solely with a view to preventing collision between human purposes, all of which must be considered to be equally ultimate, uncriticizable ends in themselves.[9]

Given individual freedom and governmental neutrality as its goals, liberal politics has adopted a variety of strategies to accomplish its aims. As can be expected, the particular strategy chosen at any given moment depends upon a prior analysis of what the theorist believes actually constitutes the greatest threat to freedom.

In its classical period, the seventeenth and eighteenth centuries, liberalism tended to see the power of the state itself as the most obvious threat to human liberty. Accordingly, classical liberal theorists worked to develop various means by which the scope of governmental activity could be restricted. By attempting to differentiate between the political sphere proper and other related but essentially distinct spheres of human activity, classical liberal theorists attempted to limit the issues that justified state action. For example, in his *First Letter Concerning Toleration* (1689), John Locke attempted to distinguish between the "business" of the civil government and that of the churches in an effort to establish a proper boundary between the two. According to Locke, religion is concerned with the salvation of one's soul. It thus is inwardly directed and must ultimately rely upon the power of persuasion and belief. Politics, on the other hand, occurs in the world of "outward things." Consequently it may employ the instruments of compulsion and force and is, in turn, concerned exclusively with such "civic interests" as the pursuits of life, liberty, and property. Given this distinction, Locke argued, the liberal state should refrain from interfering in the affairs of the church. Rather than enforcing the beliefs of a particular sect, the liberal state is to respect the religious freedom of all and thereby tolerate the spiritual preferences of each.

Similarly liberal economic theorists such as Adam Smith (1723–90) attempted to distinguish between the realms of politics and economics. According to this tradition of argument, politics is essentially an open field which is to be structured according to those principles implicit in the actions and decisions of the government. Political laws, therefore, express the values, commitments, and beliefs of that particular society which creates them. Economics, on the other hand, is a form of activity already structured by certain "natural" laws derived from the very nature of the production and exchange process itself. Unlike political laws, the laws of the marketplace are discovered, not created, and, as a consequence, exist independently of the particular values of any given society. A well-ordered liberal state would be one that respects the autonomy of the economic realm. Unlike the traditional doctrines of mercantilism, which subordinated the economic activity of society to the dictates of a political calculation concerning the national interest, liberal laissez-faire policy argued that any substantive interference by the state could only disrupt the natural harmony of an otherwise efficient economic system.

By distinguishing between the political realm on one hand and the economic realm on the other, liberal theory attempted to differentiate between political and civil society. The former is the domain of the state, while the latter is that of private commercial enterprise. By establishing an independent sphere of nonpolitical social cooperation, classical liberalism hopes to limit the exercise of state authority and thereby provide a sanctuary for human freedom. Representing this position, the contemporary economist Milton Friedman has written:

> The existence of a free market does not of course eliminate the need for government. On the contrary government is essential both as a forum for determining the "rules of the game" and as an umpire to interpret and enforce the rules decided on. What the market does is to reduce greatly the range of issues that must be decided through political means, and thereby minimize the extent to which government need participate directly in the game. . . . By removing the organization of economic activity from the control of political authority the market eliminates this source of coercive power. It enables economic strength to be a check to political power rather than a reinforcement.[10]

A third attempt to limit the scope of political activity can be found in the liberal doctrine of human rights. Whereas the first two strategies attempt to limit the role of the state by referring to the intrinsically nonpolitical nature of certain activities, the theory of natural rights bases its argument on an appreciation of the inviolable dignity of the human individual. For example, the United States Constitution lists specific individual rights that the government may not violate—even if it believes that it is in the national interest to do so. The First Amendment is but one example:

> Congress shall make no law respecting an establishment of religion, or prohibiting the free exercise thereof; or abridging the freedom of speech, or of the press; or the right of the people peaceably to assemble, and to petition the Government for a redress of grievances.[11]

Students of U.S. constitutional history are aware of the difficulty that the Supreme Court has had in attempting to apply this teaching to specific cases. Nonetheless the general logic of the argument appears to be clear. The doctrine of human rights attempts to protect individual initiative and freedom by creating a sphere into which the government cannot enter. For example, freedom of speech, as defined, is neither a privilege that must be earned nor a policy that may be changed. As a right, it presents an absolute claim, and as such it must be respected unless the government is willing to undermine its own standard of legitimacy. By positing the existence of certain *natural* rights, liberal politics secures a grounding for the worth and dignity of the individual, which is believed to exist independently of any specific social custom.

As we have seen, classical liberal politics assumed that the power of the state was potentially the greatest threat to the exercise of individual liberty. Given this analysis, it attempted to define quite narrowly the boundaries of the political realm. At the same time, however, classical liberalism was also concerned that the state be carefully restricted even while remaining entirely within its proper sphere. Arbitrary rule, even if limited to but a portion of the public realm, was by its very nature a clear threat to liberal freedom.

In an effort to prevent the possible abuse of an otherwise legitimate power, classical liberalism carried forward the traditional principles of constitutionalism. It argued that every society should establish a fundamental law whose provisions would serve as a safeguard against the abuse of political power. As we have seen, John Locke had argued that every legitimate society is necessarily based upon an implicit contract that outlines the powers and purposes for which the government was created. If for some reason a government were to violate the principles of its constitutive contract, it would, according to Locke thereby forfeit its claim to legitimacy. In such cases, the people would be free to dispose of those in power and to erect a new government in their place. For liberalism in general and Locke in particular, political power is always entrusted and never simply ceded to the government. If a government fails to retain the trust of its citizens because it has violated the very principles it was originally intended to uphold, it loses as a result both its authority and its ability to govern.

The threat of revolution as a way of enforcing a penalty against those who would rule arbitrarily is an extreme and therefore somewhat ineffective measure. Consequently classical liberalism has developed even further the traditional principles of medieval constitutionalism by establishing sanctions which, although short of force, are nevertheless able to secure the legal rights of citizens. Examples of such efforts can be found in such provisions of the U.S. Constitution as trial by jury, the equal protection of the laws, and the right to vote.

Finally, classical liberal politics has attempted to further restrain the power of the state by insisting that political sovereignty ultimately rests with the people. Again John Locke's arguments are typical of this approach. As we have seen, Locke argued that every legitimate government is created by the consent of the governed. Inasmuch as there is no principle of hierarchy operative in the state of nature, authority can arise only in the case of agreement. A people may agree to entrust their power to the government, but in doing so, they necessarily retain their right to recall it. For liberalism, then, popular sovereignty can be delegated but never forfeited. The liberal demand for required and periodic elections is a constant reminder of this fact. By forcing the politician to be accountable to the people, liberal politics establishes a powerful restraint upon the exercise of public authority.

The classical liberal attitude toward the state was first formulated in the seventeenth and eighteenth centuries, and it has continued to find supporters up to the present. However, as we shall see in chapter 11, a variant of the liberal tradition often referred to as modern liberalism began to develop in the nineteenth and twentieth centuries. Associated with such thinkers as T. H. Green (1836–82), L. T. Hobhouse (1864–1929), and John Dewey (1859–1952), modern liberalism advocates a much more activist role for the state.

The Assertion of the Self

Whereas at one time the classical liberal argued that the state was the greatest threat to individual freedom, the modern liberal chooses to focus upon the existence of other equally inhibiting limitations and constraints. For example, the modern liberal argues that one's individual freedom is limited just as much by the power of private organizations as it is by the policies and practices of the government itself. Similarly, liberal thinkers have noted that such objective conditions as ignorance, disease, and poverty have the effect of limiting one's life choices just as surely as if one lived under the rule of an arbitrary leader. Given this, some liberals have changed their traditional attitude toward the state. Rather than being an object of fear, the state now appears as a possible means for the enhancement of individual liberty. Indeed, through its regulatory powers the state can control the often arbitrary and harmful policies pursued by private interests. Similarly, through public-service programs, the state can combat the stultifying effects of poverty, ignorance, and disease and thereby free the individual citizen for a richer and more promising life. No longer victimized by forces or conditions over which they have no real control, the liberated citizens of the modern welfare state are now free to determine their own fate. From this perspective, then, the state becomes a means for, rather than an obstacle to, the development of individual autonomy and human self-worth.

Unlike the theory of the minimalist state envisioned by classical liberals, modern liberalism proposes an activist state as an agent of social reform. Justifying state intervention in terms of "the prevention of a hindrance to the capacity for rights"[12] modern liberalism has introduced those strategies that are typical of the contemporary welfare state.

As a political program, therefore, liberalism has created two markedly different and even opposed theories of the state. At the theoretical level, however, it has remained true to its original commitment of serving the needs of the autonomous self. Whereas the classical "soul" sought participation, the liberal "self" requires emancipation. As a consequence, the politics of the liberal era is inevitably a politics of liberation.

Notes

1. Thomas Aquinas, *On the Governance of Rulers*, trans. Gerald Phelan (New York: Sheed and Ward, 1938), pp. 97–98.
2. J. Huizinga, *The Waning of the Middle Ages*, trans. F. Hopman (Garden City, N.Y.: Doubleday, 1954), p. 58.
3. Pico della Mirandola, *On the Dignity of Man*, trans. Charles Glenn Wallis (Indianapolis: Bobbs-Merrill, 1965), pp. 4–5.
4. John Stuart Mill, "On Liberty," in *John Stuart Mill: Utilitarianism, On Liberty, Essay on Bentham*, ed. Mary Warnock (New York: New American Library, 1962), p. 197.
5. John Locke, *Two Treatises of Government* (New York: New American Library, 1963), p. 321.
6. C. B. Macpherson, *The Political Theory of Possessive Individualism: Hobbes to Locke* (New York: Oxford University Press, 1962), p. 3.
7. Locke, *Two Treatises*, pp. 374–75.
8. Jeremy Bentham, "Introduction to the Principles of Morals and Legislation," in *A Fragment on Government with an Introduction to the Principles of Morals and Legislation by Jeremy Bentham*, ed. Wilfred Harrison (Oxford: Basil Blackwell, 1967), p. 126.
9. Isaiah Berlin, *Four Essays on Liberty* (New York: Oxford University Press, 1969), p. 153.
10. Milton Friedman, *Capitalism and Freedom* (Chicago: University of Chicago Press, 1962), p. 15.
11. As printed in Graham and Graham, *Founding Principles of American Government* (Chatham: Chatham House Publishers, 1984), p. 382.
12. T. H. Green, *Lectures on the Principles of Political Obligation* (Ann Arbor: University of Michigan Press, 1967), p. 209.

Recommended Readings

Berlin, Isaiah. *Four Essays on Liberty*. New York: Oxford University Press, 1969.

Cumming, Robert Denoon. *Human Nature and History: A Study of the Development of Liberal Political Thought*. 2 vols. Chicago: University of Chicago Press, 1969.

Dahrendorf, Ralf. *The New Liberty: Survival and Justice in a Changing World*. Stanford, Calif.: Stanford University Press, 1975.

Dewey, John. *Individualism: Old and New*. New York: Capricorn Books, 1962.

Dunn, John. *The Political Thought of John Locke.* New York: Cambridge University Press, 1969.

Hobhouse, L. T. *Liberalism.* New York: Oxford University Press, 1964.

Laski, Harold. *The Rise of European Liberalism.* London: George Allen & Unwin, 1962.

Minogue, Kenneth. *The Liberal Mind.* New York: Random House, 1968.

Pirenne, Henri. *A History of Europe: From the End of the Roman World in the West to the Beginnings of the Western States.* Translated by Bernard Miall. Garden City, N.Y.: Doubleday, 1958.

Sandel, Michael. *Liberalism and the Limits of Justice.* New York: Cambridge University Press, 1982.

Strayer, Joseph. *On the Medieval Origins of the Modern State.* Princeton, N.J.: Princeton University Press, 1970.

Tarcov, Nathan. *Locke's Education for Liberty.* Chicago: University of Chicago Press, 1984.

C H A P T E R 6

Marxism and the Discovery of the Social Self

Introduction

In their effort to break from the traditional restraints of Western feudal Christendom, liberal political thinkers had emphasized the freedom and dignity of the autonomous individual. In the eyes of liberalism's critics, however, this apparently exclusive concern for the development of human autonomy could easily result in a one-sided and therefore distorted understanding of human nature.

For example, the French philosopher Jean Jacques Rousseau (1712–78) argued that the liberal understanding of our basic needs and capacities had proven to be an inadequate foundation for the development of a well-ordered society. Specifically, according to Rousseau, liberalism's appeal to the principle of enlightened self-interest is simply insufficient:

> Is it really such a wonderful thing to have made it impossible for men to live together without mutual bigotry, mutual competition, mutual deceit, mutual treason, and mutual destruction? How careful must we be, henceforward, never to see ourselves as we are! After all, for every two men whose interests converge, there are perhaps one hundred thousand who are adversaries; and there is but one way to succeed in deceiving or ruining all these thousands. Here is the deadly source of violence, of the betrayals and perfidies, of all the other horrors necessary in a condition where each—in pretending to work for

the fortune and reputation of others—seeks in truth, at the expense
of others, only to enhance and enlarge his own.[1]

Thus like other more conservative critics such as Edmund Burke,
Rousseau believed that the doctrine of liberal individualism fails to
account for the more universal and truly cooperative aspects of the
human personality. A similar argument can be found in the radical
criticism of Karl Marx.

Marx's Criticism of Bourgeois Man

In his "Preface to *A Critique of Political Economy*," published in
1859, Karl Marx summarized his understanding of historical materialism in the following passage:

> In the social production of their life, men enter into definite relations
> that are indispensable and independent of their will, relations of
> production which correspond to a definite stage of development of
> their material productive forces. The sum total of these relations of
> production constitutes the economic structure of society, the real
> foundation, on which rises a legal and political superstructure and
> to which corresponds definite forms of social consciousness. The
> mode of production of material life conditions the social, political,
> and intellectual life process in general. It is not the consciousness of
> men that determines their being, but, on the contrary, their social
> being that determines their consciousness. . . . With the change of
> the economic foundations, the entire immense superstructure is
> more or less rapidly transformed.[2]

As we have seen, Marx believed that the economic substructure of
Western society had evolved through at least three distinct phases.
Each phase, in turn, was characterized by its own particular form of
social consciousness. With this insight, Marx was, as a consequence,
able to argue that liberal political theory is in essence that form of social consciousness that corresponds in a particular way to the capitalist mode of production. Those who fail to appreciate this historical
relationship, according to Marx, are prone to make a serious theoretical miscalculation. Rather than acknowledging the time-bound quality of their own beliefs, such theorists assume that the "self-evident
truths" of their own day are, in fact, universal propositions valid for

all people and at all times. For example, liberal thinkers such as John Locke and Adam Smith believed that the motives and interests of their contemporaries were in fact the universal principles of human nature itself.

From Marx's perspective, such an analysis suffers from an inadequate appreciation of human historicity. As an essentially historical species, humanity changes as its needs evolve, and those who refuse to acknowledge this change are, as a consequence, oblivious to the reality of historical progress.

Marx's critique of the liberal view of human nature is based upon this insight. In general, according to Marx, liberal thinkers assume that the specific characteristics of the bourgeoisie are in fact equivalent to the principles of human nature as such. As a consequence, liberal social theory mistakenly portrays the capitalist way of life as both natural and universally valid. Inasmuch as Marx had argued that capitalism was but one of several stages within history, he resisted what he believed to be the liberal attempt to reify the present. Indeed, just as capitalism is but a prelude to communism, so, too, according to Marx, is the bourgeois understanding of human nature simply a partial and hence insufficient expression of humanity's historically developing potential.

In his *Communist Manifesto*, written with Friedrich Engels in 1848, Marx assessed both the accomplishments and limitations of the capitalist era. On one hand, capitalism represented a truly progressive force. For example, by encouraging scientific and technological innovation, capitalism had succeeded in improving dramatically the productive capabilities of the economy. Similarly, by promoting the growth of manufacturing and creating large industrial facilities, capitalism also contributed to the development of the modern city as a commercial, political, and cultural center. Finally, in seeking international markets for its products, capitalism succeeded in creating a worldwide commercial network that produced for the first time both a world history and a world literature. In short, according to Marx:

> The bourgeoisie, historically, has played a most revolutionary part. . . . It has been the first to show what man's activity can bring about. It has accomplished wonders far surpassing Egyptian pyramids, Roman aqueducts, and Gothic cathedrals; it has conducted expeditions that put in the shade all former Exoduses of nations and crusades.[3]

In spite of these accomplishments, however, Marx insisted that the bourgeois era is rightfully at an end. Although capitalism at one time may have represented the forces of progress vis-a-vis the traditions of the feudal past, according to Marx, it currently functions as an entrenched obstacle to further development. Originally the free-market system was an efficient and successful way of organizing the forces of production. As these forces developed, however, they "outgrew" the capitalist institutions that originally nurtured them, and as a consequence they can no longer expand at an appropriate rate. For Marx, the current crises of capitalism are primarily the results of this fundamental mismatch between the advancing forces of production on one hand and the outdated techniques by which they are organized and administered on the other. According to Marx, the solution to this problem is the creation of a new and more appropriate form of social organization—i.e., the communist society.

Marx's evaluation of the liberal or bourgeois theory of human nature is analogous to his assessment of capitalism in general. Specifically, according to Marx, the liberal understanding of the autonomous self represents a partially correct yet essentially outdated and hence incomplete comprehension of human needs and capacities. When it first emerged, the liberal vision of the person as an autonomous self functioned as a needed corrective to the conventional restraints of feudal society. However, inasmuch as this view allows for only a partial emancipation, further progress requires that society move beyond the traditional liberal preoccupation with the needs of the individual self.

Marx's most complete assessment of the liberal view of human nature can be found in an early essay entitled, "On the Jewish Question." Written in response to several essays on political emancipation by Bruno Bauer, Marx's "On the Jewish Question" presents his analysis of both the achievements and the shortcomings of political liberalism as represented in the American and French Revolutions.

On one hand, the liberal revolution accomplished an important and necessary task. By removing religious qualifications for citizenship, liberalism created a realm of universal and equal political rights. Thus, unlike the practices of feudalism whereby certain religious groups were denied the right of full political participation while others, such as the clergy, were allowed special privileges, liberal society grants all citizens equal rights. To this extent, liberalism is a progressive force because it frees citizens to participate in the political sphere regardless of their religious affiliation. At the same time, Marx insisted that the freedom gained by the liberal revolutions is limited. Although liberalism can rightfully claim to have achieved *political* emancipation, it nonetheless fails to recognize the larger and more difficult task of human emancipation:

> To be *politically* emancipated from religion is not to be finally and completly emancipated from religion because political emancipation is not the final and absolute form of human emancipation. . . . The limits of political emancipation appear at once in the fact . . . that a state may be a *free state* without man himself being a *free man*.[4]

According to Marx, the very technique by which liberalism first achieved political emancipation had the simultaneous effect of preventing society from progressing any further towards the goal of full human emancipation. As we have seen, liberal theorists distinguish between the political realm (the state) on one hand and the economic and social realm (civil society) on the other. By differentiating between these two spheres, liberal theory is able to abstract the political realm from the activities of everyday life. In doing so, it can remove from the political realm qualifications and conditions typical of social existence. Although individuals in society are still divided and treated according to such considerations as their religious affiliation, wealth, ethnic background, or education, as citizens—i.e., as actors in the political realm—they are able to demand the recognition of their universal political rights. Citizens as political beings are liberated from those constraints that arise from their membership within a particular group, but as social beings, i.e., in their everyday life, such limitations still determine their historical fate. According to Marx, therefore, the final stage of human emancipation can only be achieved when the universal attributes of the liberal state are reintroduced back into civil society. As a result, civil society will be reordered so as to manifest that very same universalism that has hitherto been restricted to the realm of the abstract liberal state.

Marx's critique of the liberal theory of human nature is directed against its assumption that the condition of the individual in civil society is in some way equivalent to the human conditions per se. As we have seen, liberal theorists assume that it is only natural for one to act according to the principle of enlightened self-interest. Marx, on the other hand, argues that the liberal understanding of human nature is in fact the result of the particular historical situation created by life in bourgeois civil society. In short, the autonomous individual is essentially a product of capitalism. Inasmuch as capitalism is a system of competition and exploitation rather than one of cooperation and nurture, it forms it citizens accordingly. For Marx, the liberal individual is distorted: "regarded as an isolated monad, withdrawn into himself," understood as "egoistic man, separated from other men and from the community."[5] Just as liberalism has confused the concept of human nature with that of the bourgeois egoistic self, so too does its notion of natural rights fail to transcend the particular limitations of the capitalistic perspective:

> None of the supposed rights of man, therefore, go beyond the egoistic man, man as he is, as a member of civil society; that is an individual separated from the community, withdrawn into himself, wholly preoccupied with his private interests and acting in accordance with his private caprice. Man is far from being considered, in the rights of man, as a species-being; on the contrary, species-life itself— society—appears as a system which is external to the individual and as a limitation of his original independence. The only bond between men is natural necessity, need, and private interest, the preservation of their property and their egoistic persons.[6]

According to Marx, the liberal view of human nature is the result of that particular form of false consciousness produced by the economic and social dislocations of capitalism. Inasmuch as each stage in the development of a society's economic substructure is both superior to what preceded it and at the same time inferior to that which follows, so, too, the liberal view of human nature is only partially correct. Liberalism is correct in its recognition of human individuality because postfeudal persons did in fact achieve an awareness of themselves as individuals. At the same time, however, it is equally true that individuals are conscious of themselves as sharing in a common human nature and are, as a result, aware of the fact that they are both individuals and members of the human species. Whereas liberalism emphasizes our individuality, Marx, in turn, attempted to reaffirm the importance of our "species-being." Individuals are species-beings not only in the sense of requiring the existence of others for the satisfaction of their practical and cultural needs but also inasmuch as they are able to conceive of the species as such and thereby make it an end for their actions. Indeed for Marx a person is most authentically human when he or she acts deliberately as a species-being. However, given both the competitive nature and class structure of capitalism, such species-regarding actions are all but impossible. According to Marx, therefore, capitalism represents a denial of the very possibility of actualizing one's true humanity. This situation is most carefully analyzed in Marx's discussion of human alienation.

Marx and the Analysis of Human Alienation

Marx's understanding of historical materialism has led some scholars to argue that he does not, in fact, believe in the existence of a constant human nature. Although there is evidence to support this position, it is nonetheless true that in his so-called early writings (1837–44), Marx developed an understanding of human alienation that, by its very place in his argument, seems to imply a specific interpretation of the individual as a potentially nonalienated being. The resolution of this debate as to whether there is a concept of human nature in the work of Marx ultimately depends upon the weight one gives to these early texts. Those who are generally referred to as "socialist humanists" argue that Marx's early writings are extremely important since they reveal the essential moral doctrines that inform all his later work. In any case our discussion of Marx's understanding of human nature will be based upon these earlier sources.

When discussing the development and structure of capitalism, Marx was always careful to acknowledge the real achievements of the bourgeoisie. In particular, he pointed to capitalism's commitment to economic growth, which allows humanity to conquer the age-old problem of natural scarcity. For the first time in history, the world's people are able to produce enough to satisfy all their true needs. At the same time, though, the market system of distribution by which these products are made available to the consumer depends upon an exchange of money and, as a consequence, necessarily fails to meet the needs of the very poor. Consequently, as important as capitalism's achievements are, one must not ignore the reality of its darker side. Specifically, according to Marx's analysis, capitalism's very success depends upon the systematic and brutal exploitation of the proletariat—a process that has resulted in the total dehumanization of the laboring class. On one hand, capitalism represents the near perfection of our productive capacities, but on the other it has created a form of society that dehumanizes and eventually destroys its most productive members.

Marx used the term *alienation* to describe the specific situation of the proletariat within modern capitalist society. In general it refers to that condition in which workers perceive their true humanity as being either external to or entirely removed from the reality of their everyday lives. Rather than experiencing their potential as the continuing perfection of real attributes, alienated workers see their humanity as "other" or "alien" to their actual lived condition. According to Marx, humanity consists in the ability to work in a free and creative manner. Although all animals labor, only the human can do so creatively, and it is this creative ability to transform the world and thereby transform itself as part of the world that sets the human species apart from all others.

Potentially each individual is a free and creative laborer. Historically, however, no one has ever realized the full promise of this potential, and as a consequence everyone has always experienced some degree of alienation. Originally in precapitalist societies, people were prevented from laboring freely because of the external constraints imposed upon them by the continual threat of natural scarcity. Rather than being able to labor when and how they pleased, the ancients were forced to labor in response to nature's demands. In capitalism, however, nature has finally been conquered by technology, and as a result the individual is liberated from the rule of necessity. Tragically, however, because of the very way in which capitalism has organized the laboring process, the industrial worker is actually more alienated than were any of his or her predecessors. Ironically, the modern worker has become the first totally alienated being. Fully deprived of the possibility of creative labor, the modern proletarian has been transformed into an animallike creature of instinct:

> We arrive at the result that man [the worker] feels himself to be freely active only in his animal functions—eating, drinking, and procreating, or at most also in his dwelling and in personal adornment—while in his human functions he is reduced to an animal. The animal becomes human and the human becomes animal.[7]

Inasmuch as the industrial laborer represents the actual antithesis of full human potential, it is possible to arrive at an understanding of Marx's conception of the human as a species-being by examining the negation of this quality through alienation. In particular there are four distinct yet related aspects to this phenomenon.

1. *Within capitalism, the natural relationship between the workers and the objects they produce is destroyed by the alienating effects of the market system.* Naturally, according to Marx, laborers are capable of experiencing a certain joy in their work because the objects they produce eventually embody the skills, qualities, and values of the individual who has produced them. It is as if a worker "objectifies" a certain aspect of her or himself by transforming the materials of nature into an object for human use. Just as a painting is more than simply pigment and canvas but also a representation of the artist, so that we can come to know him or her by examining such a work, so too do the objects of material labor represent more than simply the "stuff" out of which they are made. By working, people externalize their ideas, give them shape and substance, and thereby "humanize" their natural environment.

In capitalism, however, this natural relationship is destroyed by the system of production and exchange. Rather than being a direct end intended by the process of production, the object produced is transformed into a mere means created, not for its own sake, but for the sake of what it can secure, i.e., money. In capitalism laborers work because they have to. In order to satisfy their needs, workers require money, and the only way in which they can earn money is by selling their labor power to the capitalist, who then uses it to produce the goods, which are in turn sold on the market. According to Marx, this series of transactions results in the actual transformation of the object of labor itself. Rather than being an end having its own worth as a manifestation of the skills and personality of the worker, it is now simply a means whose actual value is determined by its role in the service of capital. Indeed, this transformation is of such a radical nature that the object actually becomes a power that exists independently of the worker and eventually poses as a threat to his or her very existence. Within capitalism, the object is simultaneously both a means and an obstacle to the procurement of money. It is a means inasmuch as its production allows workers to receive their wages; it is an obstacle, however, because these workers will not receive their wages unless it is first produced. In a certain sense, the object stands between the workers and that which they truly need. Consequently, rather than delighting in their products, workers come to fear and resent them. They perceive them as an alien power that exists independently of themselves and whose value is created by their own personal devaluation. By objectifying their labor within capitalism, workers create material wealth for others at the cost of their own personal impoverishment.

2. *Just as workers became alienated vis-à-vis the products of their laboring activity, so, too, are they alienated from the actual process of production itself.* In a truly nonalienated society, each person would work according to his or her ability and receive according to his or her needs. Inasmuch as a person's basic needs would be satisfied regardless of the quality, type, or amount of work produced, each individual would work only because he or she wanted to and inasmuch as he or she found personal satisfaction in performing the task at hand. In a somewhat romantic description of the work situation in a future communist society, Marx wrote:

> . . . in a communist society, where nobody has one exclusive sphere of activity but each can become accomplished in any branch he wishes, society regulates the general production and thus makes it possible for me to do one thing today and another tomorrow, to hunt in the morning, fish in the afternoon, rear cattle in the evening, criticize after dinner, just as I have a mind without ever becoming hunter, fisherman, shepherd, or critic.[8]

In capitalism, according to Marx, this potentially creative and spontaneous relationship between the workers and their own activity is destroyed by the alienating effect of both the division of labor and the private property system. The division of labor requires that each worker specialize in the performance of a single task. Rather than being an individual able to enjoy a variety of activities, the worker is forced by the discipline of the laboring process to concentrate exclusively upon a single task. Such an individual becomes, in the words of Marx, either a hunter, a fisherman, a shepherd, or a critic. With the introduction of mechanization into the manufacturing process, the actual tasks the laborer must perform become increasingly simplified and repetitive in nature. Consequently the work process itself is depersonalized and the worker is no longer able to identify with his or her own activity.

Since capitalism is a private-property system, the product the worker makes is owned exclusively by the capitalist who was paid the laborer's wages and purchased the original raw materials. As a result, the worker creates wealth by transforming raw materials into a usable product and thereby establishing their value as a commodity, but this wealth is eventually transferred to another and ultimately antagonistic class. Given this transfer of value, workers experience their own laboring activity as something done solely for the sake of another. In this situation, the very activity of laboring itself appears as a process of estrangement whereby workers are forced to give to another that which they themselves have created.

3. *The third form of alienation distorts one's species-consciousness.* As we have seen, Marx believed the individual is properly a species-being. Accordingly each individual has as his or her own goal the nurture and support of the common species-life. To argue otherwise is to assume that the individual and society are in some way fundamentally opposed. For Marx such an assumption is patently false:

> Therefore the *social* character is the universal character of the whole movement; *as* society itself produces *man as man*, so it is *produced* by him. Activity and mind are social in their content as well as in their *origin*; they are *social* activity and social mind. The *human* significance of nature only exists for *social* man, because only in this case is nature a *bond* with other men, the basis of his existence for others and of their existence for him. . . . Thus *society* is the accomplished union of man with nature, the veritable resurrection of nature, the realized naturalism of man, and the realized humanism of nature.[9]

In short, for Marx, in a nonalienated society such traditional dichotomies as those that separate citizen from society, person from nature, and individual from individual would be transcended as one's species-consciousness became aware of the common ground which does in fact unite such apparent opposites. In capitalism, this insight is not yet available because the normal relationships between the individual and the species have been reversed. Rather than encouraging the individual to contribute to the advancement of the common species-life, the egoistic and competitive quality of bourgeois existence forces people to treat their community as simply a means to the fulfillment of their own private ends. In liberalism, society is intended to serve the material interests of its members. Given this, one's individual life inevitably becomes more important than that of the species, because the former is eventually transformed into the purpose of the latter.

4. *Finally the alienation of the modern proletariat is manifested in the individual's estrangement from other humans.* Inasmuch as workers are alienated from the product of their labor (i.e., nature), from their own self-defining activity (i.e., work), and from their common species-existence (i.e., society), it follows necessarily, according to Marx, that they are eventually alienated from one another. Living amidst structures perverted by the processes of capitalistic accumulation, the individual's relationship with others is affected accordingly. Competition replaces cooperation as the struggle for scarce resources undermines any natural inclination towards solidarity or mutual aid. In such a situation, the individual necessarily encounters each fellow worker as an alien and ultimately threatening "other."

Marx's analysis of human alienation was based upon his understanding of the actual conditions of his day. Within capitalism all are alienated, he argued—even the capitalists themselves. Given the fact that capitalists are neither poor nor frustrated in their labor, they do not experience the full tragedy of the modern condition. The proletariat, on the other hand, does, and its condition symbolizes the complete negation of our humanity. By negating this negation (i.e., by imaginatively removing the effects of capitalism from a description of the laboring process) Marx was able to create an image of what he believed nonalienated or truly human labor would be like:

> Supposing that we had produced in a human manner; each of us would in his production have doubly affirmed himself and his fellow men. I would have (1) objectified in my production my individuality and its peculiarity and thus both in my activity enjoyed an individual expression of my life and also in looking at the object have had the individual pleasure of realizing that my personality was objective, visible to the senses and thus a power raised beyond all doubt. (2) In your enjoyment or use of my product I would have had the direct enjoyment of realizing that I had both satisfied a human need by my work and also objectified the human essence and therefore fashioned for another human being the object that met his need. (3) I would have been for you the mediator between you and the species and thus been acknowledged and felt by you as a completion of your own essence and a necessary part of yourself and have thus realized that I am confirmed both in your thought and in your love. (4) In my expression of my life I would have fashioned your expression of your life, and thus in my own activity have realized my own essence, my human, my communal essence.
>
> In that case our products would be like so many mirrors out of which our essence shone.[10]

Marx's analysis of truly "human" labor is important for several reasons. First it is obvious that, according to Marx, the rewards of human labor are not of a strictly material nature. Indeed, in a communist society the people would not receive wages for their work. On the contrary, Marx foresaw that in a truly nonalienated society, individuals would want to work because the laboring process itself would become a means of human self-fulfillment. Just as today an artist may paint even if his or her paintings are not meant to be sold for a profit, so, too, in a communist society people would work even if their needs were satisfied regardless of the value they produced. In short, work itself would become a true human need rather than simply remaining the means by which other more "real" needs are to be satisfied.

Second, if properly organized, work would become a means of establishing and sustaining mutually supportive relationships among the members of society. Individuals would work not only for the personal satisfaction they would find in the creative objectification of their personality but also for the sake of the interpersonal relationships that labor makes possible. Inasmuch as one's work is able to satisfy the needs of another, the two are brought together through labor into a relationship of mutual support and recognition. Indeed, Marx even speaks of this as the beginning of a love relationship. Although Marx believed that in communism there would be no enforced division of labor, he was still confident that the necessary work of society would be done. In a specific situation one may choose to undertake certain apparently "undesirable" tasks because of a conviction that in doing so one was contributing to the good of others. For Marx, with the overcoming of alienation, people would no longer be motivated solely according to their own narrow calculation of what appears to be their immediate selfish interest. In effect, the utilitarian ethics of the bourgeoisie will have been replaced by the higher standards of an ethics of social consciousness.

Finally, with the transcending of alienated labor, mankind itself will have achieved a new stage in its historical existence. At one point, Marx referred to all of history prior to the communist revolution as the prehuman or animal stage of history. Although the slave, feudal, and capitalist forms of society differ from one another in significant ways, they are all characterized by the presence of alienation and thus equally prehuman. With the emergence of communism, however, alienation will cease, and as a result mankind will achieve its truly human form:

> The supersession of private property is, therefore, the complete *emancipation* of all the human qualities and senses. . . . For it is not

only the five senses, but also the so-called spiritual senses, the practical senses (desiring, loving, etc), in brief human sensibility and the human character of the sense, which can only come into being through the existence of *its* objects, through humanized nature. . . so the fully constituted society produces man in all the plenitude of his being, the wealthy man endowed with all the senses, as an enduring reality. It is only in a social context that subjectivism and objectivism, spiritualism and materialism, activity and passivity cease to be antinomies and thus cease to exist as such antinomies.[11]

Following the example of traditional Christianity, Marx had adopted a fundamentally dramatic view of history. From this perspective, the general movement of history tells a story and the importance of specific events is determined by their contribution to the unfolding of the meaning of the whole. For Marx, history is the story of humanity's effort to overcome its alienation and thereby realize its full potential as a species. From his perspective, communism's superiority vis-à-vis the other forms of society is not simply due to its improved economic capabilities. On the contrary, as the culmination of mankind's historical mission, the communist order represents the very completion of history itself.

Marx's Politics

Although he was confident that the future communist society would be free from the distorting effects of alienation, Marx was extremely cautious about predicting the exact structure of the communist order. The proletariat would form the new society only after experiencing the purgative effect of its revolution against capitalism. Thus to predict the exact nature of the resultant society prior to the actual event was an impossibility, according to Marx.

Having said this, however, Marx was willing, nonetheless, to describe certain general features. For example, the introduction of communism would be accomplished in two phases. The first phase, referred to by Marx as either "socialism" or "crude communism," would be a relatively short yet brutal period in which the proletariat would exercise dictatorial powers in its efforts to purge society of the remnants of capitalism. The second phase, "mature communism," on the other hand, represented the positive fulfillment of Marx's expectations. With the abolition of the private ownership of the means

Human Nature and Politics

of production, all traditional class distinctions would disappear once and for all. At the same time, the wage and market systems that capitalism had used to govern the production and distribution of goods would be replaced by the well-known regulative principle "from each according to his ability, to each according to his needs." Similarly, as the private-property system disappeared, so, too, would the division of labor and with it the state. Communism, according to Marx, would be a true anarchy, and the people, united as a single society, would be in a position collectively to determine its own fate.

The abstract and ambiguous quality of Marx's description of the future communist society has created certain problems for those modern regimes that claim to be inspired by his thinking. For example, in discussing the public ownership of the means of production, Marx never fully developed the precise institutional arrangments by which this could be accomplished. As a consequence, in regimes such as the Soviet Union, private ownership of the means of production has, in most cases, been replaced by a form of state ownership—even though this, in turn, has created a huge bureaucracy whose legitimacy is problematic in view of Marx's democratic and anarchist intentions. Similarly Marx never indicated how a society was to determine the true needs and abilities of its citizens. Without such a determination, however, the principle "from each according to his ability, to each according to his needs" remains but a vague and appealing formula. As a result, the Soviet Union has continued to rely upon a wage system and permits market forces to operate in selected areas of the agricultural economy.

Given this situation, it is interesting to compare the current Soviet society with Marx's own understanding of the future communist order. Some commentators have used such a comparison in an attempt to illustrate the utopian features of Marx's program. In doing so, however, one must first acknowledge that the circumstances that led to the revolution in Russia were not the same as those that Marx himself envisioned. Thus the Soviet Union is not a "pure" case study. Nonetheless it is interesting to note that today the Soviet Union does not yet claim to be fully communist. On one hand, it argues that it is no longer a dictatorship of the proletariat (and thus no longer simply socialist) because it has transcended the class structure upon which such a dictatorship must necessarily be based. On the other hand, the Soviet Union is not yet fully communist because it retains such noncommunist features as a wage system and a state. Given this, Soviet theorists have invented a new classification that cannot be found in

Marx's own writings. According to this scheme, the Soviet Union is officially in the stage of "building communism." At the same time, the Marxist societies of Eastern Europe are classified as "building socialism," while China is seen as "building capitalism." Given both this proliferation of conceptual categories and the mixing of Marxist, nationalist, and geopolitical concerns in the practice of contemporary communist regimes, it is difficult to derive an understanding of Marxist politics through an investigation of current policy. If, however, one returns to the theory of Marx himself, two important characteristics of his political thinking become quite clear. First the politics of humanity as species-beings is a politics of liberation. In this sense, it appears as a continuation of that emancipatory project first introduced by the liberal tradition during the seventeenth century. At the same time, however, socialist politics also promises, and even demands, a significant transformation of the human condition. In this it is much more akin to similar arguments associated with the classical Greek and Christian perspective. Whether such traditions can be brought together to form a harmonious whole is a question whose answer ultimately depends upon one's understanding of human nature and its needs.

Marx's critique of the bourgeois forms of liberal freedom was not intended as a critique of freedom as such. Like liberalism, Marxism is essentially a politics of emancipation and to this extent it continues that mission first announced in the American and French revolutions. Yet, as we have seen, Marx believed the liberal understanding of freedom to be a partial one at best. Based upon an understanding of the person as an essentially autonomous individual, liberalism, especially in its classical form, typically defined freedom as a state of independence from the arbitrary will of another. From Marx's perspective, although such an understanding may have protected one from a potential abuse of political power, it did so at the cost of transforming one's political or species-life into the mere means for satisfying the needs of the private or egoistic self. For Marx such a fundamental transformation represented both an inversion of the preferred order and a diminution of the full meaning of freedom. Freedom properly understood is more than simply the freedom of being left alone. Its expanded sense, according to Marx, must necessarily include the species's ability to rationally control both its natural and social environment. A truly free humanity, therefore, is one that is liberated from the domination of things. Traditionally such domination has assumed two forms—physical necessity and reified social relationships. As a consequence, the full realization of human freedom presupposes two forms of sovereignty. First, humanity must learn to control the forces of nature, and second, it must assume the leadership and direction of society itself.

The ability to control the forces of nature depends upon the development of the forces of production. As we have seen, Marx praised the bourgeoisie for having overcome the problem of natural scarcity. Communism, according to Marx, would build upon and extend this victory over nature. Unlike such socialists as the Frenchman Charles Fourier (1772–1837) who rejected industrial civilization on behalf of a more simplified, agriculturally based life-style, Marx never envisioned communism as a return to some preindustrial utopia. Human freedom presupposes a mastery of nature, and for this reason, communism is committed in principle to the development of a modern industrial society. The development of such a society, in turn, appears to require a substantial amount of planning and centralized coordination. Consequently, as in the West, Marxist societies have developed large scientific and governmental bureaucracies and thereby have fostered the emergence of a new technological elite. Whereas from the perspective of Western liberalism, a "rule by experts" can easily be seen as a threat to autonomous freedom, from the perspective of Marxism it can also be understood as a necessary means for extending rational control over the otherwise impersonal and ultimately arbitrary forces of nature.

Second, according to Marx, freedom from the domination of things requires the assumption of rational control over the various forces which together determine humanity's economic and social fate. Under capitalism, the laws of the marketplace, which are in fact institutions and practices created by concrete individuals, appear to operate as "things" independent of human control. In this situation, economic and social policies are the result of an interplay among preferences and decisions made by particular agents who are acting only with their own short-term interests in mind. For example, in capitalism the judgment of independent consumers, each choosing only for himself or herself, has the cumulative effect of determining the total social product. As a consequence, a shift in buying habits will eventually force a reallocation of resources, including that of labor, which from the perspective of society as a whole or from that of those individuals who are adversely affected by such shifts may appear to be both unwanted and arbitrary. Although its individual corporations and businesses are carefully organized and rationally administered,

capitalism as a whole, according to Marx, is both irrational and chaotic. Inasmuch as no one is charged with consciously planning for the
needs of the system as a whole, its individual participants are subject
to changes and forces that appear to be acting according to their own
impersonal logic:

> The social character of activity, and the social form of the product, as
> well as the share of the individual in production, are here opposed to
> individuals as something alien and material; this does not consist in
> the behavior of some to others, but in their subordination to relations
> that exist independently of them and arise from the collision of indif-
> ferent individuals with one another. The general exchange of activi-
> ties and products, which has become a condition of living for each
> individual and the link between them, seems to them to be some-
> thing alien and independent, like a thing. . . . The individuals are
> subordinated to social production which exists externally to them,
> as a sort of fate; but social production is not subordinated to the indi-
> viduals who manipulate it as their communal capacity.[12]

Ironically, the very mechanisms that capitalism first created in its
effort to free people from the vicissitudes of nature have at the same
time produced an institutional environment that imposes its own
form of social control upon the isolated individual. The market appears to operate independently of the wishes of its participants. As a
consequence, according to Marx, capitalism oscillates between periods of deflationary overproduction and inflationary underproduc-
tion according to a set of economic laws that no one, in fact, autho-
rized or even intended. Given this, freedom, as the ability to control
one's collective fate, requires that capitalism's traditional market
mechanisms be replaced by a production system that can be regulated
according to the explicit plans of the socialized individual:

> In fact, the realm of freedom actually begins only when labour which
> is determined by necessity and mundane considerations ceases. . . .
> Freedom in this field can only consist in socialized man, the associ-
> ated producers, rationally regulating their interchange with Nature,
> bringing it under common control, instead of being ruled by it as by
> the blind forces of Nature. . . .[13]

Because Marx understood the extension of rational control over
the forces of both nature and society as part of the project of human

emancipation, Marxist politics is, in this sense, a continuation of the liberal tradition. Accordingly both the liberal and the Marxist views of human nature require that individuals seek to assert themselves vis-à-vis the established traditions of the Western order. In this sense, each is a decidedly modern phenomenon.

At the same time, however, there is something distinctively illiberal within Marx's perspective. As we have seen, liberalism bases its program upon an understanding of the person as properly an autonomous self. Liberal political theory therefore calls for a degree of separation between the state and civil society that allows individuals to maintain an essentially private sphere. Within this sphere they may live as they see fit. Liberalism seeks to protect individuals by ensuring their freedom rather than attempting to transform them by promoting their virtue. Marxism, on the other hand, both foresees and advocates a fundamental transformation in the human condition. Not only would communism repair those particular distortions of the psyche that are rooted in the competitive individualism of the capitalist era but it would, at the same time, correct the condition of human alienation in general. In short, the real result of the communist revolution is the formation of a "new socialist person." Describing this transformed individual, Marx wrote:

> It [communism] is, therefore, the return of man himself as a *social*
> i.e. really human, being, a complete and conscious return which as-
> similates all the wealth of previous development. . . . It is the defini-
> tive resolution of the antagonism between man and nature, and be-
> tween man and man. It is the true solution of the conflict between
> existence and essence, between objectification and self-affirmation,
> between freedom and necessity, between individual and species. It
> is the solution to the riddle of history and knows itself to be this solu-
> tion.[14]

Marx's understanding of a fully transformed mankind is seen by some as an uncharacteristically romantic element within what is otherwise a scientifically rigorous analysis. Nonetheless it is true that it is this vision of a new and ultimately reconciled humanity that gives Marxism its moral appeal. The future will not simply be different but actually better, and its improvement will not simply be due to an increased level of material consumption but rather to the expanded opportunity for human development and fulfillment. This humanistic aspect of Marx's vision is nowhere more clearly expressed than in this statement by Leon Trotsky, one of the leaders of the Russian Revolution. Referring to the future communist person, Trotsky wrote:

> Man will become immeasurably stronger, wiser, and subtler; his body will become more harmonized, his movements more rhythmic; his voice more musical. The forms of life will become dynamically dramatic. The average human type will rise to the heights of an Aristotle, a Goethe, or a Marx. And above this ridge new peaks will rise.[15]

According to Marx, history is more than simply the history of class warfare or the story of increasing productive capacities. It is, at the same time and more importantly, the story of humanity's becoming whole. In a certain sense, then, Marx's view is similar to the traditional Christian understanding of history as the epic story of human movement away from an initial condition of estrangement and towards a state of ultimate reconciliation. Whereas for Christianity this drama concerned estrangement from and eventual reconciliation with God achieved through the agency of Christ, for Marx, on the other hand, it is a purely immanent movement. Rather than relying upon the gratuitous exercise of transcendental or divine powers, humanity itself was understood by Marx as fully capable of determining its own fate. It could do so, according to Marx, because of its radically historical character. In his *Theses on Feuerbach*, Marx argued that, as an historical species, the human race is formed by the conditions of its day; yet at the same time, Marx insisted that humanity itself actually makes these very conditions. Thus inasmuch as society makes history and inasmuch as history makes society by making history, people are in fact, indirectly shaping themselves. Being both the subject and the object of history, humanity alone is capable of that radical transformation that Marx understood as the ultimate promise of socialism:

> Since, however, for socialist man, the *whole of what is called world history* is nothing but the creation of man by human labor, and the emergence of nature for man, he, therefore, has the evident and irrefutable proof of his *self-creation*, of his own origins.[16]

This vision of a transformed human nature may account, in part, for the moral appeal that Marxism has for many people. Yet it is nonetheless an element within his system that stands in a certain tension vis-à-vis his more traditionally liberal concern for human freedom.

Human Nature and Politics

As we have seen, both the classical Greek and Christian view of human nature understood politics as an activity that, if properly done, would allow individuals to actualize the higher possibilities of their nature. They, too, sought to achieve a certain type of human transformation and emphasized, as a consequence, the priority of virtue to freedom. In its understanding of politics as the revolutionary self-transformation of the species, Marxism is somewhat akin to these older traditions. At the same time, though, Marx clearly wished to retain his commitment to the value of human freedom. Thus a certain ambiguity seems to exist at the core of Marx's political teachings, and this ambiguity, in turn, may help to account for the variety of forms Marxism has assumed since the beginning of the twentieth century.

Notes

1. Jean-Jacques Rousseau, "A Preface to Narcisse," trans. Benjamin Barber and James Forman, *Political Theory* 6, no.4 (November 1978), 549.
2. Karl Marx, "A Preface to *A Contribution to the Critique of Political Economy*," in *The Marx-Engels Reader*, 2d ed., ed. Robert C. Tucker (New York: W. W. Norton & Co., 1978), pp. 4–5.
3. Karl Marx, "The Communist Manifesto," in Tucker, *Reader*, pp. 475–76.
4. Karl Marx, "On the Jewish Question," in Tucker, *Reader*, p. 32.
5. Marx, "Jewish Question," p. 42.
6. Marx, "Jewish Question," p. 43.
7. Karl Marx, "Economic and Philosophical Manuscripts," in *Karl Marx: Early Writings*, ed. T. B. Bottomore (New York: McGraw-Hill, 1964), p. 125.
8. Karl Marx, "The German Ideology," in Tucker, *Reader*, p. 160.
9. Marx, "Manuscripts," p. 157.
10. Karl Marx, "On James Mill," in *Karl Marx: Selected Writings*, ed. David McLellan (New York: Oxford University Press, 1977), pp. 121–22.
11. Marx, "Manuscripts," pp. 160–62.
12. Karl Marx, *The Grundrisse*, trans. & ed. David McLellan (New York: Harper & Row, 1971), pp. 66, 68.
13. Karl Marx, "Capital," in Tucker, *Reader*, p. 441.
14. Karl Marx, "Manuscripts," p. 155.

15. Leon Trotsky, *Literature and Revolution*, trans. Rose Strunsky (Ann Arbor: University of Michigan Press, 1960), p. 256.

16. Karl Marx, "Manuscripts," p. 166.

Recommended Readings

Avineri, Shlomo. *The Social and Political Thought of Karl Marx*. New York: Cambridge University Press, 1970.

Berlin, Isaiah. *Karl Marx: His Life and Environment*. New York: Oxford University Press, 1963.

Fetscher, Iring. *Marx and Marxism*. Translated by John Hargreaves. New York: Herder & Herder, 1971.

Heilbroner, Robert L. *Marxism: For and Against*. New York: W. W. Norton Co., 1980.

Hunt, R. N. Carew. *Theory and Practice of Communism*. Baltimore: Penguin Books, 1963.

Kamenka, Eugene. *Marxism and Ethics*. London: Macmillan, 1969.

Kolakowski, Leszek. *Main Currents of Marxism*. Translated by P. S. Falla. 3 vols. New York: Oxford University Press, 1978.

Lobkowicz, Nicholas, ed. *Marx and the Western World*. Notre Dame, Ind.: University of Notre Dame Press, 1967.

McLellan, David. *Karl Marx: His Life and Thought*. New York: Harper & Row, 1973.

Meszaros, Istvan. *Marx's Theory of Alienation*. New York: Harper & Row, 1972.

Ollman, Bertell. *Alienation: Marx's Conception of Man in Capitalist Society*. New York: Cambridge University Press, 1971.

Rubel, Maximilien, and Margaret Manale. *Marx without Myth*. New York: Harper & Row, 1976.

PART TWO: Summary

If one were to listen only to the everyday rhetoric of politicians, one might conclude that politics is only concerned with the formulation of acceptable answers to specific and relatively technical policy problems. Indeed, much of the ongoing activity of any well-established government is devoted to such tasks. However, during periods of extreme crisis, as in the case of war or revolution, the more serious nature of political life soon becomes apparent. At such times it becomes clear that politics is ultimately the means by which a given people organizes itself for action in history. It does so not only because its members wish to live, but also because they wish to live in a certain way—a way they believe to be both desirable and humane. Ultimately political societies exist in an attempt to establish or preserve a specific way of life. At this most fundamental level, then, the most important political questions are, How should one live? and How should society be organized so as to make such a life possible?

Before it is possible to answer the question of how one should live, one must reach an understanding of who one is. In the individual chapters of part 2 we examined three particularly influential perspectives on this issue. It would have been possible to select others. For example, Freudianism, existentialism, and behaviorism have developed understandings of the human condition that have obvious political implications. Yet none of these have achieved the political influence within the West of the Greek-Christian, liberal, or Marxist traditions.

The Greek-Christian understanding of the human soul has had a unique influence upon the practice of Western politics. Although it enjoyed its greatest influence prior to the Renaissance, it continues to be a vital element within twentieth-century culture. Its understanding of the human soul as ordered by the principles of its transcendent destiny has had a somewhat ambiguous effect upon the Western conception of the good society. On one hand it has limited the power of society by reminding people that they are called to a higher destiny and must therefore be left free to observe principles superior in kind

129

to those of the political realm. At the same time, however, this tradition also argues that the transcendent destiny of each is already given in a common ordering for all. As a consequence, society is empowered to exercise its authority in an effort to bring about the necessary moral and psychic transformation of its citizens. From this perspective, the purpose of politics is the education of the virtuous person.

The liberal understanding of human nature is both a continuation of and a reaction against the principles of the traditional view. Developing the traditional understanding of human dignity, liberalism further emphasizes the freedom of individuals and therefore seeks to preserve their moral and personal autonomy. Possessing natural rights, people are to be allowed to develop as they themselves best see fit. Thus the liberal understanding of the good society reacts against the traditional emphasis upon moral and social conformity. Believing that the true person is the authentic or self-legislating individual, the liberal society is dedicated to the promotion of freedom as the condition of all virtues. As such it does not seek to promulgate any preferred virtue in particular.

The Marxist view of human nature both extends and rejects the liberal order. It extends liberalism, for it too is a theory of human emancipation: it seeks to liberate humanity from its subjection to history. At the same time, however, Marxism rejects the liberal tradition to the extent that, from the Marxist perspective, the liberal emphasis upon individualism fails to appreciate the truly social dimension of human existence. Nonalienated persons need one another in order to achieve their common interest in gaining social control over the forces of both nature and society. A Marxist society seeks social freedom and through this an end to human alienation.

The fact that all three traditions we have discussed build upon certain elements found in one another explains in part why a given society may incorporate elements of each. There is no perfectly Christian, liberal, or Marxist society, and today's regimes are typically a blending of principles drawn from each perspective. Yet, to the extent that such traditions are in some ways opposed to one another in principle, there exists a certain tension at the heart of modernity. By examining the views of human nature contained in these three chapters, a student of politics will gain some appreciation of the directions in which these tensions are pulling.

PART
THREE

Political Ruling:
The Basis of
Authority

C H A P T E R   7

Who Should Rule?
The Claim of the Powerful

Introduction

Although the anarchist tradition has retained its advocates throughout the modern age, its practical influence has been relatively small.
Except for a brief period of about sixty years in which anarchism existed as a revolutionary force in nineteenth and twentieth century
Spain, the anarchist movement, in general, has been unable to generate any significant political momentum.

Such theorists as Vilfredo Pareto (1848–1923) and Gaetano Mosca
(1858–1941) have explained this failure by arguing that the creation
of a political and social hierarchy is a necessary prerequisite for all
social life. Although all do not accept Pareto's assertion that the rise
and fall of political elites can be explained with a lawlike precision, it
is true that most political theorists have acknowledged both the fact
and the desirability of political rule. Societies appear to require a hierarchical ordering and, given this, it is necessary for every community
to develop some mechanism by which it can select, train, and empower its leadership. This, in turn, presupposes that it is possible for
a society to decide which skills and qualities its leaders should possess if it is going to prosper under their rule. In short, a basic question
of political existence is the simple one "Who should rule?"

The Sophists

Within the tradition of Western political thought one of the most obvious answers to this question is that which has argued that the strong should rule. From this perspective, politics is seen as a struggle for power, and the conditions of such a struggle seem to dictate that only the powerful can succeed. Power, force, and violence can contribute to the creation of order, and no society, even the most just, can exist without a minimum of order. Similarly all visions of the "good life" presuppose the possibility of "mere life," and in a world of competition for inevitably scarce resources, mere life itself often requires the use of force.

It is not surprising that those theorists who were the most important advocates of a rule by the powerful often lived through periods of profound political disorder. Having experienced social and political unrest, these individuals were particularly sensitive to the delicate nature of any civilization. As their communities became increasingly vulnerable to foreign invasions and internal discord, they focused upon power as the *sine qua non* of political order. As strength became a virtue, so too did the rule of the powerful become a necessity.

The argument that the powerful should rule can be traced back to the teachings of the Greek Sophists in the fifth and fourth centuries B.C. As a group the Sophists were professional educators who traveled from city to city and met their expenses by teaching for a fee. Although they did not develop a common program of studies, the Sophists in general were advocates of the art of rhetoric and offered it as a skill essential for the practice of democratic politics. Our knowledge of the Sophistic teachings is limited because their work is available only in fragments or in loose paraphrases attributed to them by other authors, who in many cases were not sympathetic with their efforts. Among the best known of the Sophists are Protagoras, Gorgias, Prodicus, Hippias, and Antiphon.

One of the central teachings most often associated with the Sophistic tradition is the distinction between nature (*physis*) and custom (*nomos*). Typically the terms were understood to be opposed and at the same time mutually exclusive. In applying these categories to political and moral matters, the Sophists attempted to differentiate between something that was artificially contrived (*nomos*) and therefore perhaps false, and something that existed according to nature (*physis*) and was as a result necessarily true. By suggesting that the laws of a particular society were conventional rather than natural, the

135

Who Should Rule? The Claim of the Powerful

Sophists succeeded in challenging the apparent legitimacy of the traditional order. For some, such as Protagoras, such a challenge could easily be met by appealing to the social and cultural progress that conventional law alone made possible. For others, however, the unnatural quality of all conventional morality implied that it was unavoidably arbitrary and necessarily futile. This position is most dramatically represented in the arguments of Callicles as portrayed in Plato's *Gorgias*.

There is no independent historical evidence that Callicles actually existed. He is, however, portrayed by Plato as a wealthy, young, and politically ambitious aristocrat who has invited the Sophist Gorgias to his house. Given Gorgias's reputation as a teacher, Socrates initiates a discussion concerning the appropriate education of a statesman. After encountering both Gorgias and his pupil, Polus, Socrates is confronted by an angry Callicles, who challenges the Socratic claim that it is better to suffer an injustice than it is to commit one. From Callicles's perspective, such an argument is typical of those offered by faint-hearted and weak individuals who fear the strength of the powerful. In order to protect themselves against the ambitions of the aggressive few, the weak, who are the majority, restrain the strong by creating conventional understandings of justice that oppose their actual interests. Conventional law is, as a consequence, simply a defensive weapon created by the weak in order to shelter themselves from the natural superiority of the strong. This effort, according to Callicles, is not only futile but actually immoral because it violates that principle of nature (*physis*) which teaches that the selfish interests of the strong should always prevail. Inasmuch as nature intends that individuals should give free play to their passions, might makes right:

> But my [Callicles] opinion is that nature herself reveals it to be only just and proper that the better man should lord it over his inferior: it will be the stronger over the weaker. Nature, further, makes it quite clear in a great many instances that this is the true state of affairs, not only in the other animals, but also in whole states and communities. This is, in fact, how justice is determined: the stronger shall rule and have the advantage over the inferior.[1]

Callicles's appeal to the principles of nature was intended primarily as a criticism of the principles of the city. He assumed that the natural order should serve as the dominant model for political order and that consequently, when the conventions of a society violate the principles of nature, they lose their binding authority. In his response to this charge, Socrates does not deny the priority of the natural order. His disagreement, rather, is with Callicles's understanding of nature itself. For Socrates a fully adequate analysis would reveal that nature is in fact structured by the principles of the true, the good, and the beautiful and consequently that the natural order, containing as it does a spiritual element, actually requires the rule of the philosopher rather than that of the tyrant. For his part Callicles rejects such an interpretation as both childish and cowardly.

Callicles's understanding of nature as a justification for the rule of the stronger is an essentially individualistic argument. Nature, according to Callicles, provides a standard that, if properly understood, liberates the individual from the binding constraints of social convention. In such situations the rule of the stronger exclusively benefits those few individuals who are the most powerful, while the vast majority of citizens are left essentially unprotected. In this situation the actual interests of the few cannot in fact be reconciled with the common interests of the many. Indeed nature may intend that the strongest rule, but unless a community is convinced that such a norm can serve its common interest, it is doubtful that this standard will ever be freely adopted as a principle of social order. If the rule of the powerful is to succeed as a *political* teaching, it must first be capable of demonstrating its larger social and political utility. In short the rule of the strong must serve the common interest, and Callicles's inability to appreciate this requirement seriously limited the effectiveness of his argument. From society's perspective, the strong must be made to serve the interests of the state and in the history of western political thought no one has represented this perspective more forcefully than has the Italian Renaissance theorist Niccolo Machiavelli.

Machiavelli

As in the case of Callicles, Machiavelli's appreciation of the fundamental importance of political power can be explained in part by the perilous character of his own time. As a Florentine citizen, Machiavelli (1469–1527) lived through a period of severe political unrest. At the most general level, all of Europe was experiencing the political and social dislocation necessarily associated with the collapse of the traditional feudal order. Beginning as early as the twelfth cen-

137

Who Should Rule? The Claim of the Powerful

tury, the integrity of European Christendom, organized according to the universalistic principles of the Holy Roman Empire and the Roman Catholic Church, was being challenged by a whole variety of divisive and particularistic movements. As the traditional institutions of feudalism weakened, alternative forms of political organizations soon emerged to take their place. While the Holy Roman Empire became increasingly ineffective, local princes attempted to organize their own territories along nationalistic lines. Eventually the feudal territories of England, France, and Spain emerged as independent nation-states, while the Holy Roman Empire itself became ever more a fiction maintained by a coalition of German princes and the leadership of the Roman Catholic Church.

The European movement away from feudalism and toward the secular societies of the modern nation-state was both gradual and uneven. Whereas such areas as England, Spain, and France were developing the centralized hierarchies associated with the modern nation-state, others, such as Germany and Italy, remained both undeveloped and disorganized. Rather than being organized under the authority of a single center of power, the Italian peninsula was actually a composite of local fiefdoms and principalities which coexisted with one another in an uneasy balance of power. Although some rulers—for example, Pope Julius II—dreamed of uniting all of Italy under their leadership, none of the five major city-states (Florence, Milan, Venice, the Papal States, and the Kingdom of Naples) was strong enough to impose its will upon all the others.

This same condition of military and political weakness that prevented the internal unification of Italy also accounted for her external vulnerability. Lacking the abundant resources available to the leaders of the larger nation-states, the individual Italian city-states were incapable of adequately defending themselves against foreign invasion. Both France and Spain were able to invade at will, and their armies successfully occupied and plundered large sections of the Italian peninsula. In response, the city-states began to hire foreign mercenaries, but this in turn simply exposed them to roving bands of Swiss, German, and Albanian fortune seekers who exploited the weakness of their own employers.

As the military and political capital of Tuscany, Machiavelli's Florence was unavoidably affected by these tragic events. Ruled for three generations by the Medici family, the Florentines expelled the incompetent Pietro di Medici in 1494 and established thereby a republican form of government. In 1502 Machiavelli was invited to join the government of Pietro Soderini and served in the Florentine diplomatic corps until the downfall of the republic ten years later. In 1511 Pope Julius II formed an alliance with Spain in order to drive the French from Italy. Inasmuch as Florence was unwilling to defy the French, it in turn was attacked by Spain, and in 1512 the Medici family, supported by both Spain and the papacy, reoccupied the city and once again established its autocratic rule. Implicated in an attempted counterplot, Machiavelli was arrested, convicted, and punished as a traitor. Withdrawing from public life, Machiavelli went into exile and during this time wrote his most famous work, *The Prince*.

Given this experience of political and personal disorder, it is not surprising that Machiavelli believed it necessary to radically rethink the principles of political efficacy. The collapse of feudalism had demonstrated the inadequacy of the traditional understanding of political order. As Italy struggled to find a form of political organization adequate to the challenges of the new age, the first and most obvious question was "Who should rule?" In his *Prince*, Machiavelli attempted to answer this question by creating an image of the ideal leader. According to Machiavelli the true prince would be one whose personal qualities and political skills made it possible to create and secure a new form for the Italian state. Given this, Machiavelli argued that the strong should rule—not for their own selfish interest as Callicles had argued, but rather because their rule would serve the common good of the entire Italian nation. In a well-ordered society the power and strength of the prince would invigorate the entire body politic in such a way that the prince's personal excellence would in fact contribute to the overall excellence of society itself.

Machiavelli developed his understanding of the ideal prince by recalling the example of past successful leaders. In particular he referred to the heroic deeds of Moses, Cyrus, Romulus, and Theseus. Each was a true political master because each ". . . owed nothing to fortune but the opportunity which gave them matter to be shaped into what form they thought fit; and without that opportunity their powers would have been wasted, and without their powers the opportunity would have come in vain."[2]

Fortune, as referred to in the above statement, was, according to Machiavelli, capable of both benevolent and malevolent actions. Pictured as a woman, she would bestow her gifts only on those who please her, and pleasing her, according to Machiavelli, was essentially a matter of strength and power. If individuals were weak and incapable of resisting her fury, fortune would punish them by under-

139

Who Should Rule? The Claim of the Powerful

mining their attempts to achieve success. If, however, they were bold and forceful, she would succumb to their charms and respond accordingly:

> I certainly think that it is better to be impetuous than cautious, for fortune is a woman, and it is necessary, if you wish to master her, to conquer her by force; and it can be seen that she lets herself be overcome by the bold rather than those who proceed coldly. And therefore, like a woman, she is always a friend to the young, because they are less cautious, fiercer, and master her with greater audacity.[3]

The picture of the successful prince that Machiavelli offered as a model emphasizes the heroic virtues of strength, courage, and decisiveness. Success in politics requires that one be virtuous, but the virtue recommended is that of the warrior and not that of the saint.

Machiavelli's reputation as the first "modern" political scientist rests in part on this distinction. Traditionally classical and Christian political science had developed a fairly consistent understanding of those virtues or qualities necessary for political success. During Machiavelli's own time, this understanding included the four "cardinal" virtues of wisdom, courage, moderation, and justice and the three "princely" virtues of liberality, magnanimity, and honesty. Together these virtues were understood as producing individual moral excellence on one hand and general political efficacy on the other.

Rejecting the cardinal and princely virtues as being both unrealistic and politically ineffective, Machiavelli offered a new understanding of morality which emphasizes the efficacy of human strength and vigor. Consequently the virtuous, according to Machiavelli, are the powerful and it is their willingness to act forcefully that is most able to serve the interests of the state. Whereas such Greek thinkers as Plato and Aristotle had argued that the primary task of the politician is to oversee the moral and intellectual education of the citizens, Machiavelli believed, on the contrary, that the essential obligation of the politician is to nurture and care for the state itself. For Machiavelli, statecraft had replaced soulcraft as the politician's art.

Machiavelli's teaching is clearly based upon an appreciation of the heroic. Given his experience of the general disorder of the age, he used his writings in order to evoke an image of the heroic prince who would serve as the savior of Italy. Having created such an image, however, Machiavelli could then only hope that someone would in fact respond to his appeal and subsequently undertake the historical task he had set forth. Given what such a project would require, the founding prince would have to be an individual of exceptional strength and power who would be willing to use every means necessary for the creation of a stable state. For Machiavelli the difficulty of achieving such a goal justified the most extreme measures. In his *Discourses* he wrote:

> . . . and a wise man will never censure any one for having employed any extraordinary means for the purpose of establishing a kingdom or constituting a republic. It is well that when the act accuses him, the result should excuse him; and when the result is good . . . it will always absolve him from blame. For he is to be reprehended who commits violence for the purpose of destroying, and not he who employs it for beneficient purposes.[4]

As we have seen, Machiavelli believed that the personal excellence or *virtú* of the founding prince could expand in such a way as to create a field of power within which the state would eventually emerge. Once having been founded, however, every society must seek its own preservation, and those skills that allow one to be a successful founder are not necessarily the same as those that serve the goal of preservation. For example the Greeks had institutionalized the practice of ostracism whereby truly exceptional citizens would be expelled from the city not because of any crime or shortcoming but rather because their very excellence and ability could undermine the harmony and stability of the regime. Similarly Machiavelli argued that, although the virtues of the heroic prince are required for the creation of political order, they are not necessarily suitable for its preservation:

> Besides although one man alone should organize a government, yet it will not endure long if the administration of it remains on the shoulders of a single individual; it is well, then, to confide this to the charge of many for thus it will be sustained by the many.[5]

Whereas according to Machiavelli the creation of a political order requires the heroic actions of an exceptionally strong prince, its preservation actually presupposes such "republican" traits as wisdom, prudence, moderation, and the love of liberty. It would appear, then, that the very qualities required for creating the state eventually pre-

141

Who Should Rule? The Claim of the Powerful

vent the prince from assuming his rightful place as a full citizen within a peaceful and prosperous community of free persons. In time the prince becomes the victim of his own success; and, although the rule of the powerful is necessary, it is at the same time necessarily short. Whereas Callicles had advocated that the strong be allowed to rule for their own selfish interests, Machiavelli hoped to inspire them to sacrifice themselves for the good of the many. In both arguments, therefore, the political tension between the few and the many remains. This, in turn, undermines any effort to establish the rule of the powerful, because such a rule is inevitably opposed to the interests of an important segment of society. The many, who are weak, would resist the arguments of Callicles, while the powerful, who are few, would resist Machiavelli's call to self-sacrifice. Before everyone could consent to the rule of the powerful, both the few and the many would have to see that it was in their interest to do so. Perhaps the argument that most successfully demonstrates this calculation is that which is found in the work of the English philosopher Thomas Hobbes.

Thomas Hobbes

Thomas Hobbes (1588–1679) lived during a period of profound social, intellectual, and political change. Upon leaving Oxford in 1607 he was employed as a private tutor and studied with interest the revolutionary developments in the new mathematical and natural sciences. Rejecting the official Aristotelianism professed in the English schools of his day, Hobbes made an effort to acquaint himself with the work of such contemporary natural scientists as Bacon, Descartes, and Galileo. In time, however, Hobbes became increasingly interested in current political developments. As a tutor he had worked with the son of William Cavendish, the Earl of Devonshire, and for a brief period had taught the young prince of Wales who eventually became King Charles II. This turn toward the political is not surprising, however, especially in view of the general situation of English political life during the seventeenth century. During this period there were on-going and serious political tensions between the monarchy on the one hand and the parliament on the other, as the issue of national sovereignty had not yet been satisfactorily resolved. At the same time these tensions were compounded by significant religious and philosophical disagreements among the Roman Catholic, Puritan, and Anglican communities. Finally the whole situation became even more difficult since the political and military leadership of England was preoccupied with its efforts to extend and secure its imperial rule over the neighboring territories of Scotland and Ireland. These numerous tensions eventually culminated in that series of events commonly referred to as the English Civil War. From Hobbes's perspective this war appeared as a great cycle of violence and suffering during which political sovereignty was passed from pretender to pretender until it returned to its original and proper location in the office of the king. In summarizing his understanding of the revolution, Hobbes wrote:

> I have seen in this revolution a circular motion of the sovereign power through two usurpers . . . from the late King to this his son . . . For . . . it moved from King Charles I to the Long Parliament; from thence to the Rump; from the Rump to Oliver Cromwell; and then back again from Oliver Cromwell to the Rump; thence to the Long Parliament; and thence to King Charles II, where long may it remain.[6]

It was Hobbes's belief that this movement away from order through disorder and back to order again could be analyzed in such a way as to provide for an understanding of both the causes of and eventually the cure for political unrest. England, according to Hobbes, could serve as a case study illustrating the general and universal principles of political order. At the same time Hobbes also believed that these principles could be discovered and best demonstrated by following a method of inquiry modeled after that of the mathematical sciences. By beginning with established preliminary definitions, and by following the laws of logic, Hobbes sought to build a system of argument whose conclusions would exhibit the self-evident character of a geometrical proof. In short, he believed that political unrest was ultimately due to the influence of wrong opinion and consequently that the true purpose of political science was to correct such opinions and thereby secure peace and prosperity for all.

Although he published a number of political works, Hobbes's most systematic treatment of politics is found in his 1651 publication *Leviathan*. In the dedication of this work to Francis Godolphin, Hobbes indicated quite clearly that the central concern of his new political science was that of understanding the nature and function of political power:

143

Who Should Rule? The Claim of the Powerful

Besides, I speak not of the men, but, in the abstract, of the seat of power, (like to those simple and unpartial creatures in the Roman Capitol, that with their noise defended those within it, not because they were they, but there), offending none, I think, but those without, or such within, if there be any such, as favour them.[7]

Like both Callicles and Machiavelli, Hobbes understood the exercise of power as the characteristic feature of political existence; yet at the same time there is an important difference between his argument and those of his predecessors. Both Callicles and Machiavelli advocated the rule of the powerful, and both assumed the existence of certain individuals who were naturally powerful and thus rightfully destined to rule. In short, both Callicles and Machiavelli believed in the existence of a natural hierarchy among persons that could serve, in turn, as the model for a political hierarchy among citizens. Each, therefore, first attempted to describe the essential characteristics of these naturally powerful individuals (Callicles's man of ambition and pleasure; Machiavelli's man of *virtu*) and then having done so argued on behalf of acknowledging their superiority within society. Hobbes, on the other hand, offered a radically different argument. According to his understanding of nature there are no natural hierarchies precisely because nature itself is incapable of differentiating among the various goods of life. Nature is truly neutral; and given this it is impossible to distinguish between that which is higher and that which is lower or that which is appropriate and that which is not. Lacking such a set of natural classifications, the political scientist cannot designate any specific set of qualities that naturally entitles one person to rule another. As a consequence, rather than attempting to legitimate the superiority of any particular group of individuals, Hobbes was concerned simply with justifying the fact of political rule itself. Inasmuch as nature does not establish the existence of a power elite, it is necessary for society to create one. And it was Hobbes's task to show that such a creation, even though fundamentally arbitrary, is nevertheless in the best interest of each and every individual.

Even though Machiavelli is understood by some to be the first modern political scientist, he also continued to share several important assumptions with his classical predecessors. One of these is his belief in natural inequality. Hobbes, on the other hand, is a truly contemporary thinker inasmuch as he begins with the modern assumption that all individuals are naturally equal. Obviously Hobbes was aware of the existence of certain physical and intellectual differences, but from his perspective these distinctions are of such a type that they are incapable of establishing the existence of a truly qualitative difference among people. For example, although some individuals are physically more gifted than others, no one is strong enough to be totally immune from the threats or plots of his or her neighbors. According to Hobbes, even the weakest person is capable of killing the strongest and consequently the threat of violent death serves as an equalizer that negates all apparent differences based solely upon physical attributes. Similarly at any given moment some individuals are intellectually more adept than others; but in most cases, according to Hobbes, such traits are simply the results of experience. Therefore, given equal time, all individuals are equally capable of eventually achieving a common level of prudential insight. According to Hobbes, then, rather than differentiating among persons, nature in fact establishes their fundamental equality. This condition, however, creates a serious political problem. If persons are by nature equal, how, then, is it possible to justify the fact that some are empowered to rule over others? Given the fact of natural equality, it would appear that the consent of the ruled is the only possible justification for political authority. However this answer only introduces a further question. Why would individuals agree to abandon their original state of natural equality in order to impose upon themselves a condition of conventional inferiority? In attempting to answer this question Hobbes turned once again to an examination of nature.

Political life requires some agreement regarding those principles by which a given society will both coordinate its efforts to achieve certain common goals and decide upon strategies for the proper distribution of its necessarily limited resources. As we have seen earlier, classical political science, as developed by Plato and Aristotle, assumed that nature itself and human nature in particular provided such standards. The task of the political scientist is to attune the conventions of society according to the principles of nature. Consequently, nature itself provides a solution to the problem of creating political order. For Hobbes, on the other hand, the meaning of nature had changed. Influenced by the discoveries of modern science, he no longer believed that nature is a structured whole exhibiting both purpose and direction. To the extent that it is simply matter in motion, nature lacks both design and purpose and, lacking a design, it is devoid of any characteristic that would enable one to designate a "higher" and a "lower" or a "better" and a "worse." In this situation nature cannot serve as a

145

Who Should Rule? The Claim of the Powerful

model for political order because nature itself is unordered. Thus rather than being a solution to the problem of political disorder, nature actually reinforces it. Living in an unstructured and unprincipled nature, mankind, according to Hobbes, finds itself in a natural situation wherein life is "solitary, poor, nasty, brutish, and short."[8] To escape, then, requires an artificial or conventional solution—the creation of political order.

Hobbes's analysis of mankind's natural condition was based upon several important assumptions. First, as we have seen, he assumed that all individuals are equal, and by this he meant that no one can claim any benefit for which another may not also contend. Given natural equality, there can be no "mine" and "thine" and, consequently, everyone has an equal claim to everything. Since resources are scarce, the condition of equality breeds contention and, given the pleasure that some feel in the defeat of others, it is also possible that the struggle over resources will continue far beyond that point where one's immediate needs are satisfied. Finally, even when the fighting and violence have stopped, one must continue to prepare for its eventual renewal, inasmuch as no settlement can ever be established that is either rightful in principle or binding on another. Indeed for Hobbes mankind's natural condition is a state of continual war and ever present fear:

> So that in the nature of man, we find three principal causes of quarrel. First, competition; secondly, diffidence; thirdly, glory. The first, maketh men invade for gain; the second, for safety; and the third for reputation.[9]

Given this condition Hobbes argued that it is in the self-interest of all to create a political society and thereby leave the state of nature. To do so, each must simply agree to create and then obey a common political sovereign. By entering into such a contract individuals create that which nature cannot, i.e. a being whose power is so compelling as to be able to impose a single will upon the otherwise diverse wills of all:

> The only way to erect such a common power . . . is, to confer all their power and strength upon one man, or upon an assembly of men, that may reduce all their wills, by plurality of voices, unto one will: which is as to say, to appoint one man, or assembly of men, to bear their person; and every one to own and acknowledge himself to be

author of whatsoever he that so beareth their person, shall act or cause to be acted, in those things which concern the common peace and safety; and therein submit their wills, every one to his will, and their judgments, to his judgment.[10]

Although in Hobbes's judgment a monarchy would be the least problematic form of government, his arguments can also be applied to either an aristocracy or a democracy. According to Hobbes, neither the character nor the number of those who constitute the sovereign is important. The only important fact is that there is a sovereign as such. As the above quotation indicates, the sovereign must possess sufficient power so as to impose both its will and its judgment upon all the members of the body politic. In short it will provide those principles, arbitrary as they may be, by which a society will determine standards of cooperation and distribution. Since there is neither "good" nor "bad" in nature and inasmuch as, according to Hobbes, "true" and "false" are simply names assigned to ideas with no substantive content, it is necessary, if people are to live together, to find some way of agreeing as to what is good, true, and just. Given nature's silence on these issues, they must be settled by convention. And given the fact that one person's conventional understandings of these things are by nature no better than those of another, people must agree for the sake of peace to submit to the orthodoxical authority of the sovereign.

From Hobbes's perspective the sovereign's authority cannot be explained by the fact that its opinions are in some objective sense more accurate than those of another. Rather the sovereign's legitimacy is established solely by the individual's need for an agreed-upon public orthodoxy. According to Hobbes, it is in the selfish interest of each individual that there be only one set of authoritative opinions. Consequently each agrees to relinquish his or her natural equality and submit to the will and judgment of the sovereign in order to avoid the life-threatening inconveniences of the natural order:

The final cause, end, or design of men, who naturally love liberty, and dominion over others, in the introduction of that restraint upon themselves, in which we see them live in commonwealths, is the foresight of their own preservation, and of a more contented life thereby; that is to say, of getting themselves out from that miserable condition of war, which is necessarily consequent . . . to the natural passions of men when there is no visible power to keep them in awe

147

Who Should Rule? The Claim of the Powerful

and tie them by fear of punishment to the performance of their covenants.[11]

Given Hobbes's argument that the efficacy of the sovereign's power is both its sufficient and necessary justification, it is not surprising that he spends most of his time advising the sovereigns about those techniques by which they may keep their power intact. The sovereign's principal obligation as a sovereign is to retain absolute authority and power. Thus, according to Hobbes, the wise sovereign does not delegate political power to others, subordinate it to the law, limit it by acknowledging the absolute rights of the regime's subjects, or submit it to the moral and religious judgments of its critics. In short the power of the sovereign must remain absolute and unlimited.

By these arguments Hobbes attempted to persuade his fellow citizens that it was in their own personal interest to consent to the rule of the English monarchy. Although individuals may remove themselves from the original state of natural equality by consenting to the rule of a sovereign, they do not thereby succeed in changing the very structure of their own nature. Even living within society a person still retains natural passions and, if these passions are allowed their full expression, they will inevitably reproduce the very conditions of war and fear that characterized prepolitical existence. According to Hobbes, then, everyone wishes to satisfy his or her own passions but none, in turn, desires to live in a situation where others may do the same. Consequently it is in the interest of each that the others be bound. At the same time the only way of assuring each individual that the others will remain bound is to have the sovereign remain sufficiently powerful to bind them all. Thus Hobbes argued that it is in everyone's interest that the powerful should rule—even if this power is only the result of an arbitrary agreement. For Hobbes each individual's personal fulfillment presupposed the existence of a functioning public order, and given the harsh reality of human nature the only possible source of such an order remains that of power itself.

Notes

1. Plato, *Gorgias*, trans. W. C. Hembold (Indianapolis: Bobbs-Merrill, 1952), pp. 51–52.
2. Niccolo Machiavelli, *The Prince and the Discourses*, ed. Max Lerner (New York: Random House, 1950), pp. 20–21.
3. Machiavelli, *The Prince and the Discourses*, p. 94.
4. Machiavelli, *The Prince and the Discourses*, pp.138–9.
5. Machiavelli, *The Prince and the Discourses*, p. 139.
6. Thomas Hobbes, *Behemoth or the Long Parliament*, ed. Ferdinand Toennies (New York: Barnes & Noble, 1969), p. 204.
7. Thomas Hobbes, *Leviathan*, ed. Michael Oakeshott (New York: Collier Books, 1962), p. 5.
8. Hobbes, *Leviathan*, p. 100.
9. Hobbes, *Leviathan*, p. 99.
10. Hobbes, *Leviathan*, p. 132.
11. Hobbes, *Leviathan*, p. 129.

Recommended Readings

Butterfield, Herbert, *The Statecraft of Machiavelli*. New York: Collier Books, 1960.

Champlin, John, ed. *Power*. New York: Atherton Press, 1971.

Guthrie, W. K. C. *The Sophists*. New York: Cambridge University Press, 1971.

Jaeger, Werner. *Paideia: The Ideals of Greek Culture*. Vol. 1. Translated by Gilbert Highet. New York: Oxford University Press, 1939.

Lukes, Steven. *Power: A Radical View*. London: Macmillan, 1974.

Macpherson, C. B. *The Political Theory of Possessive Individualism: Hobbes to Locke*. New York: Oxford University Press, 1962.

Parel, Anthony, ed. *The Political Calculus: Essays on Machiavelli's Philosophy*. Toronto: University of Toronto Press, 1972.

Russell, Bertrand. *Power: A New Social Analysis*. New York: W. W. Norton, 1969.

Skinner, Quentin, *Machiavelli*. New York: Hill & Wang, 1981.

Strauss, Leo. *The Political Philosophy of Hobbes: Its Basis and Genesis*. Chicago: University of Chicago Press, 1952.

Tuck, Richard. *Natural Rights Theories: Their Origin and Development*. New York: Cambridge University Press, 1979.

Wrong, Dennis. *Power: Its Forms, Bases, and Uses*. New York: Harper & Row, 1980.

CHAPTER 8

Who Should Rule? The Claim of the Wise

Introduction

In the past the rule of the strong and the powerful has typically favored the establishment of an aristocracy, since only the wealthy few were able to meet the expense of maintaining an adequately equipped military force. As we have seen, the image of the aristocratic warrior-hero dominated the myths of early Greek culture and to a certain extent reflected the political reality of the post-Mycenaean and pre-Homeric age. It is also true, however, that this domination was soon challenged by others. In particular, one can find in early Greek poetry certain attempts to replace the rule of the strong with a regime founded upon the rule of the wise. The first example of such a challenge is found in a poetry of the peasant Hesiod (eighth century B.C.). As a peasant, Hesiod could not claim any distinction based upon either family or heritage. Yet unlike other poets who were content to simply interpret the saga tradition, Hesiod wished to influence the society of his day and therefore presented himself to his own community as its leader. In doing so, he became the first Greek poet to speak to the people of his own time in his own person.

Hesiod's claim to leadership was based upon his claim to knowledge. As a spiritual prophet, he claimed to possess the knowledge by which to interpret the ways of the gods. Such a knowledge was necessary because the Muses "know how to tell many falsehoods that seem real: but we [the Muses] also know how to speak truth when we wish to."[1] It is not enough for one to simply obey the gods because they, in turn, do not always speak the truth. Thus, rather than rely upon the oracles, an individual must develop that knowledge by which it is possible to distinguish between the truth on one hand and those "many falsehoods that seem real" on the other. For his part, Hesiod claimed to have developed such a knowledge and, as a consequence, was willing to use it for the benefit of his fellow citizens: "They [the Muses] breathed into me their divine voice, so that I might tell of things to come and things past. . . ."[2] In these simple lines, we see the first attempt to establish a necessary connection between leadership on one hand and insight on the other. In time that connection became the basis for the claim that the best society is the one in which the wise and knowledgeable are allowed to rule.

Plato

Perhaps the most influential argument on behalf of the rule of the wise is that which is found in the political works of Plato in general and in his *Gorgias* and *Republic* in particular. In the early dialogues written prior to the *Gorgias*, Plato had used the arguments of a skeptical Socrates in order to challenge many of the basic assumptions naively held by the Athenians of his day. For example in the *Charmides*, *Laches*, and *Lysis*, Plato examined various beliefs about the meaning of such commonly acknowledged virtues as temperance, courage, and friendship in order to reveal the degree of ignorance that characterized Athenian public opinion. Having exposed this condition, he then developed the arguments of the *Gorgias* and *Republic* and therein advocated the rule of the philosopher-king.

On one level, the *Gorgias* is a debate between teachers. The teacher Gorgias and his pupils, Polus and Callicles, represent the school of rhetoric and sophistry, while Socrates represents the school of philosophy. At the same time, however, the dialogue is also a political debate to the extent that the question being debated is, Who should be allowed to teach the next generation of Athenian political leaders?

Gorgias's claim is based upon his belief in the ultimate efficacy of rhetoric. Rhetoric, or the art of making public speeches, allows one who has mastered its techniques to persuade others and thereby gain their obedience. This manipulative power is so great, in fact, that its practitioners can actually persuade their audiences to follow error instead of truth. Rhetoricians deal with images and beliefs, and it is this facility, according to Gorgias, which will guarantee their political success. Thus he argues:

151

Who Should Rule? The Claim of the Wise

And I make the further declaration that if a rhetorician and a physician should come to any city you please and have the occasion to debate which of them ought to be elected public physician, the doctor would be utterly eclipsed, and the capable speaker would, if he chose, be elected. And likewise in a contest with any other craftsman whatsoever, the rhetorician would win his own election against all opposition of any kind; for not a single craftsman is able to speak in a crowd, on any subject in the world, more persuasively than the rhetorician. This is to show you how great and how splendid is the power of the art.[3]

In opposing the claim of Gorgias, Socrates does not deny the power of rhetorical speech. Rather he acknowledges the efficacy of rhetoric and, at the same time, provides an interesting account of its effect. According to Socrates, the power of rhetoric is due primarily to its ability to give pleasure. By using words carefully and saying only those things the audience wishes to hear, the rhetorician is able to please his or her listeners and thereby earn their affection. As a cook can prepare a meal to satisfy those who eat it, so too a rhetorician can employ words to please those who listen. From Socrates's perspective, therefore, the practices of rhetoric, cookery, and cosmetology are essentially equivalent because each, in its own way, is primarily concerned with the giving of pleasure—the pleasure derived from either words, food, or physical appearance.

As a representative of the art of philosophy, Socrates denies Gorgias's political claim on the basis of his own prior understanding of the nature of politics. Rhetoric may be efficacious, but given both the nature and the needs of the political community, it is insufficient and thus inappropriate as the sole ruling art. At this point, Socrates's argument depends upon his ability to establish the very purpose of politics itself, and he does this by suggesting an analogy between medicine and politics. The art of medicine, according to Socrates, is concerned with promoting the good of the body, i.e., its health; and the art of politics is concerned primarily with promoting the good of the soul, i.e., justice. Just as the doctor must know the nature of the body in order to minister to its needs, so too the politician must know the nature of the soul in order to foster its excellence. As a composite creature possessing both a body and a soul, the human person has a variety of needs—each of which must be satisfied if that person is to fulfill the full range of his or her human potential. The needs of the body are essentially of a material nature and, according to Greek practice, were cared for primarily within the confines of the household. The needs of the soul, on the other hand, are primarily of a spiritual, intellectual, and moral nature, and their nurture was the essential responsibility of the city-state. In short, politics for Plato is primarily an educational activity in which the character of the citizen is formed in such a way that it can achieve its own right order.

This task of achieving the right order of the soul is complicated by the very nature of the soul itself. The soul, as an erotic center, desires a variety of goods, and these desires, if left undisciplined, can actually rend the soul by pulling it in a number of different directions at the same time. Consequently by giving free reign to all the passions an individual may in fact fail to satisfy any of them adequately. Given this innate tendency towards an inherently chaotic condition, the soul, according to Socrates, is in need of the harmonizing influence of philosophy. Only the practice of philosophy can establish the love of wisdom as one's dominant passion and thereby subordinate all other desires to this highest of pursuits. Socrates understood the well-ordered soul to be the "just" soul and pictures the life of justice as the most desirable of human achievements. Properly ordered, an individual's soul is capable of realizing its highest potential and in doing so it achieves that natural excellence constitutive of true human happiness:

> So that the self-controlled man, Callicles, as we have defined him, just and brave and holy, must of necessity be completely good; and that the man must do well and fairly whatever he does; and that since he does his work well, he must be happy and blessed by the gods; and that, on the contrary, the wicked evil-doer must be wretched. Such a man will be one whose make-up is precisely opposite to that of the self-controlled man. . . .[4]

Just as the soul requires philosophical knowledge in order to achieve its properly harmonious order, so does the prosperity of the city-state depend upon the wisdom and virtue of its leaders. According to Socrates, society is like the human soul, since it too has a variety of interests and needs that necessarily compete with one another for scarce resources. Those in a position of leadership must know what is truly good for society or, lacking such knowledge, they will simply attempt to satisfy the most obvious interests of the most influential of its members. Lacking a knowledge of what is good for society and failing to appreciate the true nature of political justice, the leaders of a disorganized society are incapable of serving the common

153

Who Should Rule? The Claim of the Wise

good and seek instead simply to satisfy their own selfish needs. According to Socrates, however, a society dedicated exclusively to the pursuit of pleasure is, in fact, spiritually ill and requires, therefore, leaders who have an understanding of the principles of spiritual and political health. According to Socrates, it had been Athens's misfortune that such leaders had not been readily available to her. Like the rhetoricians of Socrates's own day, the Athenian leaders of the past sought only to please the people rather than to improve them.

> . . .you [Callicles] praise men who wined and dined our fellow citizens and crammed them full of what they desired. Men say that they made our city great, not perceiving that it is swollen and ulcerous because of its ancient counselors. With no regard for self-control or justice they stuffed our state with harbors and docks and walls and tribute-money and all such nonsense; so when this presumed attack of illness finally comes, they will blame the advisors who happen to be about at the time while praising to the skies Themistocles and Cimion and Pericles, though they were the true authors of the trouble.[5]

Just as the Socratic analogy comparing philosophy with medicine suggests that the sick soul seek the guidance of the philosopher if it truly wishes to be cured, so, too, does it imply that the pathologically ill state will become healthy only if and when the philosophers acquire political power. This implication, only hinted at in the *Gorgias*, is the explicit teaching developed fully in Plato's *Republic*. There, for the first time, Plato called for the rule of the philosopher-king.

The *Republic* is Plato's most complete political writing because it takes those themes first announced in the *Gorgias* and sets them within a larger metaphysical and epistemological framework in order to establish their essential philosophical validity. Central among these themes is the Platonic distinction between pleasure and the good. It was necessary for Plato to establish the legitimacy of this distinction because it, in turn, was the basis for such other important distinctions as that between philosophy and rhetoric on one hand and that between health and illness on the other. If the good and pleasure were the same, then Plato's effort to differentiate between the harmonious and the pathological soul would have been unsuccessful. And, if that were the case, it would have been equally impossible for him to distinguish between those effects that necessarily arise from the practice of philosophy and those that appear to accompany a commitment to the principles of rhetoric.

Plato's distinction between the reality of pleasure on one hand and the existence of the good on the other was one that he believed was given in the very structure of human experience itself. As a bodily creature, each person experiences the reality of the material world. Yet as a rational or *noetic* creature, each person also experiences a spiritual reality whose principles cannot be reduced to those of the former. In his famous "Allegory of the Cave," Plato attempted to portray this simple fact. The "realm of the cave" is composed of images and things. It is essentially of a material nature and offers one those pleasures desired by that passionate element of the soul that is attuned to the needs of the body. The "realm outside the cave," on the other hand, is an essentially "intellectual" or nonmaterial reality that contains both the 'Ideas' or 'Forms' and the very ground of being itself, which was called by Plato the 'Good' or the *Agathon*. The realities of this realm satisfy the soul's search for "that which is," and thus they appeal to its wisdom-loving or philosophical element.

The implications of Plato's dualistic metaphysics are many and varied; however for our purposes it is necessary to emphasize only one point. According to Plato the 'Good'(*Agathon*), as the principle of the intellectual realm, and pleasure, as a principle of the material, exist as two distinct poles within a highly differentiated reality. Each has its own proper sphere and each exists according to its own distinctive mode. For example, according to Plato, pleasures change; the 'Good' does not. As a consequence, from Plato's perspective that which is good and that which gives pleasure are not necessarily the same thing. Once this has been established, the role of the Platonic philosopher becomes quite evident.

If that which is good and that which gives pleasure were the same, one could simply follow pleasure as an infallible guide to the good. In such a situation, our bodily senses would give us all the information we would need in our effort to realize the good life. Yet given Plato's insistence that the good and pleasure are not the same, one can no longer simply rely upon the pursuit of material interests. An awareness of the good requires something else; and that for Plato was philosophical knowledge.

The philosopher, according to Plato, is the one who is devoted to the study and pursuit of the good. Given the fact that the good exists as an intellectual reality, its pursuit requires both the exercise of *noetic* reasoning and the concomitant disciplining of the bodily passions. As we have seen in the *Gorgias*, Socrates referred to this philosophic condition as one of justice. Consequently if a city seeks for

155

Who Should Rule? The Claim of the Wise

itself just rulers, it must necessarily seek the rule of the philosopher-king. According to Plato, it is the philosopher-king alone who can achieve that degree of personal and social harmony necessary for the attainment of human and political prosperity:

> Unless . . . the philosophers rule as kings or those now called kings and chiefs genuinely and adequately philosophize and political power and philosophy coincide in the same place, while the many natures now making their way to either apart from the other are by necessity excluded, there is no rest from ills for the cities, . . . nor I think for human kind, nor will the regime we have now described in speech ever come forth from nature, insofar as possible, and see the light of the sun.[6]

The phrase "the regime we have now described" refers to Plato's description of a model city in which the philosopher's knowledge has replaced the opinion of the many as the governing principle of society. Opinion, according to Plato, is the result of one's self-conscious encounter with the realm of appearances. Thus its authority characterizes a regime in which policies are made in terms of what *appears* to be good for the city rather than in terms of what *is* actually so. Knowledge, on the other hand, is the result of the philosopher's self-conscious encounter with pure being itself. Thus the regime of the philosopher-king would be one based upon an actual understanding of the city's true good rather than upon opinion concerning that which simply seems so. As pleasure can be distinguished from the good, so, too, being can be distinguished from appearance. And it is the philosopher's ability to knowingly draw such distinctions that, according to Plato, justifies the claim to rule. In the Platonic perspective, the obligation of the ruler is to improve the city; yet inasmuch as one cannot make something better without at first knowing what makes it good, the nature of political ruling itself would seem to require the rule of the wise.

Lenin

Plato's comparison of the philosopher with the medical doctor was only one example of the various analogies he used in his attempt to justify the rule of the wise. On other occasions, he compared the philosophical statesman with a pilot of a ship, a weaver of cloth, or a carpenter. In each case, the appeal was to a craftsman who possessed a definite set of skills based upon a specific body of knowledge. If the practice of politics were an art or a craft similar in nature to the practices of carpentry, clothmaking, or sailing, then those craftsmen who had mastered the principles of such an art could rightfully claim to have authority over the unskilled apprentice. This Platonic attempt to establish the craftlike quality of political rule has had many supporters. One of the more recent and influential was Vladimir Lenin (1870–1924), the Russian revolutionary leader and statesman. Writing in 1902, Lenin suggested his own analogy to the crafts, based upon the practice of architecture, wherein he likened the creation of a socialist society to the construction of a large and complex building:

> Pray tell me, when bricklayers lay bricks in various parts of an enormous, unprecedently large structure, is it "paper" work to use a line to help them find the correct place for the bricklaying; to indicate to them the ultimate goal of the common work; to enable them to use, not only every brick, but even every piece of brick which, cemented to the bricks before and after it, forms a finished, continuous line? And are we not now passing through precisely such a period in our Party life when we have bricks and bricklayers, but lack the guide line for all to see and follow?[7]

Lenin's position was similar to that of Plato to the extent that both argued that the creation and maintenance of a just society required the leadership of one who possessed a craftsman's vision of the whole. Unlike Plato's, however, Lenin's own understanding of this vision was based upon a Marxist analysis of history. For Plato and the Greeks in general, the philosopher's wisdom is due to an understanding of those universal principles that structure an essentially unchanging nature. According to Plato, the 'Good' (*Agathon*) and the 'Forms' are that part of reality that belongs to the realm of 'Being,' pure and simple. As such, they do not change, and thus our knowledge of them can be used to gauge those changes that do occur in our everyday experience. The realm of history, on the other hand, is the realm of fluidity and flux. Whereas the realm of 'Being' is timeless and metaphysically stable, the realm of history is one of becoming and consequently incapable of generating anything more than mere opinion. For Plato, true knowledge requires that one transcend the realm of history in order to participate in the metaphysical reality of an essentially ahistorical or unchanging 'Good.'

157

Who Should Rule? The Claim of the Wise

Lenin, on the other hand, was influenced by the arguments of Karl Marx; and Marx, following in the tradition of the German philosopher Georg Hegel, had claimed to achieve a scientific understanding of the very meaning of history itself. According to Marx, historical change is neither arbitrary nor accidental. On the contrary, history is understood to evolve according to a necessary and set pattern. Those who can decipher this pattern possess thereby a true knowledge of the past, present, and future. Whereas the Greeks typically believed that history is the realm of contingency and flux and therefore without purpose or principle, Marx believed that historical change is evolutionary in nature and thus by design and on behalf of a goal. In the eulogy he delivered at Marx's graveside, Friedrich Engels, his companion, said, "Just as Darwin discovered the law of development of organic nature, so Marx discovered the law of development of human history."[8]

This law which was the basis of Marx's *scientific* socialism was summarized by Marx and Engels somewhat differently on different occasions. One occasion arose when they were asked to write the party manifesto for the Communist League which was being reorganized in 1847. The result of their collaboration on this project was the *Communist Manifesto*; it began with the subsequently famous lines, "The history of all hitherto existing society is the history of class struggles."[9] With this statement Marx was arguing that the pattern of historical change within the West would become sufficiently clear once one fully understood the logic of the antagonistic relationship that necessarily existed among the classes. Marx was not the first analyst to discover the existence of distinct classes within society; nor was he the first to suggest that the interests of such classes were unavoidably in conflict with one another. Rather his discovery was one that equipped him to foretell the necessary outcome of this tragic situation. According to Marx, the history of past and present class struggle reveals the inevitability of a successful communist revolution. In a letter written in 1852, Marx claimed:

> . . . And now as to myself, no credit is due to me for discovering the existence of classes in modern society or the struggle between them. Long before me bourgeois historians had described the historical development of this class struggle and bourgeois economists the economic anatomy of the classes. What I did that was new was to prove: (1) that the existence of classes is only bound up with the particular historical phases in the development of production, (2) that the class

struggle necessarily leads to the dictatorship of the proletariat, (3) that this dictatorship itself only constitutes the transition to the abolition of all classes and to a classless society. . . .[10]

This knowledge that history is inevitably moving first through a period of "crude communism," which requires the exercise of dictatorial power by a united proletariat, and then into a period of "mature communism," in which the state will wither away and society will exist as a naturally harmonious anarchy, is an insight capable of directing the actions of those who learn its lesson. In short, a knowledge of history promises political success, and those who possess such a knowledge appear to have an obvious claim to leadership.

In Marx's own writings, it is not always clear whether he accepted the assumption that a scientific understanding of the laws of history necessarily entitles a select group of individuals to rule over others. On one hand, it is true that Marx understood his own writings as having a necessary authority and that he vigorously opposed the efforts of others, such as the anarchists, to formulate principles for the communist movement of his day. Although appealing to the special role of the proletariat, Marx himself was not a member of the working class and consequently claimed to bring to it something that it had not yet discovered for itself. In an 1843 letter, Marx wrote:

We develop new principles to the world out of its own principles. . . . We only show the world what it is fighting for, and consciousness is something that the world *must* acquire, like it or not.[11]

At the very least it would appear that Marx understood himself as leading the world to consciousness at least to the extent that his work was making explicit those principles that were already operating implicitly within history itself.

At the same time, there are a number of passages throughout his writings in which Marx appears to support the view that consciousness is nothing but the reflection of an actual situation and, consequently, that the proletariat knows what its role is because it directly experiences the "proletarian condition." If a true insight into the direction of history arises spontaneously because of the very nature of proletarian existence, there would appear to be little justification for a select group of intellectuals to claim that it is entitled to rule the working class. According to Marx, the very structure of the proletarian

159

Who Should Rule? The Claim of the Wise

condition requires that the proletariat assume its fateful role in history. The proletariat does not have to be taught to destroy capitalism because its very nature requires it to do so. In 1843 Marx wrote:

> When the proletariat announces the *dissolution of the existing social order*, it only declares the *secret of its* own existence, for it *is* the *effective* dissolution of this order.[12]

This argument, which is based upon Marx's understanding of superstructure and substructure, may explain why Marx himself never founded a political party and why he was only a member of an existing party for several years. If the proletariat can achieve its knowledge of history spontaneously, it needs neither a party nor an individual, like Marx, to lead it. The contemporary French Marxist Maximilien Rubel has written somewhat ironically:

> Did the proletariat need Marx? . . . we might say that this question would have appeared absurd to Marx and no doubt he would have replied in the negative.[13]

Given these various arguments, there is some ambiguity in the writings of Marx concerning the relationship between knowledge and political leadership. There is, however, no such ambiguity in the work of Lenin. Throughout his writings, Lenin argued repeatedly that a successful proletarian revolution presupposed that the working class submit itself to the authority of a select group of highly organized and professionally trained party regulars. According to Lenin, the Communist party was to be composed of selected intellectuals and workers who were to serve as the vanguard of the proletariat and in that capacity lead the working class in the direction Marx had foretold. This argument was most forcefully expressed in his 1902 pamphlet *What Is to Be Done?*

At the beginning of the twentieth century, Lenin and his followers were but one of several political groups actively committed to a political struggle against the czarist regime of Russia. In addition to Lenin's own Bolshevik wing of the Russian Social-Democratic Workers' Party, there were also its Menshevik wing, the Socialist Revolutionaries, and the Constitutional Democrats. These parties disagreed with one another on a whole range of tactical and strategic issues. Within the Marxist tradition in particular, the major disagreement between the Bolsheviks and the Mensheviks was concerned with the proper relationship of the party to the proletariat. In general, the Mensheviks accepted the arguments of the Russian Marxist Georgi Plekhanov, who resisted the Bolsheviks' effort to introduce socialism to the workers from above.

According to Plekhanov, the proper tactic for the Social Democratic Party was to join with the liberals in an effort to overthrow the czarist autocracy and establish thereby the free institutions of a bourgeois democracy. In this liberalized environment, the Russian economy would develop and thus permit a growing industrial proletariat to strengthen its political position. Eventually, according to Plekhanov, the workers would make their political revolution and do so without the tutelage of a patriarchal or authoritarian party.

Lenin labeled the Menshevik position as "tailism," by which he accused it of following the proletariat rather than leading it. The problem with following the proletariat, according to Lenin, was that, if left on its own, the proletariat would fail to develop that level of revolutionary consciousness necessary for decisive political action. He argued that the working class had to be raised to the level of the party rather than allowing the party to descend to the level of the workers:

> We have said that there could not have been Social-Democratic consciousness among the workers. It would have to be brought to them from without. The history of all countries shows that the working class, exclusively by its own efforts, is able to develop only trade union consciousness, i.e. the conviction that it is necessary to combine in unions, to fight the employers, and strive to compel the government to pass necessary labour legislation, etc. The theory of socialism, however, grew out of the philosophic, historical, and economic theories elaborated by educated representatives of the propertied classes, by intellectuals. . . . [I]n Russia the theoretical doctrine of Social-Democracy arose altogether independently of the spontaneous growth of the working-class movement; it arose as a natural and inevitable outcome of the development of thought among the socialist intelligentsia.[14]

Rather than follow the proletariat, the party, according to Lenin, was to work both "to combat spontaneity" and "to divert the working-class movement."[15] This conclusion was required by Lenin's prior belief that only two types of ideology were possible at that time—either bourgeois or socialist. Given the argument that

161

Who Should Rule? The Claim of the Wise

there could be no third or middle way, all forms of consciousness that were not sufficiently socialist were, as a consequence, inevitably bourgeois in nature. Quite ironically, therefore, the spontaneous or natural form of proletarian consciousness was, according to Lenin's analysis, only a perverted form of bourgeois ideology. Whereas Marx had argued that the conditions of proletarian life in and of themselves created the necessary prerequisites for a revolution, Lenin maintained that unless the workers' movement were subordinated to the authority of the Socialist party, it would remain an essentially bourgeois phenomenon. Commenting on this analysis, the former Polish communist Leszek Kolakowski wrote:

> . . . the working-class movement, i.e. a political revolutionary movement, is defined not by being a movement of workers but by possessing the right ideology, i.e. the Marxist one, which is "proletarian" by definition. In other words the class composition of a revolutionary party has no significance in determining its class character.[16]

According to Lenin, the party, understood as the vanguard of the proletariat, is to become "the teacher, the guide, the leader of all the working and exploited people. . . ."[17] It is prepared to do so because it alone possesses that certain knowledge of history and society that is based upon a correct Marxist analysis. In his writings, Lenin offered several examples of this understanding. Whereas the workers' spontaneous trade-union consciousness leads them to organize in an effort to achieve better terms for the sale of their labor power to the capitalists who own the factories, the party's analysis of capitalism shows that one must work for the total abolition of that very social system that requires for its own operation the buying and selling of labor power as if it were a mere commodity. Similarly genuine political consciousness can be differentiated from spontaneous working-class consciousness inasmuch as the former is trained to give a materialist analysis of the situation of every class or group within society rather than simply focusing upon the immediate economic concerns of a particular trade or occupation. Finally, according to Lenin, a "real" Marxist is one who not only acknowledges the necessity of the class struggle but also understands the reasons why such a struggle will necessarily result in the dictatorship of the proletariat. These and similar insights are, in Lenin's view, the result of the theoretical work accomplished by Marx and his followers. Consequently a knowledge of these insights and an appreciation of the theoretical analysis that produced them can alone serve to justify the rule of the many by the few.

Karl Popper

The differences between Platonic thought and Marxism-Leninism are significant and should not be underemphasized. Plato's view of reality acknowledges the existence of both a worldly and a transcendent dimension and his political teachings are based upon a metaphysical distinction between the pleasures of the material realm and the goods of a spiritual existence. Marxism-Leninism, on the other hand, posits a strictly immanentist understanding of reality, and its fundamental political teaching is based upon a radical distinction between the experience of the past and the promise of the future. Yet in spite of such substantive differences, there do exist certain formal similarities between these two traditions. Both assume that it is possible for human reason to comprehend those basic principles that define the true order of political and social existence. Similarly, both argue that those who have learned to recognize these principles are thereby rightfully entitled to rule over others. In short, both Plato and Lenin advocated a form of political elitism based upon a particular understanding of scientific insight.

In 1945, the Austrian philosopher Karl Popper published the two volumes of his work *The Open Society and Its Enemies*. Whereas the first volume is a critique of Platonic political thought, and the second focuses upon Marxism and its Idealist predecessors, the work as a whole was intended as a criticism of any attempt to justify the existence of a political elite by appealing to the principles of scientific reasoning. According to Popper, a correct understanding of the principles of scientific discovery justifies only one form of political order, i.e., the open society of a truly democratic community.

Born in Vienna in 1902, Popper emigrated to New Zealand in 1937 in order to escape the Nazi annexation of Austria. After the war he went to England and taught at the University of London. As a philosopher, Popper has been primarily concerned with the philosophy of science, and his scholarly work in this field (such as *The Logic of Scientific Discovery* and *Conjectures and Refutations*) is considered by many to constitute one of the most influential critiques of logical positivism in contemporary thought. As a youth in Vienna, Popper

163

Who Should Rule? The Claim of the Wise

was a Marxist; yet his experience with left-wing politics and, more important, his encounter with right-wing fascism drove him to examine the phenomenon of totalitarian politics and eventually resulted in the publication of his two most important political works, *The Open Society and Its Enemies* (1945) and its sequel *The Poverty of Historicism* (1957). Like Plato and Lenin, Popper answered the question Who should rule? by referring to the principles of scientific reason; yet unlike theirs, his understanding of science was methodological rather than substantive, and it resulted in an emphasis upon critical institutions rather than upon the wisdom of specific enlightened individuals.

In his political analysis, Popper argued that the authoritarian elitism of both the Platonic and the Marxist-Leninist traditions was essentially proto-totalitarian in nature. According to Popper, this work represented a crude reaction to the inevitability of social change and attempted to either arrest or control it by the imposition of totalitarian restraints. This project, in turn, was based upon what Popper considered to be a false rationalism or pseudorationalism, which must be contrasted with the true rationalism of the modern scientific spirit. True rationalism, Popper argued,

> . . . is the awareness of one's limitations, the intellectual modesty of those who know how often they err, and how much they depend on others even for this knowledge. It is the realization that we must not expect too much from reason; that argument rarely settles a question, although it is the only means for learning—not to see clearly, but to see more clearly than before.[18]

Pseudorationalism, on the other hand, is "the immodest belief in one's superior intellectual gifts, the claim to be initiated, to know with certainty, and with authority."[19]

Whereas such enemies of the open society as Plato and Marx embodied the spirit of pseudorationalism, Popper believed that the spirit of true rationalism is most clearly expressed in the practices of the modern scientific community. For Popper, the scientific community becomes the model for the political community; and, since the former is essentially critical, tolerant, and open, it creates an essentially democratic paradigm.

Popper's *The Logic of Scientific Discovery* begins with the following statement:

> A scientist, whether theorist or experimenter, puts forward state-
> ments, or systems of statements, and tests them step by step. In the
> field of the empirical sciences more particularly, he constructs hy-
> potheses, or systems of theories, and tests them against experience
> by observation and experiment.[20]

This seemingly simple statement contains the core of Popper's understanding of modern science; its simplicity, however, belies the truly nontraditional nature of its claims.

For example, according to Popper's formulation, the work of the scientist typically results in the offering of hypotheses rather than in the establishment of settled truths. Rather than producing a system of absolutely certain and irrevocably true statements, science actually produces a series of inconclusive and therefore relative hypotheses which only reflect the development of scientific progress to that point. As progress continues, established hypotheses are likely to be superseded. As a consequence, scientific progress itself is more accurately described in terms of the discovery of error than in terms of the discovery of truth. In short, science proceeds by correcting its past mistakes.

Given this method of operation, it is essential that the results of every scientific inquiry be formulated in such a way that under testing their mistakes will eventually become apparent. For Popper it is logically impossible to verify the claims of empirical science because such claims are based upon an examination of many "singular" cases. Even though the number of singular cases may be large, according to the rules of logic, a set of true singular statements can never yield a universal statement that is necessarily true. For example, even though every swan that has ever been seen has been white (a set of singular observations), it is still logically incorrect to assume from this that all swans are therefore necessarily white (a universal state-ment). Yet by denying the possibility of verification, Popper is not thereby denying the possibility of all forms of testing. As we have seen, testing plays a central role in his conception of science; and, even though we may not be able to test for the verifiability of a statement, we can, according to Popper, test for its falsifiability. Although universal statements can never be derived from singular statements, they can, in fact, be contradicted by them. For Popper it is this possibility of falsification that establishes the truly scientific character of empirical research. Scientific statements are different from, or in Pop-

165

Who Should Rule? The Claim of the Wise

per's terms "demarcated from," all other types of statements because they alone are required to be put into a logical form that allows for their eventual falsification:

> But I shall certainly admit a system as empirical or scientific only if it is capable of being *tested* by experience. These considerations suggest that not the verifiability but the *falsifiability* of a system is to be taken as the criterion of demarcation. In other words I shall not require of a scientific system that it shall be capable of being singled out, once and for all, in a positive sense; but I shall require that its logical form shall be such that it can be singled out, by means of empirical tests, in a negative sense: *it must be possible for an empirical scientific system to be refuted by experience.*[21]

Popper's emphasis upon falsifiability and his understanding of scientific progress in the negative sense of correcting past mistakes rather than in the positive sense of discovering new truths have several important consequences. First, the "scientific character" of any particular set of statements is not due to the actual content of such statements but rather to the form in which they are expressed and to the method by which they were derived. For Popper, science is characterized by its procedural methods, not by its substantive content; as a consequence, those who wish to be scientific or truly rational must be more committed to the critical procedures of the scientific process than to any of its substantive principles in particular. The essence of the scientific method is its spirit of free criticism, which subjects every established orthodoxy to the tests of observation and experimentation. This, in turn, requires the constant checking and rechecking of each scientist's work against the work of another. Inasmuch as science progresses as one person corrects the mistakes of another, scientific reasoning is dependent by its very nature upon that level of mutual criticism possible only in a free community of practicing scientists. The legitimacy of any scientific work is established only after it is repeatedly tested and confirmed by the work of others. Its worth is attested to by its acceptance within the community of scientists, and it is this approval rather than any particular excellence or virtue on the part of its discoverer that justifies its claim to our attention:

> [Scientific objectivity] . . . is a matter of scientific method. And ironically enough, objectivity is closely bound up with the *social aspect of the scientific method*, with the fact that science and scientific ob-

jectivity do not (and cannot) result from the attempts of an individual scientist to be "objective," but from the co-operation of many scientists. Scientific objectivity can be described as the intersubjectivity of scientific method.[22]

This analysis of science replaces the traditional and fundamentally fiducial understanding of reason with a modern and essentially critical one. At the formal level at least, both Plato and Lenin argued that the many must ultimately trust the few because of some particular insight (Plato's *noetic* experience or Lenin's true proletarian consciousness) which historically has been available only to a relative few. Popper, on the other hand, replaces trust with skepticism and, in calling for the repeated testing of all received opinion, suggests thereby the self-critical and essentially egalitarian nature of the scientific community.

If one wishes to establish a rational political community (and Popper admits that the choice to pursue a rational politics rather than a politics of irrationality is itself a moral decision based upon faith, not reason), then the scientific community provides the most appropriate model for the political order. Given the fact that scientific statements are both hypothetical and relative, all attempts to introduce reason to society should be done on a piecemeal and pragmatic basis. Holistic ideologies that attempt to transform the whole of the social order assume that their own principles are absolute, no longer in need of testing, and therefore beyond criticism. Such an assumption, however, is typical of that form of pseudorationalism which Popper associates with the work of Plato and Marx. A true rationalism, on the other hand, acknowledges the hypothetical nature of science and therefore welcomes the continued testing of all of its propositions. Social policies and ideas should be introduced on a limited basis, tested thoroughly, and held open to the possibility of an eventual reform. As our knowledge of the social world improves, new policies will inevitably be substituted for the old; and they, in their turn, should be exposed to the rigors of an ongoing critical analysis. Summarizing Popper's understanding of the open society, the philosopher Brian Magee wrote:

> Rationality, logic, and a scientific approach all point to a society which is "open" and pluralistic, within which incompatible views are expressed and conflicting aims pursued; a society in which everyone is free to propose solutions; a society in which everyone is

167

Who Should Rule? The Claim of the Wise

free to criticize the proposed solutions of others, most importantly those of the government, whether in prospect or application; and above all a society in which the government's policies are changed in the light of criticism.[23]

As we have seen, Popper understands science to be characterized by its methods rather than by its results. In other words, science exists as a process and not as a set of select or absolute truths. Similarly, Popper understands the "open society" as one that is characterized by its institutions and processes rather than by any particular set of principles or beliefs held by its members. In short, a democracy exists where free institutions are preserved, and in the modern work the preservation of free institutions often requires the large-scale intervention of the state. For example, Popper argues that an unrestrained capitalistic market system will eventually destroy the economic freedom of the poor. In order to prevent this and thus preserve economic freedom, the state must be willing to intervene in the economic process and attempt to minimize the amount of avoidable suffering.

Having established this, however, a certain dilemma appears. On one hand, Popper advocates free institutions, while on the other he realizes that the maintenance of such institutions often requires an exercise of state power and compulsion. This, in turn, raises the possibility that those in power will either overstep their proper bounds or fail to act aggressively enough in their effort to protect society's basic institutions. Either too much or too little state intervention may be a threat to human freedom. How, then, can a proper balance be achieved?

Popper's response to this dilemma once again emphasizes the importance of testing and criticism. Those in power should be subject to criticism, and their policies should be reevaluated on a continuing basis. Consequently, government leaders should be held strictly accountable for what they do; and, because it is possible that their policies may be "falsified" by their undesirable consequences, there should be an established and efficient way to peacefully remove them from power:

But this leads to a new approach to the problem of politics, for it forces us to replace the question: *Who should rule?* by the new question: How can we so organize political institutions that bad or incompetent rulers can be prevented from doing too much damage?[24]

Like Plato and Lenin, Popper resolves the issue of political sovereignty by appealing to the model of science. Unlike the former, however, his is an understanding of science as process not as substance, and consequently the elitism of the principled few is replaced by the democratic processes of the "open society."

Notes

1. Hesiod, *Theogony*, trans. Norman O. Brown (Indianapolis: Bobbs-Merrill, 1953), p. 53.

2. Hesiod, *Theogony*, p. 54.

3. Plato, *Gorgias*, trans. W. C. Hembold (Indianapolis: Bobbs-Merrill, 1952), p. 15.

4. Plato, *Gorgias*, p. 83.

5. Plato, *Gorgias*, p. 97.

6. Plato, *The Republic*, trans. Allan Bloom (New York: Basic Books, 1968), pp. 153–54.

7. Lenin, "What Is to Be Done?" in *The Lenin Anthology*, ed. Robert C. Tucker (New York: W. W. Norton, 1975), p. 101.

8. Friedrich Engels, "Speech at the Graveside of Marx," in *The Marx-Engels Reader*, 2d. ed., ed. Robert C. Tucker (New York: W. W. Norton, 1978), p. 681.

9. Karl Marx and Friedrich Engels, "The Communist Manifesto," in Tucker, *Reader*, p. 473.

10. Karl Marx, "Letter to Weydemeyer, 5 March 1852," in *Karl Marx: Selected Writings*, ed. David McLellan (New York: Oxford University Press, 1977), p. 341.

11. Karl Marx, "For a Ruthless Criticism of Everything Existing," in Tucker, *Reader*, pp. 14–15.

12. Karl Marx, "Contribution to the Critique of Hegel's *Philosophy of Right: Introduction*," in Tucker, *Reader*, p. 65.

13. Maximilien Rubel, "Did the Proletariat Need Marx and Did Marxism Help the Proletariat?" in *Marx and the Western World*, ed. Nicholas Lobkowicz (Notre Dame, Ind.: University of Notre Dame Press, 1967), p. 48.

14. Lenin, "What Is to Be Done?" in Tucker, *Anthology*, pp. 24–25.

15. Lenin, "What Is to Be Done?" in Tucker, *Anthology*, p. 29.

16. Leszek Kolakowski, *Main Currents of Marxism: The Gold Age*, trans. P. S. Falla (New York: Clarendon Press, 1978), pp. 389–90.

17. Lenin, "The State and Revolution," in Tucker, *Anthology*, p. 328.

169

Who Should Rule? The Claim of the Wise

18. Karl Popper, *The Open Society and Its Enemies*, vol. 2 (New York: Harper & Row, 1963), p. 227.

19. Popper, *Society*, vol. 2, p. 227.

20. Karl Popper, *The Logic of Scientific Discovery* (New York: Harper & Row, 1965), p. 27.

21. Popper, *Logic*, pp. 40–41.

22. Popper, *Society*, vol. 2, p. 217.

23. Bryan Magee, *Karl Popper* (New York: Viking Press, 1973), p. 74.

24. Popper, *Society*, vol. 1, p. 121.

Recommended Readings

Althusser, Louis. *Lenin and Philosophy*. Translated by Ben Brewster. New York: Monthly Review Press, 1978.

Dilman, Ilham. *Morality and the Inner Life: A Study in Plato's Gorgias*. Totowa, N.J.: Barnes & Noble, 1979.

Guthrie, W. K. C. *Socrates*. New York: Cambridge University Press, 1971.

Irwin, Terrence. *Plato's Moral Theory*. New York: Clarendon Press, 1977.

Lukacs, Georg. *Lenin*. Translated by Nicholas Jacobs. Cambridge: M.I.T. Press, 1971.

Luxemburg, Rosa. *The Russian Revolution & Leninism or Marxism?* Ann Arbor: University of Michigan Press, 1961.

Magee, Bryan. *Karl Popper*. New York: Viking Press, 1973.

Meyer, Alfred. *Leninism*. New York: Praeger Publishers, 1972.

Randall, John Herman, Jr. *Plato: Dramatist of the Life of Reason*. New York: Columbia University Press, 1970.

Schlipp, Paul, ed. *The Philosophy of Karl Popper*. 2 vols. LaSalle, Ill.: Open Court, 1974.

C H A P T E R   9

![black bar]

Who Should Rule? The Will of the People

Introduction

In 1774 the English philosopher and politician Edmund Burke spoke before a group of his constituents gathered in Bristol, England, and told them:

> Your representative owes you, not his industry only, but also his judgment; and he betrays, instead of serving you, if he sacrifices it to your opinion. . . . If government were a matter of will upon my side, yours without question, ought to be superior. But government and legislation are matters of reason and judgment, and not of inclination; and what sort of reason is that, in which determination precedes the discussion, in which one set of men deliberate, and another decide; and where those who form the conclusion are perhaps three hundred miles distant from those who hear the arguments? . . . Parliament is not a *congress* of ambassadors from different and hostile interests; which interests each must maintain, as an agent and advocate, against the other agents and advocates; but parliament is a *deliberative* assembly of *one* nation, with *one* interest, that of the whole; where, not local purposes, not local prejudices ought to guide, but the general good, resulting from the general reason of the whole.[1]

Burke's statement is often cited as an attempt to distinguish between two possible roles for the elected representative. As delegates,

171

Who Should Rule? The Will of the People

elected representatives are expected to articulate the interests and wishes of their constituents; but, as trustees, they are entrusted to act according to their own reasoned assessments. The latter role obviously provides for much more discretion and independence on the part of elected officials, while the former emphasizes their accountability and responsiveness. Burke's justification of the trustee model was based upon his prior understanding of the nature of English politics. Like such classical thinkers as Aristotle and Cicero, Burke believed that politics was a matter of prudential judgment—not of will. Accordingly, he assumed that all political activity ought to pursue naturally determined objective ends and consequently that a practical knowledge of these ends was a necessary prerequisite for those who wished to rule. According to Burke, the English political tradition simply required that the voters be allowed to designate those members of the "natural aristocracy" in whose judgment they had come to rely.

Burke's understanding of politics was a typically artistocratic one that presupposed that society was a natural and organic unity of orderly ranks. Yet in the seventeenth and eighteenth centuries, a radically different interpretation of the social order was being propounded in the writings of the so-called social contract theorists. Thinkers such as Thomas Hobbes (1588–1679), John Locke (1632–1704), and Jean-Jacques Rousseau (1712–78) argued that all legitimate societies resulted from a contract among individuals who, by agreeing to certain basic procedural principles, actually "willed" society into existence. This understanding of the political order implied a conception of politics quite different from that of Burke. In summarizing this newer view, the contemporary political theorist Michael Walzer has written:

> The people's claim to rule does not rest upon their knowledge of truth. . . . The claim is most persuasively put, it seems to me, not in terms of what the people know but in terms of who they are. They are the subjects of the law, and if the law is to bind them as free men and women, they must also be its makers. . . . The argument has the effect of making law a function of popular will and not of reason as it had hitherto been understood, the reason of wise men, sages, and judges. The people are the successors of gods and absolute kings, but not of philosophers. They may not know the right thing to do, but they claim a right to do what they think is right (literally, what pleases them).[2]

Political Ruling: The Basis of Authority

If one accepts this understanding of politics and thereby acknowledges the essential importance of popular sovereignty, the rule of the wise must of necessity be replaced by a regime founded upon the will of the governed. Within Western political thought, the writings of the theorist Jean-Jacques Rousseau have done more to demonstrate the necessity of this conclusion than any other single set of teachings.

Jean-Jacques Rousseau

Born in Geneva, Switzerland, in 1712, Rousseau moved to Paris to seek his fortune at the age of twenty-nine. He soon met a number of the Enlightenment intellectuals who had come to the French capital in order to write and publish Diderot's *Encyclopedia*, the first great experiment in popular education. While living in Paris and enjoying the patronage of certain French aristocrats, Rousseau began to write and publish his own political and social commentaries. The most important of these were *The Discourse on the Sciences and Arts* (1750), *The Discourse on the Origin of Inequality* (1755), and *The Social Contract* (1762). In 1762, Rousseau also published his treatise on education, the *Emile*. Certain passages in this book were perceived as theologically suspect and caused it to be banned by the city magistrates of Paris, Geneva, and Bern. Fearing arrest, Rousseau fled Paris and traveled throughout Europe. Convinced that there was a worldwide conspiracy against him, he returned to Paris in 1767 and was forced to enter a poorhouse. He remained there, copying music and working on a series of autobiographical writings until his death in 1778.

Before Rousseau's work was published, the concept of democracy often carried with it the implication of political instability and moral chaos. Given this, ancient and early modern thinkers attempted to restrain the democratic tendencies of political regimes by constructing various constitutional checks and balances to the popular will. Beginning with Rousseau, however, a new attitude emerged that not only favored democratic self-government but also made the stronger argument that all nondemocratic regimes are essentially illegitimate. It is generally considered that Rousseau's *Social Contract*, more than any other single work, was responsible for this fundamental shift in political sentiment.

Rousseau's writings present an essentially romantic critique of the cultural and social practices of his own day. In his *Discourse on the Sciences and Arts*, he used the occasion of a public essay contest

173

Who Should Rule? The Will of the People

to criticize some of the central tenets of the newly emerging bourgeois civilization. For example, the popular ideal of the rational, self-interested, and emancipated individual appeared to Rousseau to offer a seriously distorted understanding of humanity's true potential. Rousseau believed that, although at one time people were both virtuous and authentic, modern civilization with its inordinate emphasis upon the cultivation of scientific and literary talent has had an essentially corrupting effect. "Civilized" peoples had assumed a degree of inauthenticity that not only allowed them to hide behind their roles and functions but also deprived them of their individuality and intrinsic creativity. Rather than developing the human personality, modern culture, Rousseau wrote, has actually weakened and perverted it:

> Civilized peoples, cultivate talents: happy slaves, you owe to them that delicate and refined taste on which you pride yourselves; that softness of character and urbanity of customs which make relations among you so amiable and easy; in a word, the semblance of all virtues without the possession of any.[3]

In a similar manner, Rousseau intended his *Discourse on the Origin of Inequality* to be a critique of the political and economic conditions of modern Europe. Writing during the era of French despotism, Rousseau compared the degree of economic and political inequality characteristic of his own time with the condition of liberty and equality that typified life in the state of nature before the creation of society. Although men and women are free and equal by nature, in modern society they have come to accept those radical inequalities that differentiate the rich from the poor and the powerful from the weak. In short, Rousseau believed that modern society is both corrupt and unnatural.

Some commentators argue that Rousseau was a "primitivist" inasmuch as they understand him to suggest that one can escape the evils of modernity by returning to the more primitive life-style of the far-distant past. Yet it seems quite clear that this was not in fact his intention. First, Rousseau explicitly denied that he wished to "destroy societies, annihilate thine and mine, and go back to live in forests with bears."[4]

Second, and more important, he was confident that he had discovered a strategy that made it possible to go forward to a better future by correcting the failures of the present. The inadequacies of a modern culture based upon the assumptions of hedonism, individualism, and rationalism could be corrected by implementing a new educational program that incorporated a more adequate understanding of human nature and its needs. In an effort to demonstrate this, Rousseau published his educational treatise, the *Emile*, which he believed could foster such qualities as confidence, discrimination, self-reliance, honesty, and public-spiritedness. Having thus provided an understanding of a reformed human nature, it then became necessary for Rousseau to develop the model for a reformed society that would, in turn, allow such natures to prosper.

The economic and political inequalities of modern life were, according to Rousseau, the inevitable results of the creation of civil and political society. However, rather than advocate the "primitivist" solution that modern society be destroyed, Rousseau attempted to improve the state by securing its moral legitimacy:

> Man is born free, and everywhere he is in chains. One believes himself the master of others, and yet he is a greater slave than they. How has this change come about? I do not know. What can render it legitimate? I believe that I can settle this question.[5]

The creation of a state entails the establishment of a hierarchy among individuals whereby certain persons are given the exclusive power to enforce the laws of society. Since this hierarchy does not exist in nature, according to Rousseau, it must be created by convention. Given the fact that individuals can agree to cooperate for unworthy purposes, the founding convention itself must be in accordance with some prior moral principle. Specifically the terms of agreement by which a political society is created must be of such a kind that they do not violate the fundamental principles of human nature:

> To renounce one's liberty is to renounce one's quality as a man, the rights and also the duties of humanity. For him who renounces everything there is no possible compensation. One such renunciation is incompatible with man's nature; for to take away all freedom from his will is to take away all morality from his actions.[6]

Earlier in his *Second Discourse*, Rousseau attempted to distinguish between animal nature and human nature. Traditionally this

175

Who Should Rule? The Will of the People

distinction was made by referring to mankind's ability to reason. Yet according to Rousseau's analysis of the state of nature, a human's ability to experience and combine ideas is different from that of an animal only in degree, not in kind. Consequently, Rousseau rejected the traditional argument that it is mankind's rational capabilities that define the unique and specifically human quality of our species. Instead Rousseau preferred to emphasize the importance of free will:

> Therefore it is not so much understanding which constitutes the distinction of man from animals as it is his being a free agent. Nature commands every animal, and the beast obeys. Man feels the same impetus, but he realizes that he is free to acquiesce or resist, and it is above all in the consciousness of this freedom that the spirituality of his soul is shown . . . in the power of willing, or rather in choosing, and in the sentiment of this power are found only spiritual acts about which the laws of mechanics explain nothing.[7]

Given Rousseau's understanding that it is the exercise of liberty alone that can secure our humanity, any attempt to justify either the enforcement of a law or the establishment of a hierarchy must be done in such a way as to preserve the actuality of human freedom. In view of this demand, Rousseau rejected two of the most common arguments used to justify the existence of political authority.

First, as we have seen, one tradition in Western political thought has argued on behalf of the rule of the strongest. In his own day, Rousseau understood this tradition to be best represented in the writings of the Dutch jurist Hugo Grotius (1583–1645). Earlier Grotius had maintained that the right of conquest actually established the right to rule. Yet conquest is a matter of force, and according to Rousseau:

> Force is a physical power; I do not see what morality can result from its effects. To yield to force is an act of necessity, not of will; it is at most an act of prudence. In what sense can it be a duty? . . . Let us agree, then, that might does not make right, and that we are obliged to obey only legitimate powers.[8]

The second defense of political hierarchy, that Rousseau considered was related to that tradition of speculation that favored the rule of the wise. In his *Politics*, Aristotle had argued that some individuals lacked a sufficient degree of reason to rule themselves and so were destined to be ruled by those who were their intellectual superiors.

Political Ruling: The Basis of Authority

These arguments pointed to a class of "natural slaves" and justified the institution of slavery as required by nature itself. Although Rousseau acknowledged that certain people do in fact live in a truly slavish manner, he denied that their own nature requires this. Those who appear slavish are so because of the conditions within which they live. Consequently, although some may be born *in* slavery, no one is born *for* slavery.

Rousseau rejected these traditional arguments on behalf of political rule because he believed that they had failed to adequately appreciate the significance of free choice. Human beings are what they are precisely because they possess a free will. Therefore, the only obligations or systems of authority that can exist without simultaneously denying an essential principle of our humanity are those that are freely accepted by the individuals involved. In short, legitimate political authority can only emerge in accordance with the principles of a properly constructed social contract:

> To find a form of association which may defend and protect with the whole force of the community the person and property of every associate, and by means of which each, coalescing with all, may nevertheless obey only himself, and remain as free as before. Such is the fundamental problem of which the social contract furnishes the solution.[9]

Rousseau envisioned a procedure whereby each individual would transfer all rights to the newly formed political association through the mechanism of the social contract. To the extent that one's rights have been given over to the community as a whole rather than to any of its members in particular, no individual is thereby subordinated to the will of another. Similarly, inasmuch as each associate transfers all rights originally possessed, no one retains any particular privilege, and each citizen becomes thereby the moral and political equal of every other.

In differentiating humans from all the other animal species, Rousseau emphasized the fundamental importance of the human will. Unlike other animals, humans choose to act the way they do. Each person as an individual typically wills to act on behalf of his or her own specific and concrete interests. Yet since the faculty of free choice is shared by all humans and thus indicates that a specific individual is, at the same time, a member of the general species, humanity, the human will has both a universal and a particular interest. As a member

177

Who Should Rule? The Will of the People

of the human species, each individual shares in its condition and benefits from its existence. A person who chooses to act primarily for the sake of his or her own particular interest is choosing according to private will. However, one who chooses on behalf of the universal good of the associated species as a whole is acting according to the general will and thus expressing the intention to further the interest of all. In short, the general will intends the good of all and as a consequence includes the interest of each. In a well-ordered political community, the general will is sovereign and its decisions are binding upon all the members. Yet, since each individual member, in obeying the general will, is actually obeying what he or she chooses as a true associate of the community, in obeying the law, the individual is actually following his or her own dictates. By agreeing to a properly designed social contract, the individual leaves the state of nature where power and appetite determine the quality of life in order to enter into a civil society where the general will both establishes moral duty—i.e., universal law—and at the same time preserves human freedom—i.e., self-imposed regulation. Inasmuch as "obedience to a law one prescribes to one's self is freedom," the creation of a democratic society "renders man truly master of himself."[10]

In describing the terms of the social contract, Rousseau was aware that he was not describing an actual state. In order for the general will to become truly effective, there has to exist an egalitarian community in which each citizen has a vote and in which the actions of society have an equal effect upon all. For Rousseau, true law exists only when all the people act on something that concerns the entire community. Consequently a law that only serves the interests of a specific or select group is not an example of the general will because the general will can, by definition, only intend the universal.

Similarly a law enacted by only a portion of society or its selected representatives is not an example of the general will because respect for human freedom requires that each citizen obey only those laws that he or she individually has actively prescribed. For Rousseau, therefore, duty and freedom presuppose the institutions of a participatory democracy wherein the citizen body as a whole meets to determine those principles that will guide the policies of the state. For Rousseau it is the assembled citizenry alone that is sovereign. Those political systems that have established a form of representative democracy err, since to do so is to delegate sovereignty to a few select individuals. Government officials, even if elected democratically, cannot legislate for others without at the same time violating the oth-

ers' fundamental moral autonomy. Commenting on the English parliamentary system of representative government, Rousseau wrote:

> Sovereignty cannot be represented for the same reason that it cannot
> be alienated; it consists in the general will and the will cannot be
> represented. . . . The deputies of the people, then, are not and can-
> not be its representatives; they are only its commissioners and can
> conclude nothing definitely. Every law which the People in person
> have not ratified is invalid; it is not law. The English people thinks
> that it is free, but it is greatly mistaken, for it is so only during the
> election of Parliament; as soon as they are elected, it is enslaved and
> counts for nothing.[11]

Rousseau's answer to the question Who should rule? was quite
clear: the people themselves. He arrived at this answer through a
prior analysis of our human nature. Given his belief that our humanity is constituted by the exercise of our free will, any system of government other than direct self-rule negates the very purpose of political
life itself. Society is created to benefit humanity and thereby serve the
human good. Yet unless it is structured as a participatory democracy,
it can only destroy that which it was intended to serve.

Rousseau's teaching is both radical and demanding. It is radical
because it implied that all the existing societies of his day were in fact
morally illegitimate. It is demanding because, at the same time, Rousseau realized that a working participatory democracy presupposes a
set of conditions that in themselves are difficult to achieve. Given the
need for the periodic and regular meetings of all the citizens, Rousseau's well-ordered society can be neither too large nor too populous.
Its economic resources must be moderate but nonetheless sufficient,
and, most important, its members must be educated so as to be capable of subordinating their individual preferences to the principles of
the general will as they engage in public deliberation. In short, Rousseau's democratic society presupposes that its citizens embody those
very educational and moral qualities that he first outlined in his
Emile. Examining his own era, Rousseau was not optimistic that
these conditions could be met; yet, given his understanding of the nature of human freedom and moral duty, he was unable to envision any
acceptable alternative to democratic self-government.

In spite of its historically radical effect, Rousseau's effort to locate
political sovereignty with the people rather than within the offices of
the state was, in fact, a guarded one. Although he argued that only the

179

Who Should Rule? The Will of the People

assembled people can be sovereign, they are not thereby free to do whatever they wish. According to Rousseau, popular rule is legitimate only to the extent that it truly embodies the general will; and, just as it is possible for an individual to prefer his or her own interests to those of society as a whole, so too is it possible for the majority of citizens to choose wrongly. Rousseau attempted to clarify this possibility by distinguishing between the general will and the "will of all":

> It follows from what precedes that the general will is always right and always tends to the public advantage; but it does not follow that the deliberations of the people have always the same rectitude. One always desires his own good, but does not always discern it. The people are never corrupted, though often deceived, and it is only then that they seem to will what is bad. There is often a great deal of difference between the will of all and the general will; the latter regards only the common interest, while the former has regard to private interests, and is merely a sum of particular wills. . . .[12]

Rousseau's distinction seems to imply that there exists a more-or-less-objective standard that defines the appropriate content of the common interest. By implying the existence of such a substantive measure, Rousseau is understood by some commentators to be contradicting his earlier argument that consent alone is the basis of political legitimacy. Apparently it is not enough that the people agree; rather it now seems that they must agree about the right thing. Commenting on this, Michael Walzer wrote:

> Rousseau says . . . [the people] . . . must will the common good and goes on to argue that the people will the common good if they are a true people, a community, and not a mere collection of egoistic individuals and corporate groups. Here the idea seems to be that there exists a single set—though not necessarily an exhaustive set—of correct or just laws that the assembled people . . . may not get right. Often enough they get it wrong and then they require the guidance of a legislator or the restraint of a judge. . . . In any case, this . . . surely raises the most serious questions about Rousseau's fundamental argument, that political legitimacy rests on will (consent) and not on reason (rightness).[13]

The categorical distinction between the general will and the will of all introduces an ambiguity at the center of Rousseau's teachings. Yet, at the same time, it is true that this ambiguity becomes less important as humanity becomes more decent. If the citizens of Rousseau's society were educated according to the principles of his *Emile*, they would exhibit those very traits that would make this distinction less bothersome. As Peter Gay writes:

> The link between Rousseau's *Emile* and *Social Contract* should be obvious. Each requires the other. . . . Once a community of Emiles has been formed, it will govern itself calmly, wisely, and generously. The key element in the citizen's activity is his participation in decision-making, and as a sound citizen he will cast his vote by listening not to his own selfish interests, but to his perception of the public weal. Of course, with the best of intentions, he may confound the two. But then the decision of the majority—not just any majority, but the intelligent, sensible, uncorrupted majority that Rousseau envisions—will recall the straying minority to its duty, to its true, larger interest. . . . In a word Rousseau seeks the virtuous citizen, who will, as he puts it in the *Social Contract*, "make virtue reign."[14]

It would appear then that Rousseau's guarded reliance upon the will of the majority was based upon his prior acknowledgment of the significant difference between the people as they are and the people as they would be if they were truly virtuous. It is clear that Rousseau believed that in the latter case the people should rule themselves. Yet, given people as they actually are, who should rule? This question is a central concern for contemporary analysts of interest-group democratic theory in general and for the political scientist Robert Dahl in particular.

Robert Dahl

The behavioral movement that came into prominence in American political science following the Second World War has concentrated much of its research effort on a comprehensive evaluation of democratic politics in general and of American democracy in particular. According to its own understanding of the scientific method, behavioralism prefers to work empirically. Consequently, rather than positing an ideal democratic order that attempts to realize certain preferred

181

Who Should Rule? The Will of the People

values, the behavioral tradition seeks instead to develop an empirically accurate description of real-world politics. By emphasizing historical experience rather than metaphysical principle, the behavioral study of democratic politics hopes to avoid certain problems associated with the more traditional theories. For example, Rousseau's analysis of a true democracy requires that one distinguish between the universal general will, on one hand, and the more selfish will of all, on the other. Yet, as we have seen, this distinction seems to imply the existence of certain objective interests whose "rightness" can then be used to differentiate between the two. The all-too-frequent failure of individuals to acknowledge such a standard, however, leads to a situation wherein certain individuals are "forced to be free" and all existing governments are denounced as morally illegitimate. For those primarily interested in understanding the world of everyday practice, such sweeping denunciations may appear irrelevant and not particularly useful. Rousseau's condemnation of existing society was the result of his insisting upon the recognition of a moral distinction between universal interests on one hand and selfish interests on the other. For the behavioral scientist, however, such a value preference—i.e., between universal and selfish interests—is both scientifically unacceptable and theoretically unnecessary. For example, while analyzing the role of specific interest groups within society, the behavioral political scientist David Truman wrote:

> Seen in these terms is an interest group inherently selfish? In the first place such judgments have no value for a scientific understanding of government or the operation of society. Schematically they represent nothing more than the existence of a conflicting interest, possibly, but not necessarily involving another group or groups. Judgments of this kind are and must be made by citizens in their everyday life, but they are not properly a part of the systematic analysis of the social process.[15]

In other words, for the behaviorally oriented political scientist the question Who should rule? can best be answered by refraining from an examination of metaphysical or moral principles. Instead, the answer one gives to this question will depend upon the empirical results one desires.

Among contemporary behavioralists who have studied democratic politics, one of the most influential has been the Yale political scientist Robert Dahl. In his 1956 publication *A Preface to Democratic*

Theory, Dahl developed his outline for a more rigorously empirical form of democratic theory. Referring to the "descriptive method," he suggested considering

> . . . as a single class of phenomenon all those nation states and social organizations that are commonly called democratic by political scientists, and by examining the members of this class to discover, first the distinguishing characteristics they have in common, and, second, the necessary and sufficient conditions for social organizations possessing these characteristics.[16]

Dahl distinguished his approach from other more traditional affairs that attempted first to "specify a set of goals to be maximized" and then to define democracy "in terms of the specific governmental processes necessary to maximize these goals or some among them."[17] As an example of this latter method, one could refer to the work of Rousseau. His goal was to provide legitimacy to the exercise of political power, while the mechanism by which he attempted to achieve this goal was the total alienation of all individual rights. Dahl gives as his own examples the maximizing approach implicit within the theory of democracy developed by James Madison in *The Federalist Papers* on one hand and the theory of democratic populism on the other.

According to Dahl, the Madisonian theory of democracy has as its goals the establishment and preservation of a nontyrannical regime. It attempts to realize this objective, first, by creating constitutional checks and institutional balances to the centralized exercise of power and, second, by relying upon the destabilizing effects of a large, diverse, and extended electorate. However, Dahl finds this theory to be clearly inadequate. First, Madisonianism is based upon a set of assumptions about human nature and the dynamics of political power that have never been established empirically and are of a highly questionable nature. Second, some of its key concepts, such as "tyranny" and "faction," are defined in such a way as to be operationally meaningless and thus incapable of empirical validation. From Dahl's perspective, Madison's understanding of democracy is both empirically and logically flawed. It fails, not only to offer a consistent set of political goals, but to explain the actual practices of the American regime. Democracy works fairly well in America, according to Dahl, but not for the reasons Madisonianism suggests.

The Madisonian concern for protecting the rights of minorities is characteristic of those traditions of democratic theory that emphasize

183

Who Should Rule? The Will of the People

the importance of liberty. However, populist theories of democracy typically emphasize the importance of equality. If all citizens are equal, then the preferences of the greatest number must be respected in each case. From this perspective, the Madisonian attempt to limit the power of the majority is equivalent to establishing a bias on behalf of the interests of select minorities. In rejecting this, populist democracy advocates the exclusive pursuit of two goals in particular: political equality and popular sovereignty. To achieve these objectives, it establishes the procedural rule that in choosing among alternatives, the alternative preferred by the greatest number must be selected.

Dahl's analysis of the theory of democractic populism is highly critical and, in developing it, he raises technical, ethical, and historical objections to its arguments. In general, however, he rejects its claim because of their essentially nonempirical character:

> . . . the theory of populist democracy is not an empirical system. It consists only of logical relations among ethical postulates. It tells us nothing about the real world. From it we can predict no behavior whatsoever.[18]

Dahl's critique of populism is interesting, not only for its evaluation of that particular tradition of democractic theory, but also because it indicates what he himself expects an empirical theory of democracy to achieve. An adequate descriptive theory, according to Dahl, should give one sufficient information to plan actual, concrete political actions. Rather than simply defining a procedural rule for the ideal attainment of political equality and popular sovereignty, Dahl expects an adequate theory to answer the question; What are the necessary and sufficient conditions for maximizing democracy in the real world?[19] Dahl's own answer to this question is found in his understanding of what he calls "polyarchal democracy."

The theory of polyarchy combines both the descriptive method and the method of maximization. Although he is reluctant to develop an explicitly ethical justification for the values he prefers, Dahl does offer as a desirable objective the maximization of both political equality and popular sovereignty. However, unlike the traditional theorists of populistic democracy, Dahl begins his argument by referring to the practices of existing democractic organizations in order to determine to what extent they actually operate according to the principle of majority rule. This approach requires that Dahl specify certain more-or-

less observable conditions which can then be used as measurements
in an effort to quantify the extent to which majority rule is operative in
any particular case. For the purposes of the book under discussion,
Dahl specifies eight such real-world conditions that would have to be
fulfilled in order to achieve the full maximization of the goals he has
set. Included are such factors as the equal weighting of each vote, the
availability of identical information to each citizen, the dominance of
the majority preference, and the faithful execution of the orders of the
elected officials. Those organizations that "score" relatively well on
these eight scales are then classified as polyarchies and are offered as
real-world examples of actual functioning democracies. Although no
organization has fully maximized political equality and popular sovereignty, Dahl argues that the American political system does provide
a relatively good example of a peaceful, moderate, and stable polyarchal democracy. Given this, Dahl's understanding of polyarchy in
general can be illustrated by looking at this analysis of America in
particular.

One of the first lessons from an examination of the American system is that in actual, operating democracies, majorities rarely rule on
matters of specific policy. In view of this, Dahl concludes that the
Madisonian attempt to prevent a tyranny of the majority is a false concern. Given the range and complexity of issues in modern politics,
majorities rarely emerge. Rather, a small core of politicians responds
to a variety of influential minorities who exert pressure upon the leadership to act on their behalf on selected issues. In this environment,
the "will of the people" does not exist as a uniform or consistent interest articulated by majority preference. On the contrary, if it exists at
all, it is the result of a decentralized, fragmented bargaining process
that involves numerous competing and overlapping minorities. Similarly, political competition and elections do not result in the formation of a majoritarian government. Although elections do allow us to
determine which political leaders are the first choice of most of the
voters who went to the polls on a given day, they do not provide significant or useful policy information beyond that. Rather than being a
device by which the majority is able to express its wishes concerning
the policies of the government, the function of elections in a polyarchy is primarily to increase the number and variety of minorities
whose preferences must be acknowledged by the politicians. According to Dahl, "the making of governmental decisions is not a majestic
march of great majorities united upon certain matters of basic policy.
It is the steady appeasement of relatively small groups."[20] If Dahl is

185

Who Should Rule? The Will of the People

correct, then, neither the Madisonian nor the populist understanding of majoritarian democracy is empirically accurate. Democracy in the modern world appears as the rule of minorities, each seeking to dominate specific areas of concern with little or no regard for the larger public good.

Even though the theory of polyarchal democracy acknowledges that minorities rule, it still insists that such rule is a true form of democractic self-government. First, polyarchy is the rule of *minorities*, not the rule of *a minority*. As a result there is a certain circulation among the elites that keeps the system relatively open and thereby distinguishes it from that closure characteristic of a dictatorship. Second, the minorities that happen to dominate a specific policy area at a specific time are prevented from abusing their power by the existence of certain self-operating limitations. As a minority, they lack those resources necessary to impose their will upon others except in the case where the great majority of competing groups is relatively apathetic. Given the apathy of most, it is possible for intense minorities to pursue their interests successfully. In view of this, it is in the self-interest of the governing minorities to encourage political apathy; and political apathy, in turn, can be most easily sustained if a nongoverning group's expectations and interests are being adequately met. In short, it is in the self-interest of the governing minorities not to frustrate the important interests of other groups. Because of this, polyarchies, according to Dahl, tend toward responsiveness, compromise, and moderation.

An important feature of Dahl's argument is his insistence that the essential checks upon the rule of minorities are social rather than constitutional in nature. As the case of Nazi Germany shows, constitutional and procedural limitations on power can be circumvented if certain groups wish to do so. The more effective check on those in power, according to Dahl, is that provided by the political culture and social mores of the society. If the people have a strong commitment to the principles of democractic self-government and demand that their leaders behave democractically, this expectation in itself will function to limit the exercise of power. As long as the leaders appear to act democractically, the majority of groups can remain apathetic. If, however, the ruling minorities fail to meet this expectation, previously apathetic groups may enter into the competition for power and thereby undermine the advantage of the ruling coalition. This possibility requires that those in government act with a certain degree of responsibility and caution. Consequently, although the American political system may fail to fully maximize political equality and popular sovereignty, it is nonetheless highly responsive to the interests of active and legitimate minority groups:

> With all its defects, it does nonetheless provide a high possibility that any active and legitimate group will make itself heard effectively at some state in the process of decision.[21]

Given this openness, polyarchal democracy appears to be a relatively stable system that is able to operate with a minimum of coercion and thereby provide maximum protection for constitutional rights. If these objectives are seen as desirable, then ruling should be entrusted to those individuals who are both committed to and successful in the process of compromise, appeasement, and coalition building. In such a system the people govern, albeit indirectly, through the rule of competing interest groups as mediated by the compromising practices of professional politicians.

Notes

1. Cited in C. B. Macpherson, *Burke* (New York: Hill & Wang, 1980), p. 25.
2. Michael Walzer, "Philosophy and Democracy," *Political Theory* 9, no. 3 (August 1981): 383.
3. Jean-Jacques Rousseau, *The First and Second Discourses*, trans. Roger D. Masters and Judith R. Masters (New York: St. Martin's Press, 1964), p. 36.
4. Rousseau, *First and Second Discourses*, p. 201.
5. Jean-Jacques Rousseau, *The Social Contract*, trans. Charles M. Sherover (New York: New American Library, 1974), p. 5.
6. Rousseau, *Contract*, p. 15.
7. Rousseau, *First and Second Discourses*, p. 114.
8. Rousseau, *Contract*, p. 11.
9. Rousseau, *Contract*, p. 23.
10. Rousseau, *Contract*, p. 33.
11. Rousseau, *Contract*, p. 161.
12. Rousseau, *Contract*, p. 45.
13. Walzer, "Philosophy," p. 384–85.
14. Peter Gay, "Introduction," in *On the Social Contract, Discourse on the*

187

Who Should Rule? The Will of the People

Origin of Inequality, Discourse on Political Economy by Jean-Jacques Rousseau, trans. Donald A. Cress (Indianapolis: Hackett Publishing, 1983), p. 9.

15. David Truman, *The Governmental Process: Political Interests and Public Opinion*, 2d ed. (New York: Alfred A. Knopf, 1971), p. 38.
16. Robert A. Dahl, *A Preface to Democratic Theory* (Chicago: University of Chicago Press, 1956), p. 63.
17. Dahl, *Preface*, p. 63.
18. Dahl, *Preface*, p. 51.
19. Dahl, *Preface*, p. 64.
20. Dahl, *Preface*, p. 146.
21. Dahl, *Preface*, p. 150.

Recommended Readings

Baskin, Darryl. *American Pluralist Democracy: A Critique.* New York: Van Nostrand Reinhold, 1971.

Becker, Carl. *Modern Democracy.* New Haven: Yale University Press, 1941.

Cassirer, Ernst. *The Question of Jean-Jacques Rousseau.* Translated by Peter Gay. Bloomington: Indiana University Press, 1963.

Cobban, Alfred. *Rousseau and the Modern State.* London: George Allen & Unwin, 1934.

Cranston, Maurice, and Richard Peters, eds. *Hobbes and Rousseau: A Collection of Critical Essays.* Garden City, N.Y.: Doubleday, 1972.

Duncan, Graeme, ed. *Democratic Theory and Practice.* New York: Cambridge University Press, 1983.

Hallowell, John. *The Moral Foundation of Democracy.* Chicago: University of Chicago Press, 1954.

Lively, Jack. *Democracy.* New York: G. P. Putnam's Sons, 1977.

Macpherson, C. B. *The Real World of Democracy.* New York: Oxford University Press, 1972.

Masters, Roger. *The Political Philosophy of Rousseau.* Princeton: Princeton University Press, 1968.

Pateman, Carol. *Participating and Democratic Theory.* New York: Cambridge University Press, 1970.

Ricci, David. *Community Power and Democratic Theory: The Logic of Political Analysis.* New York: Random House, 1971.

Simon, Ives. *Philosophy of Democratic Government.* Chicago: University of Chicago Press, 1951.

PART THREE: Summary

To rule successfully, those in authority must acquire a degree of legitimacy. Unless the numerical and/or qualitative "weight" of a society willingly complies with those in power, no regime can endure for long. Typically custom and the habit of obedience are enough to secure such a condition; however, in times of crisis or critical self-examination a regime's claim to legitimacy must ultimately appeal to the validity of its principles of order. In the chapters of part 3 we have examined three of the most important of these appeals.

The claim that the powerful should rule is more than simply a descriptive statement. Those who make this claim offer it as a moral principle. They argue that, given the nature of political reality, it is good that the strong should rule.

Similarly, those who advocate the rule of the wise do so because they understand wisdom as a key to the solution of political problems. Although political problems may not be like mathematical problems, since they have no single or final answer, they do require some form of solution, perhaps only temporary, if society is to continue. The distribution of scarce goods and the organization of society for the pursuit of common goals presuppose some principles of order. The advocates of the rule of the wise believe that such a principle can be known. Consequently, they liken politics to the practice of an art, craft, or science.

Finally, those who argue on behalf of the will of the people do so because of their prior understanding of the requirements of human freedom. Politics is a *human* good, and as such it must operate according to principles that reflect our distinct humanity. For many this feature is best found in the free will, and this belief in turn implies the political principles of liberty and equality. From such a perspective the task of government is to articulate and represent the will of the people. The variety of contemporary democratic institutions attest to the difficulty of this task but, given the arguments of this tradition, the necessity of the task remains beyond doubt.

The arguments developed in these three chapters reveal an inter-

Political Ruling: The Basis of Authority

esting and important aspect of political theory. The topics discussed are not easily isolated from one another. For example, to determine who should rule, one should first understand both the nature of political society and the needs of those who constitute the community. But to do so, one must be able to distinguish between adequate and inadequate opinions about these things. In short, the issues discussed in parts 1, 2, and 3 of this text mutually depend upon one another's conclusions. It is the task of the political theorist to make these relationships and dependencies as explicit and as clear as possible. This concern for the whole and the relationships among its parts is what distinguishes the arguments of the political theorist from those of the political participant. The latter is typically concerned with specific issues and particular interests, while the former wishes to understand the context of the debate as provided by that whole that is presupposed by those involved.

PART
FOUR

The Boundaries of Politics

C H A P T E R   10

![black bar divider]

The Boundaries of Politics: The Minimal State

Introduction

Whether organized as nation-states, empires, feudalities, or city-states, all political communities seek to achieve certain goals. Depending upon what these goals are, communities develop various institutions and practices designed to achieve the results the regime intends. As these goals change, so too do the institutions originally created to serve them. Given such fluidity and change, it is not surprising that different cultures have developed different understandings as to what properly constitutes the "political." For example, in medieval Christendom the political realm was understood to include religious concerns, whereas in modern Western liberalism it does not. Similarly classical Greek political theory generally treated economic issues as a strictly nonpolitical or familial affair, whereas in the seventeenth and eighteenth centuries the doctrine of mercantilism clearly regulated the economic interests of the individual in order to serve the political advantage of the nation as a whole. In viewing such a variety of understandings, the political theorist Sheldon Wolin has written:

> This poses one of the basic problems confronting the political philosopher when he tries to assert the distinctiveness of his subject-matter: what is political? what is it that distinguishes, say, political authority from other forms of authority, or membership in a political society from membership in other types of institutions? . . . Just as

other fields have changed their outlines, so the boundaries of what is political have been shifting ones, sometimes including more, sometimes less of human life and thought. . . . What I should like to insist upon, however, is that the field of politics is and has been, in a significant and radical sense, a created one. The designation of certain activities and arrangements as political . . . [is not] . . . written into the nature of things but . . . is . . . the legacy accruing from the historical activity of political philosophers.[1]

Since the French Revolution at the end of the eighteenth century, the dominant form of political organization throughout the world has become that of the nation-state. Consequently contemporary theoretical considerations concerning the "boundaries of the political" usually involve an examination of the power and authority of the nation-state. Since the political realm is now generally equivalent to the range of state activity, the traditional question, What is political? can now be rephrased to read, In what areas may the state rightly enforce obedience?

The Utilitarians

Compared with the feudalities of the medieval period, the modern nation-state represents an immense centralization and rationalization of public power. As power became increasingly concentrated in the offices of a national administration, the number of politically meaningful intermediate organizations declined. For the modern citizen the most important political relationship has become that which exists between the individual and the state. This, in turn, raises the issue regarding the proper extent of state power. How extensively should the state become involved in the private lives of its citizens? Or more precisely, where should the line be drawn that separates the private realm from the public sphere? Within the history of Western political thought there exists a tradition of speculation that has attempted to minimize the extent of state power. Beginning with the Stoics of ancient Rome and including such Christian thinkers as Saint Augustine, this tradition has consistently advocated the recognition of a relatively extended non-political sphere. Within modern political thought this argument on behalf of a minimal state has been expressed most powerfully in the writings of the nineteenth-century English utilitarians. Of these, the two most influential were Jeremy Bentham (1748–1832) and John Stuart Mill (1806–73).

Born in London in 1748, Jeremy Bentham devoted his life to creating a scientific basis for the development of political and legal philosophy. A critic of the English common-law tradition, he soon became involved in a series of political projects and gathered around himself a group of like-minded "philosophical radicals" intent upon reforming English political practice. In time the "Benthamites" became extremely influential and gradually succeeded in transforming the English Parliament into a legislative body committed to dismantling some of the outdated social and economic privileges traditionally enjoyed by the British aristocracy.

Although Bentham is generally credited with coining the term *utilitarianism*, he insisted that examples of utilitarianlike teachings could be found throughout the history of Western political philosophy. Rather than attempting to create a new or original philosophy, Bentham sought only to systematize utilitarianism's traditional teachings and present them in a philosophically rigorous form. In *An Introduction to the Principles of Morals and Legislation* Bentham defined the central principle of utilitarianism as

> . . . that principle which approves or disapproves of every action whatsoever according to the tendency which it appears to have to augment or diminish the happiness of the party whose interest is in question. . . . I say of every action whatsoever; and therefore not only of every action of a private individual, but of every measure of government.[2]

The distinctiveness of the utilitarian position becomes clear once one realizes that Bentham used the term *happiness* as an equivalent for the term *pleasure*. Consequently utilitarianism teaches that it is the experience of pain and pleasure alone that can determine the rightfulness of any particular act. To the extent that an act tends to increase pleasure and diminish pain it is morally good and should be pursued accordingly.

Bentham maintained that the superiority of utilitarianism is due primarily to its realism. Arguing that individuals are, in fact, motivated to act solely by their desire for pleasure and their corresponding dislike of pain, utilitarianism offers a psychological theory that claims to correctly explain the realities of human behavior. As a moral

The Boundaries of Politics

theory, utilitarianism at the same time claims to articulate a universal principle of right and wrong. In this, nature itself is the guide:

> Nature has placed mankind under the governance of two sovereign masters, pain and pleasure. It is for them alone to point out what we ought to do, as well as to determine what we shall do. On one hand the standard of right and wrong, on the other the chain of causes and effects, are fastened to their throne. They govern us in all we do, in all we say, in all we think: every effort we can make to throw off our subjection, will serve but to demonstrate and confirm it.[3]

As a political doctrine, utilitarianism teaches that the sole aim of government is to foster the security and pleasure of its citizens. Unlike some traditional theories that posit the existence of an organic community and charge the government with serving its particular and distinct interests, Bentham's utilitarianism regards the political community as a mere "fiction." The political community as such is simply a name given to the sum total of those individuals who compose it. As a consequence, only the sum total of their individual interests can constitute the so-called common good. In short, the purpose of government, according to Bentham, is to promote the greatest happiness of the greatest number. This, in turn, includes such subsidiary goals as maintaining security, favoring equality, providing for subsistence, and promoting abundance.

Bentham argued that this political program could be realized in several ways. First, by maintaining an ordered and rational legal code, the government is able to create for its citizens a system of rights and obligations. Such a system must be created because, according to Bentham, rights and duties do not exist in nature. Instead they are the result of a prior political decision to punish certain unacceptable acts. Based upon a utilitarian calculation, the government may decide to prohibit certain activities as harmful to the public happiness. Generally such a decision should be made only in an effort to prevent those types of pain that are so acute as to be avoided at all costs. As examples, Bentham gave starvation and death, physical harm, loss of reputation, and damage to status. Once those activities that imply such consequences are prohibited, each citizen is obligated to refrain from performing them, and every citizen acquires thereby the right to expect that everyone else will fulfill the same obligations. In this view the chief function of the government is to prevent, by the threat of punishment, those mischievous acts that may diminish the greatest happiness of the greatest number. Rather than being a truly active agent that provides society with a substantive order in an effort to coordinate its pursuit of a positive political goal, the government, in Bentham's scheme, is reduced to the somewhat negative role of threatening to impose physical punishment upon potential criminals.

In addition to a concern for the security of its citizens, a government committed to utilitiarian principles would also be concerned with the promotion of their wealth and prosperity. According to Bentham's analysis, such concerns are best met by securing for each individual the fruits of his or her labor. Consequently the government should act only to protect the property system and to enforce those contracts that regulate the economic relations of society. Although in extreme cases of poverty and suffering the government may intervene on an individual's behalf, it was Bentham's general assessment that the government could do little to improve the overall efficiency of the economic system. Like the goal of providing security, the goal of pursuing prosperity seems to require only a minimum of governmental activity.

Bentham's concern to restrict the activity of the state in general also explains his preference for organizing the state according to democratic principles. A true democracy, according to Bentham, is characterized by periodic elections and a relatively expanded franchise. In this situation it is in the self-interest of the politicians to respond to the demands of the electorate or face the possibility of being removed from office. All individuals, according to Bentham, seek power for their own selfish ends; and it is the genius of the democratic system that it alone is able to take advantage of this situation so as to restrain those who are most likely to harm others. Democracy, for Bentham, is to be preferred to all other forms of government because it is the one the least likely to inflict pain upon the governed. Thus for strictly utilitarian reasons Bentham was led to support democratic self-government as the lesser of several evils:

Q: What is the actual end actually pursued by man in general?
A: His own greatest happiness.
Q: What is the actual end of government under a democracy?
A: The greatest happiness of the greatest number.
Q: What is the actual end of government under every other form of government?
A: The greatest happiness of those among whom the powers of government are shared.[4]

Referring to Bentham's understanding of democracy as one of "protective democracy," the contemporary political theorist C. B. Macpherson emphasized its minimalist intentions:

> . . . its case for the democratic system of government was that nothing less could in principle protect the governed from oppression by the government.[5]

In the same book Macpherson also referred to the model of "developmental democracy." He described it as bringing in a new moral dimension," [as] seeing democracy primarily as a means of individual self-development."[6] Of those associated with this newer model, none was more influential than England's second-greatest utilitarian philosopher, John Stuart Mill.

Mill was both an advocate and a product of Bentham's utilitarian philosophy. His father, James Mill, was a colleague and admirer of Bentham, and together they had worked with some success to reform English politics so as to open the system to the aspirations and needs of the rising commercial class. The elder Mill's commitment to a utilitarian world view included the attempt to educate his son according to strictly Benthamite principles. To accomplish this James Mill kept John Stuart from other children and assumed the role of his tutor. By the age of three John Stuart Mill had learned Greek. Later he studied arithmetic, history, and Latin and by the age of twelve had begun the study of logic, political economy, and analytical psychology. At sixteen Mill's formal education was completed, and he joined his father in the India Service as a clerk.

Although employed full-time in the India Service, John Stuart Mill was actively involved in the cultural, literary, and political affairs of his day. He joined in founding the Utilitarian Society in 1822 and was a frequent contributor to the influential *Westminister Review*. Included among his more strictly philosophical writings are *System of Logic* and *August Comte and Positivism*. His political and ethical works included *Utilitarianism, On Liberty,* and *Considerations on Representative Government.*

As an advocate of ethical utilitarianism, Mill devoted several of his writings to a defense of its moral teachings. Bentham, in his original formulation, had reduced utilitarian morality to the simple pursuit of physical pleasure. Consequently, the morally good life, according to Bentham, was one that minimized one's experience of pain while maximizing one's enjoyment of pleasure. From this perspective more pleasure was obviously better than less, and ethics became simply a matter of calculating the amount of pleasure one could expect from following a certain course of action.

Critics of Bentham attacked his teaching both for its hedonism and for presupposing a simplistic and primitive view of human nature. By equating the good with physical pleasure and associating evil with its opposite, Bentham had appeared to reduce the person to the level of a mere animal and to treat the moral experience as a matter of basic instinct. In his defense of the utilitarian tradition, Mill attempted to introduce an expanded notion of pleasure that would allow one to differentiate among the various kinds of pleasure and distinguish thereby that which is properly human from that which is strictly animal:

> It is quite compatible with the principles of utility to recognize the fact, that some *kinds* of pleasure are more desirable and more valuable than others. It would be absurd that while, in estimating all other things, quality is considered as well as quantity, the estimation of pleasures should be supposed to depend upon quantity alone. . . . It is better to be a human being dissastified than a pig satisfied; better to be Socrates dissatisfied than a fool satisfied.[7]

For Mill the qualitatively higher pleasures are those that result from intellectual activity. Consequently even though the sheer amount of physical pleasure may be greater than the amount, intensity, or duration of a corresponding intellectual pleasure, the latter is superior in kind to the former and should be pursued accordingly. By differentiating between the intellectual and physical realms, Mill had attempted to save utilitarianism from its critics. Whether it was legitimate to make such a qualitiative distinction on strictly utilitarian grounds is an issue that has been debated by philosophers ever since. It is clear, however, that Mill himself believed that his arguments were entirely consistent with the original Benthamite position. Having "saved" the utilitarian tradition, it was then possible for Mill to use its arguments in an attempt to justify a liberal restriction on the authority and power of the state.

Mill's most famous publication, *On Liberty*, appeared in 1859. He began his argument with the following distinction:

> The subject of this Essay is not the so-called Liberty of the Will . . .

but Civil or Social Liberty: the nature and limits of the power which can be legitimately exercised by society over the individual.[8]

Although the issue of the legitimate extent of political authority had been a traditional concern for the political theorist, the problem had acquired a new complexity within modern democratic societies. Traditionally the problem of political liberty was conceived of primarily in terms of the relationship between the government and its citizens. In this sense Bentham's concerns had been quite traditional inasmuch as he had understood the problem of liberty to arise from the ultimately antagonistic nature of the relationship between the rulers and the ruled. According to Mill's analysis, however, this was no longer the issue. Constitutional remedies, such as the widespread use of institutional checks and balances, had reduced the arbitrary power of the state and transformed it into a true representative of the people. Rather than fearing the state as in the past, people now sought to further empower the regime so that it could serve as a more efficient agent of their interests. This development, according to Mill, raised the novel possibility of a tyranny of the majority. Acting with the consent of the majority, it was possible for the modern democratic state to destroy the social and civil liberties of its essentially unprotected minorities. In view of this, Mill attempted to establish a principle that would limit the exercise of state authority—even in the case where such an exercise was desired by a large majority of its citizens:

> The object of this Essay is to assert one very simple principle, as entitled to govern absolutely the dealings of society with the individual in the way of compulsion and control whether the means used be physical force in the form of legal penalities, or the moral coercion of public opinion. That principle is, that the sole end for which mankind are warranted, individually or collectively, in interfering with the liberty of action of any of their number, is self-protection. That the only purpose for which power can be rightfully exercised over any member of a civilized community, against his will, is to prevent harm to others. His own good, either physical or moral, is not a sufficient warrant.[9]

Mill admitted that his doctrine was intended to apply only to those who are "civilized" or mature. Consequently parents would be allowed to exercise authority over their children because children are not yet sovereign over their own minds and bodies. However, upon reaching maturity, each person acquires an absolute claim to his or her self. As a consequence all forms of political paternalism are strictly prohibited.

Mill's effort to minimize the realm within which the state may legitimately act was based upon his prior distinction between *other-regarding* and *self-regarding* actions. Other-regarding acts, either of commission or omission, are those whose effects directly concern the interests of other people. As such, they may be either prohibited or required, depending upon a prior utilitarian assessment of their consequences. Self-regarding acts, on the other hand, are those whose consequences directly and immediately affect either only the actors themselves or those who have voluntarily consented to associate with them. In this sphere each individual must be respected as sovereign and his or her liberty regarded as absolute. As examples of the liberties included within this category, Mill listed freedom of thought, feeling, and opinion, the liberty of taste and pursuits, and the freedom to associate with whom one pleases.

Mill's attempt to limit the sphere of governmental concern to the regulation of other-regarding actions was designed, not only to protect the established interests of the individual but also to support the the possibility of one's future development and growth. As a liberal, Mill acknowledged the importance of recognizing the dignity and moral autonomy of each adult. As a progressivist, he was also committed to the cultural and spiritual improvement of humanity as a whole. Finally, as a utilitarian, he was required to demonstrate that his restrictions on state authority would in the long run contribute to the greatest happiness of the greatest number. After having announced his preference for the minimal state, Mill proceeded to present a utilitarian justification for its acceptance. To do so, he selected as a case study one of the liberties contained within the sphere of self-regarding actions—the freedom of thought.

In building his defense, Mill began with the assumption that mankind as a whole necessarily benefits from (i.e., is made happier by) the growth of science and the enrichment of culture. He then argued that freedom of thought and expression was a necessary prerequisite for scientific progress and consequently that utilitarian morality requires that dissent be not only tolerated but actually encouraged.

To establish his argument, Mill offered three scenarios. First, it is possible to assume that the established or orthodox opinion of the day is entirely false. If this were the case, truth would necessarily be served by encouraging the expression of dissenting views. Second, it is also possible to assume that the public orthodoxy is entirely true and that all dissenting beliefs are necessarily false. Even if this were the case, however, truth would still be served by encouraging dissent because without the challenge of dissent established opinion soon becomes mere dogma and is reduced thereby to an empty formula whose rational substance is soon forgotten. The third possibility is the one most likely to occur. In this case both the orthodox and the dissenting opinions are each assumed to be partially true. In this situation it would appear obvious that through the process of criticism and debate such partial perspectives could be brought together to advance the cause of truth as a whole. In short, for Mill every situation can be improved by the presence of real and lively dissent. By encouraging a variety of opinions and by promoting a diversity of life-styles, the spirit of individualism necessarily contributes to the advancement of science and knowledge. This, in turn, contributes both to the utility of society as a whole and to the happiness of each of its members.

In succeeding chapters Mill expanded his argument to include a discussion not only of the freedom of thought but also of the freedom to live as one chooses. The very same arguments that support the freedom of opinions also require that individuals be free to live according to their own opinions and to practice their own beliefs as long as these actions are not directly injurious to the interests of others. It is clear throughout this discussion that Mill is concerned with protecting the individual whenever possible. In certain passages it even appears that individualism is treated as a value in and of itself regardless of its utilitarian consequences. For example on one occasion Mill wrote:

> If a person possesses any tolerable amount of common sense and experience, his own mode of laying out his existence is the best, not because it is the best in itself, but because it is his own mode.[10]

This concern for the promotion of individuality and creative autonomy influenced Mill's understanding of the proper role of the state. In a democratic society, the state must respond to the demands and expectations of the public. Yet, according to Mill, public opinion is inevitably mass opinion, and mass opinion is never more than collective mediocrity. In this situation, the development and preservation of individual excellence requires that state activity be kept to an absolute minimum. Not only must the enforcement powers of the state be limited to the regulation of other-regarding actions, but the state must even refrain from actively helping its citizens lest they become dependent upon its beneficence and as a consequence allow their own creative capacities to atrophy. Thus, although Mill had reformed Bentham's original understanding of utilitarianism and joined to it the positivist notion of inevitable human progress, he still remained true to the utilitarian advocacy of the minimal state.

Natural-Rights Theory

In previous chapters we have had several opportunities to examine various representatives of the natural-rights tradition. In chapter 5 John Locke's theory of natural rights was offered as an example of the traditionally liberal understanding of politics and society, and in chapter 7 we examined the more authoritarian interpretation of Thomas Hobbes. Whether the natural-rights tradition as a whole favors either the liberal or the authoritarian model of politics is a question of current scholarly debate. It is clear, however, that those who wish to work within the natural-rights tradition and, at the same time, seek to justify a minimalist conception of the state would be most comfortable beginning with Locke's assumptions. A current example of such an attempt can be found in Robert Nozick's 1974 publication *Anarchy, State, and Utopia*. Nozick summarized his own conclusion as follows:

> Our main conclusions about the state are that a minimal state, limited to the narrow functions of protection against theft, fraud, enforcement of contracts, and so on, is justified; that any more extensive state will violate persons' rights not to be forced to do certain things, and is unjustified; and that the minimal state is inspiring as well as right. Two noteworthy implications are that the state may not use its coercive apparatus for the purpose of getting some citizens to aid others, or in order to prohibit activities to people for their *own* good or protection.[11]

Like the utilitarians, Nozick rejects all forms of paternalistic politics and refuses to accept the "fiction" that a social entity is anything more than the sum of the individuals who compose it. Unlike the utilitarians, however, he reaches these conclusions through an examination of the state of nature rather than by any calculation concerning the probability of pleasure and pain. To this extent he follows in the tradition of John Locke and explicitly uses Locke's arguments in order to introduce his own case.

To make his case, Nozick must accomplish two objectives. First, in opposing anarchism he must demonstrate that the existence of a minimalist state is preferable to a condition in which there is no state at all. And second, in opposition to those who seek an extended state he must show that any state other than a minimalist one is morally unacceptable.

To establish his first point Nozick follows Locke's example by calling attention to certain inconveniences in the state of nature that cannot be remedied without the establishment of a minimal state. Specifically, in the state of nature, according to Nozick, one must personally enforce his or her own rights. Yet, given the absence of any political apparatus, a specific individual may lack the sufficient power to do so; or, in a case where it can be done, such an effort may inevitably lead to an endless sequence of retaliation and countermeasures. In view of this dilemma Nozick develops several nonpolitical strategies that might serve to remedy this situation. First, one could join in a voluntary mutual protection association or, if the circumstances permitted it, even create a dominant mutual protection association that included most of the individuals in a given geographical area. After examining these options, however, Nozick concluded that for reasons of efficiency and morality, such associations must unavoidably evolve into the minimal state. The minimal state is different from and superior to any arrangement of dominant mutual-protection associations since it alone can claim a monopoly over the legitimate use of force and at the same time extend its protection to cover all of the individuals in a given geographical area. In claiming a monopoly over the use of force, the minimal state is only recognizing the de facto imbalance of power that arises unavoidably as it seeks to achieve the objective of protecting the rights of its members. Similarly in extending its protection to all the individuals within a specific territory—even to those who don't wish to pay for such a service—the state is only following the moral principle that requires fair compensation. Individuals have a right to be compensated (by being protected) for the disadvantages they incur when the state prohibits them from certain acts. In short, Nozick believes that only a minimal state can truly solve the "inconveniences" associated with life in the state of nature and that it can do so without violating the legitimate rights of any individual:

We have discharged our task of explaining how a state would arise from a state of nature without anyone's rights being violated. . . . It [the minimal state] is not an unjust imposition of a monopoly; the _de facto_ monopoly grows by an invisible hand process and by morally permissable means. . . . And requiring the clients of a _de facto_ monopoly to pay for the protection of those they prohibit from self-help enforcement against them, far from being immoral is morally required by the principle of compensation. . . .[12]

Having justified the existence of a minimal state, Nozick proceeds to argue that a correct understanding of the natural-rights tradition prohibits the state from becoming anything more than that which has already been described. According to Nozick, anything more extensive than a minimal state will necessarily violate peoples' rights, and such violations should never be tolerated even in pursuit of such politically appealing concepts as justice or equality.

Often those who argue for an expanded state do so by appealing to the notion of distributive justice. Typically they have in mind a certain pattern of distribution they would like to see maintained by state intervention in the economy. For example, some might argue that material goods should be distributed according to the principle of moral merit; others may favor the principle of need; and still others may argue for such principles as utility or human equality. In each case, such arguments are similar, since each seeks to achieve a certain end-result pattern that conforms to a given ideal distribution. Inasmuch as the historical distribution of goods in any given society is inevitably the result of a series of independent and irreversible decisions, any attempt to adjust the actual distribution according to an ideal pattern would appear to require the almost continuous interference of the state in the daily lives of its citizens. Similarly, since the attempt to achieve an ideal pattern of distribution necessarily implies a _redistribution_ of the goods that have already been assigned, any effort on behalf of a patterned distribution must inevitably violate the individual's right to retain that which he or she has previously acquired. According to Nozick, the only principle of transfer that does not violate the entitlement rights of citizens would be one that reads, "From each as they choose, to each as they are chosen."[13]

For similar reasons Nozick rejects the arguments of those who support an expanded state for the sake of such values as equality of opportunity, enhanced self-esteem, the creation of a meaningful work situation, or the elimination of poverty. If such goals can be achieved on a voluntary basis, then there is no compelling moral reason that would prohibit such cooperation. However, if the state exercises its authority in order to achieve these ends, it will in the process necessarily violate the rights of its citizens.

Nozick bases his arguments about these and similar issues upon his understanding of entitlement. This understanding can be summarized in three propositions:

1. A person who acquires a holding in accordance with the principle of justice in acquisition is entitled to that holding.
2. A person who acquires a holding in accordance with the principle of justice in transfer, from someone else entitled to the holding, is entitled to the holding.
3. No one is entitled to a holding except by (repeated) application of 1 and 2.[14]

The third proposition in the above statement applies to states as well as to individuals. When the state pursues such a goal as the elimination of poverty, it must redistribute the goods of its citizens in such a way as to achieve this purpose. Yet since each citizen is entitled to the goods he or she has acquired through the application of principles 1 and 2, the state's attempt to rearrange the historically achieved pattern of distribution must necessarily violate the entitlements of its citizens. Given this, any state that acts to pursue goals other than those required to solve the inconveniences of the state of nature is morally illegitimate.

In view of his understanding of both the inviolable nature of human rights and the diversity of the human condition, Nozick believes that the minimal state is not only morally necessary but also politically desirable. From his perspective, it is the closest real-world approximation of an ideal utopia that can be imagined. In a true utopia, according to Nozick, everyone would be free to live according to his or her own understanding of the good life, and no one would be empowered to impose a dominant interpretation upon anyone else. A utopian environment would be open to an infinite variety of differing life-styles and supportive of the many communities that would emerge to sustain them. According to Nozick, this is exactly the environment a minimum state would make possible.

Notes

1. Sheldon Wolin, *Politics and Vision: Continuity and Innovation in Western Political Thought* (Boston: Little, Brown, 1960), pp. 4–5.

2. Jeremy Bentham, *A Fragment on Government with an Introduction to the Principles of Morals and Legislation*, ed. Wilfrid Harrison (Oxford, England: Basil Blackwell, 1967), p. 126.

3. Bentham, *Introduction*, p. 125.

4. Jeremy Bentham, "Summary of Basic Principles," in *Bentham's Political Thought*, ed. Bhikhu Parekh (New York: Barnes & Noble, 1973), pp. 295–96.

5. C. B. Macpherson, *The Life and Times of Liberal Democracy* (New York: Oxford University Press, 1977), p. 22.

6. Macpherson, *Democracy*, p. 22.

7. John Stuart Mill, *Utilitarianism, On Liberty, Essay on Bentham*, ed. Mary Warnock (New York: New American Library, 1962), pp. 258–60.

8. Mill, *Liberty*, p. 126.

9. Mill, *Liberty*, p. 135.

10. Mill, *Liberty*, p. 197.

11. Robert Nozick, *Anarchy, State, and Utopia* (New York: Basic Books, 1974), p. ix.

12. Nozick, *Anarchy*, pp. 114–15.

13. Nozick, *Anarchy*, p. 160.

14. Nozick, *Anarchy*, p. 151.

Recommended Readings

Cowling, Maurice. *Mill and Liberalism*. New York: Cambridge University University Press, 1963.

Halevy, Eli. *The Growth of Philosophical Radicalism*. Translated by Mary Morris. London: Faber & Faber, 1949.

Himmelfarb, Gertrude. *On Liberty and Liberalism: The Case of John Stuart Mill*. New York: Alfred A. Knopf, 1974.

Parekh, Bhikhu, ed. *Jeremy Bentham: Ten Critical Essays*. London: Frank Cass, 1974.

Paul, Jeffrey, ed. *Reading Nozick*. Totowa, N.J.: Rowman & Allanheld, 1981.

Plamenatz, John. *The English Utilitarians*. Oxford, England: Basil Blackwell, 1949.

Ryan, Alan. *John Stuart Mill*. New York: Pantheon Books, 1970.

Sen, Amartya, and Bernard Williams, eds. *Utilitarianism and Beyond*. New York: Cambridge University Press, 1982.

Smart, J. J. C., and Bernard Williams. *Utilitarianism: For and Against*. New York: Cambridge University Press, 1973.

Tuck, Richard. *Natural Rights Theories: Their Origins and Development*. New York: Cambridge University Press, 1979.

C H A P T E R 11

![black bar divider]

The Boundaries of Politics: The Extended State

Introduction

Since everyone is born into a series of preexisting societies, such as the family, community, and country, we often assume the stability, permanence, and objectivity of our social institutions. Individuals are born, mature, and die; but the family, city, and state appear to continue on almost indefinitely. In a certain sense every political society seems to take on a life of its own which is independent of the individual lives of its constituents. From the perspective of the individual citizen, the state exists as an "other." As such, it is an external object that can be experienced by its members as either a tool or an obstacle. Those theorists who advocate the minimal state tend to see the state as a potential obstacle which stands over and against the interests of its members and threatens to prevent the full realization of their aspirations. At the same time, there is a tradition of speculation that tends to see the state primarily as a tool or an instrument by which mankind organizes itself in order to accomplish more effectively those goals that are beyond the reach of any particular individual. It is within this tradition that one will normally find those who advocate the creation of an extended state. The classical Greek philosopher Aristotle (384 B.C.–322 B.C.) was one of the first and most influential of these advocates.

Aristotle

Aristotle's two most important works in the field of political theory are his *Nicomachean Ethics* and his *Politics*. Although they are published today as two separate works, originally they were the two halves of a single manuscript and thus demonstrate the essential relationship between politics and morality in Aristotle's world view. Whereas the *Ethics* is devoted to an examination of human happiness and the nature of the good life, the *Politics* analyzes those specific political and social conditions that make such a life possible. Their arguments build upon one another, and together they formulate the fundamental principles of Aristotelian practical science.

Aristotle begins Book 1 of the *Politics* with a discussion of the nature of the political association. As a Greek living in the fourth century B.C., Aristotle took as his model of the political association the institutions of the Greek city-state, or *polis*. He apparently assumed that the city-state was the natural or perfected form of political society and was inclined to ignore such an obvious alternative as that provided by the Macedonian empire to the north. Given this tendency, much of Aristotle's political analysis presupposes the institutional order of classical Greece and is, as a consequence, irrelevant to an examination of the modern nation-state. At the same time, Aristotle was concerned with more than merely describing the practices of his day. As a philosopher, he was also interested in the study of political reality as such and sought to understand those universal principles that serve to differentiate the political order from every other kind. Since individuals create a variety of associations in order to pursue a variety of goals, Aristotle argued that the distinguishing characteristics of a *political* society would become apparent only through an analysis of its proper and peculiar end. With this in mind, Aristotle began Book I of his *Politics* with an examination of the various "unions" created as individuals join together to pursue certain common goals.

The most elemental union Aristotle discussed is the union between a man and a woman for the purpose of reproducing the species. Added to this is that union formed between the master and the slave for the mutual benefit of each. Together these two unions create the higher union of the household which, according to Aristotle, is that institution within society that is most capable of serving the daily and recurring needs of its members.

Aristotle's discussion of the household is a prime example of his being limited by the legacy of the *polis*. The Greeks practiced slavery, and Aristotle appears to have assumed that this particular Greek custom was in some way natural and therefore morally acceptable. In his *Politics* Aristotle argued that some individuals are by nature incapable of ruling themselves and therefore require for their own good that they be ruled by others. These "natural slaves" benefit from the wisdom of their rulers, and the rulers in turn are repaid for their efforts by the labor that the physically superior slaves can contribute to the maintenance of the household. At the same time, Aristotle assumed that each union was characterized by its having a single and separate end. From his perspective the sole purpose of marriage was the reproduction of the species, and other ends, such as the mutual companionship shared by husband and wife, received little if any consideration. These and other similarly time-bound assumptions make Aristotle's discussion of the natural order of unions somewhat problematic. However this does not necessarily compromise his understanding of politics itself. Aristotle's definition of the political order attempts to set it apart from its subsidiary associations. Consequently the inadequate understanding of such subsidiary associations does not necessarily imply a failure to comprehend that which is essentially different.

In modern terms, the purpose of the Aristotelian household is primarily economic in nature. By coordinating the efforts of husband-wife, parents-children, and master-slave, the household organizes the activities of its individual members in such a way as to provide for their essential economic needs. This task is made even easier when several households come together to form a village. By pooling the resources of its constituent households, the village is able to work even more efficiently and if circumstances permit, acquire a sufficient surplus of goods to allow its members some increased leisure time. Its purpose, however, is still primarily economic in nature; the village seeks to fulfill the requirements of material life.

When several villages come together to form a political association, a qualitative distinction emerges. Whereas the household and the village pursue the essentially economic purpose of preserving and reproducing life, the political association comes into existence for the sake of a particular way of life—one referred to by Aristotle as the *good* life:

> When we come to the final and perfect association, formed from a number of villages, we have already reached the polis—an association which may be said to have reached the height of full self-

sufficiency; or rather (to speak more exactly) we may say that while it *grows* for the sake of mere life (and is so far, and at that stage, still short of full self-sufficiency), it *exists* (when once it is fully grown) for the sake of the good life. . . .[1]

According to Aristotle a truly political union is distinguished from all others by the specific nature of its goal. Human nature intends not only mere life but also the good life, and the individual's actualization of his or her full potential presupposes the functioning of a well-ordered political community. To the extent that each political association is to contribute towards the realization of the good life of its citizens, the first and most fundamental questions of politics are, What is the good life? and How can it be realized? The best formulation of Aristotle's own answers to these questions can be found in his *Nicomachean Ethics*.

Aristotle began his *Ethics* by noting the problem that, while everyone agrees that happiness is the goal of life, few can agree about the term's precise meaning or content. For example, in reviewing the opinions of his contemporaries Aristotle found that some equated the happy life with the life of pleasure and wealth. Others argued that the good life is the life of honor and thus recommended that one should embark upon a political career as the most effective means of earning the respect of others. Finally some maintained that the truly happy life is the life of contemplation and, as a consequence, they recommended the pursuit of philosophy as the most appropriate of all human activities. Given this variety of attitudes, the question of the good life was obviously a complex one and could not be answered by a simple appeal to the commonsense opinions of the day. Aristotle believed that a theoretically adequate understanding of the good life would require nothing less than an explicit philosophy of human nature in general and of the human soul in particular:

> There can be no doubt that the virtue we have to study is human virtue. For the good which we have been seeking is a human good, the happiness a human happiness. By human virtue we do not mean the excellence of the body, but that of the soul. If this is true, the student of politics must obviously have some knowledge of the workings of the soul. . . .[2]

For Aristotle the soul was understood to be the principle of life.

Consequently its nature can be studied by analyzing the various "ways of living" the soul can make possible. In the case of mankind three such ways of life are immediately apparent. At the most fundamental level the human soul enables the individual to share in the most common of life's functions—the vegetative. The human person, like all the rest of organic nature, is able to process nourishment and thereby grow. This capacity is a sign of life, and its presence separates living nature from the nonliving world. Yet, since people share this function with all living things, the vegetative component of the soul is not exclusively human, and so its operation cannot constitute true human excellence.

All living things can and must grow; yet only a portion of living nature is able to achieve that higher form of life that allows it to experience and respond to sense perceptions. This ability to experience pleasure and pain presupposes a more complex form of the soul whose vital presence raises the life of the animal above that of the merely vegetative. Like vegetative nature, animals must be able to feed and grow if they are to survive. But at the same time animals can transcend the merely organic level because they participate in an aspect of reality beyond the reach of the vegetative. The reality of the senses and the experience of pleasure and pain evoke in animals a range of appetites and needs altogether unknown within the vegetative world. Unlike plants, animals have desires. They seek to encounter pleasure, and they strive to avoid pain. As an animal, the human person pursues pleasure; yet, unlike that of the other animals, this human pursuit is not simply a matter of instinct and passion. The nonhuman animal responds to the commands of its instincts and, as a consequence, its pursuit of pleasure is both direct and unmediated. In the case of mankind, however, the pursuit of pleasure is somewhat more complex. As a rational being, the individual can instruct and inform his or her passion; in the case of a morally mature individual, such instructions are typically followed in a characteristically virtuous way. The human animal may deliberate and ultimately choose which pleasures to pursue, in what amount, and in what manner. The nonhuman animal, on the other hand, is directed in its pursuit according to the strict commands of its instincts.

Aristotle's analysis of the human soul thus revealed that it has both a vegetative and an appetitive element. A person is partly vegetative and partly animal; consequently, individuals must care for both their vegetative and animal needs if they are to live full and rich lives. At the same time, however, just as humans are more than simply vegetative, so, too, they are more than simply animal. The human soul contains a third, rational element which allows a person to transcend the reality of pleasure and pain and participate in the reality of an intellectual and spiritual existence. In short, the human soul allows the individual to lead the life of reason and, by living such a life, each person is able to rise to a distinctively human level of excellence. As the reality of pleasure and pain is closed to the vegetative soul, so the realities of the true, the good, and the beautiful are closed to that of the animal. In opening one's existence to the realm of the rational, the human soul exhibits its truly distinctive character. According to Aristotle, then, the good life for the *human as a human* is the life of reason, and the truly happy person is the one who is capable of realizing the full rational potential of the distinctively human soul:

> On these assumptions, if we take the proper function of man to be a certain kind of life, and if this kind of life is an activity of the soul and consists in actions performed in conjunction with the rational element, and if a man of high standard is he who performs these actions well and properly, and if a function is well performed when it is performed in accordance with the excellence appropriate to it, we reach the conclusion that the good of man is an activity of the soul in conformity with excellence or virtue, and if there are several virtues in conformity with the best and most complete.[3]

The full importance of Aristotle's discussion of the rational element of the soul becomes clear only when one realizes that the addition of the rational element implies a radical transformation of the prior two. The human soul is not simply a composite of three mutually independent elements that operate exclusively according to their own principles of right order. Rather it is a vital whole in which the subsidiary principles of the organic and the appetitive are transformed by their involvement with the principle of reason. Their meaning is changed inasmuch as they are now part of a larger whole to which they contribute and by which they are informed. Describing the Aristotelian understanding of human nature, the German philosopher Helmut Kuhn wrote:

> Man, it is true, is capable of achievements beyond the reach of animals. Language and rational thought are given him alone. But if we understand the ancient definition of man as *animal rationale* in that sense . . . it defines a hybrid rather than a man. Nothing is more

monstrous than an animal, living, feeding, mating, perishing as an animal but endowed with intelligence. Only a dehumanized man may approach this condition. Rather than being grafted upon animality, the distinctively human element must inform and transfigure animality. Man is human not only by virtue of his ratiocinative power. He calls his matings marriage, his begetters parents, his feeding taking meals, and, conscious of life, he foresees the oncoming death. For better or worse, he is an altogether unique being, projecting as it were, into a dimension foreign to animality.[4]

In his *Politics* Aristotle had argued that the purpose of political society was to promote the good life. In his *Ethics* he had defined the good life as the life of reason. Consequently, from Aristotle's perspective, the purpose of politics is to engender and support the life of reason among the citizens of the political association. Since such a task requires a transformation of the human condition, Aristotle's understanding of politics is one that requires the actions of a truly extended state. This implication becomes quite clear during his discussion of the moral and intellectual virtues.

Virtue, according to Aristotle, is a quality or condition that allows one to do well that which he or she is intended to do. For example, one may speak of the virtues of a wrestler as including speed, endurance, and strength, since the presence of these qualities allows one to be a more effective wrestler. Similarly one may list agility, grace, and beauty as virtues that would allow a dancer to excel in her capacity as a dancer. Just as one may designate specific virtues for the accomplishment of specific tasks, so too it is possible to designate common human virtues that contribute to the universal goals of our common humanity. Specifically, every human has the task of living his or her life. The human virtues, accordingly, would be those qualities which help one to live that life well. According to Aristotle, for a human to live well means living well the life of the appetites on one hand and, more importantly, living well the life of reason on the other. For Aristotle the former requires the moral virtues, while the latter depends upon their intellectual counterparts.

The life of the appetites is that form of life that we share with the animals. At its simplest it is a life that requires that we choose among the pleasures and pains of daily existence. Choosing well, however, implies that we do not simply rely upon our instincts but rather defer to that form of wisdom that Aristotle termed prudence, or practical knowledge. Prudence teaches that in the pursuit of pleasure a good choice is one that avoids the extremes. Either too much or too little pleasure can be harmful to the appetites, and either too much or too little pain can work against the realization of human happiness.

The morally excellent individual, for Aristotle, is the one who is moderate and thus avoids either of the two extremes. The difficulty with this arises from the fact that the middle or mean between the extreme of excess, on one hand, and that of deficiency, on the other, is not always clear. In moral matters the mean is not an arithmetical one and thus cannot be derived by simply dividing the sum of the two extremes by two. Rather, in choosing among pleasures and pains, the moral individual must calculate according to the "median relative to us." Since each of us is different from every other, what is too much of a thing for one person may, in fact, be too little of the same thing for another. Because of this, determining the moral mean can never be reduced to a formula universally applicable in every situation. Moral choice, according to Aristotle, will always require an exercise of practical judgment, and judging well becomes the defining characteristic of the morally virtuous person:

> Thus we can experience fear, confidence, desire, anger, pity, and generally any kind of pleasure and pain either too much or too little, and in either case not properly. But to experience all this at the right time, toward the right objects, toward the right people, for the right reason, and in the right manner—that is the median and the best course, the course that is a mark of virtue.[5]

According to Aristotle the human soul is not born with its appropriate virtues in effect. Rather than possessing the moral virtues innately, each individual must acquire them through habituation. Like physical skills, the moral virtues are acquired by use. For example, if one wished to become courageous, he or she may become so by imitating the actions of other courageous people until such actions become habitual in nature. When people habitually act in a courageous manner they have, in fact, become courageous. Since an individual's moral development requires the acquisition of the appropriate moral habits, the regulation of human behavior becomes an essential means for promoting the moral improvement of each person. Laws determine behavior, and good behavior breeds good character:

> Lawgivers make the citizens good by inculcating (good) habits in

them, and this is the aim of every lawgiver; if he does not succeed in doing that, his legislation is a failure. It is in this that a good constitution differs from a bad one.[6]

Aristotle understood the human soul as being rational by its very nature. However his understanding of nature was a strictly teleological one. That is to say, for Aristotle, the nature of any given reality was most clearly expressed in the perfected realization of its purpose (*telos*). Consequently the human soul is rational precisely to the degree to which it achieves or actualizes the purpose intended by the very principles of its nature. To say that the individual is rational is to say that he or she has the potential to become so. The realization of this potential, however, is not a spontaneous achievement, and thus it presupposes the acquisition of the intellectual virtues. Like the moral virtues, the intellectual virtues are those attributes that cause the appropriate part of the soul to perform its function well. Whereas the moral virtues govern the life of the appetites, the intellectual virtues facilitate the life of reason.

In Aristotle's analysis of the rational soul he distinguished between two elements in particular. In general the rational soul seeks truth. More specifically, however, its scientific element seeks to apprehend the truth of those realities whose fundamental principles are both unchanging and universal, while its calculative element attempts to know those things that admit of change and can be controlled.

The scientific element of the rational soul is that faculty by which an individual is able to understand the nature of things. For Aristotle such an understanding entailed a knowledge of material, efficient, formal, and final causation. The realities studied by scientific reason are those that cannot be other than they are and, as a consequence, are both unchanging and necessary. Aristotle mentioned theology, natural science, and mathematics as examples of scientific reasoning. In each case the reality studied—i.e., being, nature, or number—is an unchanging one. Since this is the case, the individual scientist cannot hope to manipulate such realities for his or her own immediate benefit. In pursuing scientific research the individual is motivated by a sense of wonder and the desire to know. In order for scientific inquiry to succeed, however, the individual must first acquire those rational skills provided by the intellectual virtues. If the soul is to truly know the causes of things, it must be trained and equipped to do so. In particular, Aristotle listed three necessary virtues: (1) intuitive insight (2) deductive reasoning, and (3) theoretical wisdom, which is the combination of the former two. If any of these is lacking, the soul will be impaired in its efforts to apprehend the nature of things. Since it is the rational soul's purpose to gain knowledge, each individual must acquire the necessary intellectual virtues if he or she is to realize the full potential of his or her humanity. To the extent that the intellectual virtues can be taught, the realization of our human potential presupposes that we succeed in our search for the appropriate teacher.

In the area of calculative reasoning, the soul seeks to attain truth. However, this element of the rational soul is interested only in knowing about those things that can be controlled or changed for the benefit of the individual or society. Calculative reasoning, therefore, desires knowledge exclusively for the sake of action. As examples of calculative inquiry, Aristotle listed technology, ethics, and politics.

Technology is applied knowledge, and it is important since any action can be improved when the actor is aware of the principles which govern a craft. For example a carpenter who understands the principles of carpentry is a better carpenter than one who does not. In the field of technology in general, the concern of the practitioner is with making things, and Aristotle listed as his fourth intellectual virtue that quality which allows the craftsman to make things well, i.e., the virtue of craftsmanship (techne). As a productive skill, craftsmanship can be taught to others and is learned when the apprentices submit themselves to the authority of the master craftsman.

A second form of calculative reasoning is found in the practical arts of politics and ethics. Here, too, practitioners are concerned with acting, since individuals are able to exercise some control over both their own lives and the common life of their city. Unlike the technological sciences, however, the practical arts are concerned with doing rather than with making. As a person of practice, the individual is not free, as is the carpenter, to form the material under study in any way whatsoever. A carpenter may take wood and use it as material for a home, a boat, or a cabinet. The choice is ultimately the worker's. In the practical sciences of ethics and politics, however, the material being worked with is human nature itself. In making an ethical or political decision, individuals are shaping their own lives and the life of the city. In these cases the reality being controlled is one that already has it purpose given in its very nature. Unlike a piece of wood that can take on any form without having its dignity or worth debased, the proper form of the human being is already given in its natural purpose. In short, ethical and political decisions are to be made according to those principles of conduct that will promote the perfection of human nature and provide a social environment supportive of its realization in practice. According to Aristotle the intellectual virtue that will allow one to do these things well is that of prudence or practical wisdom. Inasmuch as it is an intellectual virtue, it can be taught to others by those who have already mastered its principles-in-action.

Aristotle's discussion of the intellectual and moral virtues presents a concrete analysis of what he meant by the good life. The good life, or the life of true happiness, is that which is made possible by the development of human virtue. For a human being to live well as a human, the life of moral and intellectual excellence must become a vital reality. This, in turn, defines the goal of the political association. Politics, according to Aristotle, is that activity by which society attends to the moral and intellectual development of its citizens. The Aristotelian state is an extended state, since its concerns expand to include the most important and personal aspects of human life. For Aristotle the well-ordered political community seeks to form the very character of its members. Its essential task, therefore, is educational in nature. Aristotelian education seeks to raise human nature to its highest form, and to do this it must manipulate the very soul of the citizen itself:

> It follows on this that the legislator must labor to ensure that his citizens become good men. He must therefore know what institutions will produce this result and what is the end or aim to which good life is dedicated. . . . The legislation of the true statesman must be framed with a view to all these factors. In the first place it must cover the different parts of the soul and their different activities; and in this field it should be directed more to the higher than the lower, and rather to ends than means. In the second place it must also cover, and it must place in the same perspective, the different categories of acts.[7]

From Aristotle's perspective, the state is legitimately concerned, not only with the actions of its citizens, but also with their personal character and life-styles. Its authority is immense but not unlimited. For Aristotle, reason and virtue are capable of establishing both the goals and the limits of political power. Since the good life is defined by the objective realities of the natural order, its meaning serves as the nonarbitrary standard against which all political actions are to be measured.

T. H. Green

Aristotle's emphasis upon the pursuit of virtue was typical of the classical tradition in general. Within this tradition, the discussion of virtue presupposes the possibility of a knowledge of human nature. Without such a knowledge, the concept of human potential lacks any substantive content, and without an understanding of human potential, the very notion of virtue itself becomes somewhat problematical. One of the characteristics of contemporary political thought is the increasing reluctance of the theorist to make any universal claims regarding the meaning of human nature. The development of the historical sciences in the nineteenth century, the emergence of cultural anthropology in the twentieth, and the general influence of philosophical positivism throughout Western culture have had the combined, if unintended, result of introducing a strong note of caution into the discussion of human-nature theory. As the concept of human nature came under increasing scrutiny, so too did the traditional understanding of human virtue. Given this, many modern thinkers have moved away from an examination of human virtue and towards an analysis of human freedom. As we have seen in the previous chapter, some of these, such as John Stuart Mill, have developed an analysis of human freedom that advocates the creation of a strictly delineated state. Others, however, have used their understanding of freedom as the basis for supporting an expanded notion of the political. One of the most influential of this latter group was the nineteenth-century English philosopher Thomas Hill Green (1836–82).

Born in Birkin, England, in 1836, Green left home at the age of fourteen to attend school at Rugby and in 1855 entered Balliol College, Oxford. After considering both service in a religious ministry and the possibility of a political career, Green chose the academic life and in 1866 was named the senior dean of his college. By 1870 this position required that Green devote a significant portion of his time and energy to strictly administrative affairs. Nonetheless his thoroughness as both a teacher and scholar and his personal involvement in local partisan politics gained for him a considerable degree of influence, which went far beyond the confines of the scholarly world.

The Boundaries of Politics: The Extended State

During the nineteenth century the success of the English industrial revolution had created a number of serious social and economic problems for the urban and rural working classes. Since Green believed that the traditional laissez-faire policies of British liberalism were incapable of responding adequately to this challenge, he supported a series of important reform measures. In an effort to further democratize the political system, Green worked to provide the working classes with an opportunity for increased participation in the electoral and legislative process. He supported the Reform Bill of 1867, which almost doubled the number of citizens eligible to vote in Parliamentary elections by expanding the franchise to include previously disenfranchised male urban artisans. At the same time, Green was a strong advocate of educational reform and worked to create a public school system that would provide comparable educational opportunities for poor and rich alike. In reviewing Green's success as a reformer, the political scientist Melvin Richter wrote:

> Between 1880 and 1914, few, if any, other political philosophers exerted a greater influence upon British thought and public policy than did T. H. Green.[8]

Among Green's most important political writings are his posthumously published *Lectures on the Principles of Political Obligation*.

As a philosopher, Green is typically associated with the tradition of philosophical idealism. Influenced by the writings of Plato, Kant, and Hegel, he sought to advance a concern for metaphysical questioning within a British tradition characterized by an almost exclusive commitment to empiricism, utilitariansim, and the appeal to everyday common sense. As an idealist, Green wished to analyze that underlying spiritual principle which he believed was operative simultaneously in the realms of nature, history, and consciousness. From his perspective, the universe was a single and eternal energy, and the task of the philosopher was to make this rational unity evident so that the deeper meaning of our otherwise disparate scientific, moral, religious, and esthetic experiences could be revealed to all. Although Green's style of philosophizing was not particularly original, he did present the idealism of such thinkers as Hegel and Kant so persuasively that he was able to influence an entire generation of British philosophical thought. Among his most important philosophical

The Boundaries of Politics

works are his *Prolegomena to Ethics* and his *Introduction to Hume's Treatise of Human Nature.*

Much of Green's political writing is devoted to a critique of the liberal utilitarian tradition. Philosophically Green believed that utilitarianism presupposed a patently inadequate understanding of human nature and that this in turn raised serious questions concerning the principles of a utilitarian politics. Specifically Green argued that utilitarianism's understanding of human individuality inevitably led to a system of governance incapable of addressing the serious social problems of the day. Similarly the utilitarian advocacy of hedonism failed to provide a proper defense of democratic principles, which, according to Green, were ultimately of a spiritual nature. Finally the utilitarian understanding of society and history was a strictly immanentist one and thus incapable of acknowledging what Green believed was the necessarily beneficial role of religion in society. In short, Green argued that utilitarianism was both theoretically and morally bankrupt and that the continued existence of liberal society required the construction of a more adequate philosophical foundation. In his own attempt to provide this, Green advocated a return to a modified version of the natural-law tradition.

Green's use of the natural-law argument must be sharply differentiated from the traditional usage as seen in Aristotle. First, Green, unlike Aristotle, did not believe that the state should attempt to enforce a specific form of morality among its citizens. Whereas Aristotle wished to regulate human behavior in order to create the good life, Green argued that the very idea of a compulsory morality was a contradiction in terms. According to Green morality consists in the disinterested performance of self-imposed duties. Consequently the use of force by the state to create obligations must necessarily negate the moral character of the resulting acts:

> The 'jus naturae' . . . is at once distinguished from the sphere of moral duty, and relative to it. It is distinguished from it because admitting of enforcement by law. Moral duties do not admit of being so enforced. The question sometimes put, whether moral duties should be enforced by law, is really an unmeaning one; for they simply cannot be enforced. They are duties to act, it is true, and an act can be enforced: but they are duties to act from certain dispositions and with certain motives, and these cannot be enforced. Nay, the enforcement of an outward act, the moral character of which depends on a certain motive and disposition, may often contribute to render that motive and disposition impossible. . . .[9]

Green's distinction between law and morality does not imply, however, that the law is altogether unrelated to morality. Although law cannot create morality, it can create those social and political conditions that make morality possible. Or more precisely, in a well-ordered political community the law will provide its citizens with the opportunity for each to live the good life by removing those social and economic obstacles that would hinder such an effort. Although compulsion cannot make individuals moral, it can create an environment that gives them the freedom to become so.

A second distinction between Aristotle's and Green's use of the natural-law tradition is found in their understanding of the common good. According to Aristotle the common good is an objectively knowable reality whose content is firmly established by the unchanging principles of human nature. For Green, on the other hand, the meaning of the common good depends upon those particular aspirations and ideals recognized by the members of society at a given time as appropriate for and desirable to all its members. In short, the common good can change as people evolve in their understanding of the human ideal.

Green's modification of traditional natural-law theory was intended to prevent the emergence of political paternalism. From Green's perspective, Aristotle and classical Greek theory in general failed to adequately acknowledge the moral autonomy of the human person. As a consequence, they created regimes that were both politically static and morally deficient. In their emphasis of virtue they failed to recognize freedom.

Green's advocacy of the extended state was based upon his essentially positive understanding of human freedom. Green claimed that the English utilitarians had defined human freedom in a basically negative way. From their perspective, an individual's freedom was understood to increase as the number of unwanted external controls affecting him or her began to decrease. Freedom was essentially *freedom from* external restraint. Green, on the other hand, defined freedom in a more positive sense. For him freedom meant the positive opportunity to achieve one's potential. As people's options and choices increase, they become more *free to* explore a variety of alternative possibilities and thereby increase that power by which they are able to make the best of themselves. In this sense the growth of freedom occurs as one is increasingly empowered to act according to his or her own rational will. As willful creatures, humans act for the sake of their potential self-satisfaction; yet, at the same time, as rational creatures they are able to conceive of the perfection of their own human nature as the appropriate object for this desire. When will and reason come together, the individual is free. And it is the possibility of achieving this union that defines the purpose of social existence:

> The value then of the institutions of civil life lies in their operation as giving reality to these capacities of will and reason, and enabling them to be really exercised. In their general effect . . . they render it possible for a man to be freely determined by the idea of a possible satisfaction of himself, instead of being driven this way and that by external forces, and thus they give reality to the capacity called will: and they enable him to realize his reason, i.e. his idea of self-perfection, by acting as a member of a social organization in which each contributes to the better-being of the rest.[10]

Green's understanding of positive freedom justifies a much more activist state than does the traditional liberalism of the utilitarians. According to Green, the just state is charged with the dual responsibility of guaranteeing the material conditions for and removing the unnecessary obstacles to the moral self-development of the individual citizen. In order to meet these responsibilities the state is justified in regulating and controlling the actions of its members if such policies are necessary to further promote the growth of positive freedom:

> . . .we shall see that freedom of contract, freedom in all of the forms of doing what one will with one's own, is valuable only as a means to an end. That end is what I call freedom in the positive sense: in other words the liberation of the powers of all men equally for contribution to a common good.[11]

With these arguments Green effectively established the theoretical foundations for the modern welfare state. From his perspective the state is both to protect its citizens and at the same time create those positive conditions that will advance the general level of their welfare. To the extent that such conditions as poverty or ignorance prevent certain individuals from achieving their own self-perfection, the state is obligated to liberate them from the effects of such restraints. Thus, like Aristotle, Green believed that the state is more than a necessary evil. As the mode of human self-realization it is, in fact, a positive good.

Notes

1. Aristotle, *The Politics*, trans. Ernest Barker (New York: Oxford University Press, 1958), pp. 4–5.
2. Aristotle, *Nicomachean Ethics*, trans. Martin Oswald (Indianapolis: Bobbs-Merrill, 1962), p. 29.
3. Aristotle, *Ethics*, p. 17.
4. As quoted in *The Moral Foundations of Democracy* by John H. Hallowell (Chicago: University of Chicago Press, 1954), p. 82.
5. Aristotle, *Ethics*, p. 43.
6. Aristotle, *Ethics*, p. 34.
7. Aristotle, *Politics*, pp. 317–18.
8. Melvin Richter, *The Politics of Conscience: T. H. Green and His Age* (Cambridge: Harvard University Press, 1964), p. 13.
9. T. H. Green, *Lectures on the Principles of Political Obligation* (Ann Arbor: University of Michigan Press, 1967), p. 34.
10. Green, *Principles*, pp. 32–33.
11. T. H. Green, "Liberal Legislation and the Freedom of Contract," in *The Political Theory of T. H. Green*, ed. John R. Rodman (New York: Appleton-Century-Crofts, 1964), p. 53.

Recommended Readings

Arnhart, Larry. *Aristotle on Political Reasoning*. DeKalb: Northern Illinois University Press, 1981.

Barker, Ernest. *The Political Thought of Plato and Aristotle*. New York: Dover, 1959.

Greengarten, I. M. *Thomas Hill Green and the Development of Liberal-Democratic Thought*. Toronto: University of Toronto Press, 1981.

Hearnshaw, F. J. C., ed. *The Social and Political Ideas of Some Representative Thinkers of the Victorian Age*. London: George G. Harrap, 1933.

Jaeger, Werner. *Aristotle: Fundamentals of the History of His Development*. Translated by Richard Robinson. New York: Oxford University Press, 1962.

Mulgan, R. G. *Aristotle's Political Theory*. New York: Oxford University Press, 1977.

Murray, Robert. *Studies in the English Social and Political Thinkers of the Nineteeth Century*. Cambridge, England: W. Heffer and Sons, 1929.

Richter, Melvin. *The Politics of Conscience: T. H. Green and His Age.* Cambridge: Harvard University Press, 1964.

Sidgwick, Henry. *Lectures on the Ethics of T. H. Green.* New York: Macmillan, 1902.

PART FOUR: Summary

Following the end of World War II with its subsequent breakup of the European colonial system, the nation-state emerged as the dominant form of political organization in the modern world. Those communities that have failed to organize themselves in this fashion suffer from both an economic and a military disadvantage in their relationships with other peoples. At the same time, international law and such international organizations as the United Nations operate according to the assumption that only the nation-state is the ultimately sovereign political actor. Given this situation, one of the most important contemporary political questions concerns the extent and purpose of state power. How this question is answered is one of the elements that separates the various schools of contemporary liberalism from their more conservative counterparts.

In chapter 10 we examined several arguments on behalf of the minimal state. Although utilitarian theory and natural-rights theory begin with radically different understandings of ethics and morality, the dominant versions of each tradition agree as to the desirability of a minimal state. The state is the most highly centralized and efficiently organized concentration of power in modern society. As such it may be viewed as the most potentially dangerous threat to both individual freedom and personal happiness. Given this potential, the advocates of the minimal state seek not only to make the state more responsible to the wishes of its citizens but also to reduce its power in absolute terms. A tyranny of the majority is still a tyranny, and the easiest way to prevent its occurrence is to minimize state power.

In chapter 11 we examined the arguments of those who advocate a more extended state. Typically they assume a teleological perspective towards politics. Politics is a goal-oriented activity, and the purpose of state power is to organize a community's efforts to achieve a common objective. That objective may be a material one, or it may include such spiritual goods as virtue or freedom. In any case, the state is perceived as an instrument; and, inasmuch as one who wishes the

The Boundaries of Politics

end must at the same time wish its means, the state will appear as valuable as the good it serves.

Typically a person's attitude towards the state combines elements from both the minimalist and the extended tradition. We wish the state to be active in some areas and passive in others. The challenge, therefore, is to have a principle of differentiation that will allow us to distinguish one occasion from the other. That goal, in turn, is one of the purposes for the practice of political theory.

INDEX

Index

Index

Index

Index